Abou

Martyn Stewart is from Manchester, England. During his college education, an unforeseen incident unexpectedly led him towards psychology. The subject has been integral to his life ever since.

He has over fifteen years of experience in the field, focusing especially in human relationships and cognitive psychology. During this time, he has conducted studies into interpersonal attraction and the factors influencing relationship breakdown. Currently working as Head of Psychology at one of the world's top international colleges, he is constantly using his experiences and diverse knowledge to inspire the next generation.

In his spare time Martyn is a keen sportsman and entrepreneur. He also holds an interest in acting, music, history, films and travelling. He has contributed significantly to his local area via youth work, social inclusion and teaching.

His latest project, *'Why men REALLY cheat: The Psychological Secrets of Male Infidelity'*, has produced a series of successful international seminars culminating with the production of this book. The research findings from men all over the United Kingdom are delivered here in an informative but remarkably refreshing and entertaining manner; the hallmark of all of his enterprises.

Why Men REALLY Cheat:
The Psychological Secrets of Male Infidelity

MARTYN STEWART

Matador
9 Priory Business Park,
Wistow Road, Kibworth Beauchamp,
Leicestershire. LE8 0RX
Tel: (+44) 116 279 2299
Fax: (+44) 116 279 2277
Email: books@troubador.co.uk
Web: www.troubador.co.uk/matador

ISBN 978 1783061 280

British Library Cataloguing in Publication Data.
A catalogue record for this book is available from the British Library.

Typeset by Troubador Publishing Ltd, Leicester, UK
Printed and bound in the UK by TJ International, Padstow, Cornwall

Matador is an imprint of Troubador Publishing Ltd

ACKNOWLEDGEMENTS

To my mum, brothers and sisters for always believing in me and giving me their unwavering support. To my daughter Shauntea for always giving me a purpose to keep going!

To my two closest friends who have always believed in my potential.

To Samantha Fielding, you are going to be an amazing editor. Thank you for your eye and skill with your contributions. Also to everybody in the Troubador/Matador team that helped put this project together.

To my friends and family – near and far – thank you for the support from the beginning. It has not been forgotten.

I hope you enjoy my work.

CONTENTS

FOREWORD

From the very outset of this project people have asked me where the concept for this book came from. Why am I writing about men and cheating behaviour? As if you really need to ask. Intrigue!

Most people are probably lying to themselves if they even attempt to claim that this topic has ***never*** held any interest for them. Infidelity is so intertwined with human existence that we have all experienced it in some format at some point; whether personally or by extension. Idle gossip on the topic always perks the ears up whether you were paying attention or not.

After writing several studies into relationships during my psychology studies; constantly being the reference point for friends and colleagues with their relationship queries; and working on several different relationship projects, I soon realised that there was one question that continually surfaced. Why do men cheat?

When engaging in general discussion on the topic, a lot of people will miss the real purpose of this book. Assumptions will abound that it is doing a disservice to one, or both of the genders to write about just men and infidelity. They will disregard the objective questions which are being asked here. Why do men really cheat? Are they born to cheat or do they choose to? What is the real catalyst that triggers the behaviour?

When we ask this, we are not interested in the excuses men spout when they are caught; nor the validation that men try to glean because of the obvious differences in gender biology, but why do men ***really*** cheat?

Even women who are happy with their relationships are interested in the answer to this question (either out of apprehension or precaution).

So to get to the bottom of the debate, I decided, not only to look at the previous research, but to ask men face to face and get the answer straight from the horse's mouth. I asked modern men of today their views and experiences of cheating: 547 of them!

This study was to be different. So I visited places where women rarely go but I knew the truth would be found. Gathering information from gyms, barbershops, sports changing rooms and boys' nights out. The male safe havens where they feel safe; where they are free to express their true perspectives and experiences regarding infidelity, without fear of retribution or identification.

Now, there are many explanations already out there in the public sphere for why men cheat. These include biological, sociological and anthropological explanations amongst others. I am a psychologist, so bear in mind that the explanation in this book comes from a psychological point of view. I am not discounting the merits of other explanations. I just ask you to consider this one with an objective and open mind.

Some of my research findings were surprising. None more so than the fact that there are not one, two or three but ***at least*** twenty-seven different types of men! Twenty-seven types who think and act differently! Whose brains, thoughts and experiences have interspersed, shaping them into very distinct types. You encounter them on your daily journeys. You can meet 'a charmer' on the train or 'an opportunist' in the work canteen; 'a family man' in the office or 'an enigma' in your closest circle of friends. All men are not the same.

Naturally, lots of researchers have tried to identify differences in men. Any search on the Internet will reveal articles suggesting that there are four, eight, ten or sixteen different types of men. Interestingly, I am not the first to suggest there are twenty-seven different types. This was also identified by the famous sociologist, Dr. Stephen Whitehead; an acclaimed and prolific writer in the field of gender differences in his book '*The Many Faces of Men*'. Although we both identify the same number, that is really where the similarities end in terms of our publications.

This book focusses on an explanation for ***why*** men cheat and ***how*** these different types of men are formed. The actual number of types is just one important facet, a sub-plot to the overarching answer.

Even though we look at gender from two totally different angles, the fact that two professionals from differing fields, have independently drawn the same conclusion on the number of different types of men, provides validation and authenticity that cannot be ignored.

Prior to my research, I had deliberately stayed away from the other famous and popular books relating to relationships and gender differences. I didn't want to be unwittingly influenced by their concepts or style of writing. I wanted to produce an objective, fresh, entertaining and insightful piece which was uniquely my own – apart from the obvious similarities, that there is no getting away from.

And the result is this book. It is an entertaining and enthralling look at an ever-intriguing topic. A novel concept fusing together psychological understanding with engaging narrative; it is filled with fresh ideas and a provocative delivery. After years of research, I was convinced that this book needs to be read by the public!

However, I have had people say, why focus only on men? They are not the only ones that cheat, women do as well. Of course I am fully aware that the 'fairer' sex is known to have their own relationship indiscretions too. And although there are similarities in the patterns of behaviour, the story proceeding why the modern woman cheats appears to be entirely different to men and needs to be told separately. Perhaps a sequel beckons.

Nevertheless, not to be diverted from the topic at hand, everybody will relate to different sections of this book in their own way. They will use its contents depending on the particular stage of their life they are at. However, no matter where on life's journey they are, everybody needs to be aware of the relationship 'BETs' that they make. Do you really know the type of man you are betting on? My B.E.T. theory – the unique technique provided here to identify the patterns of behaviour of different types of men – is for everybody. It illustrates that some men may be more prone or less prone to cheating than others. This knowledge is paramount in making an informed relationship decision about any type of man. I was even able to identify my own type using B.E.T. theory, with a little unbiased soul-searching. (I wasn't Mr Perfect as I had hoped for but there is no sense lying to myself!)

Objectively, if I can gain some understanding from my own work, I believe everybody can take something valuable from it too. Whether you are a man searching for your own traits and characteristics or a female trying to identify a specific man in your life, this is for everyone. Hopefully this book will help you efficiently uncover the information that you seek!

Enjoy, *Why Men REALLY Cheat: The Psychological Secrets of Male Infidelity*

***Note – All individual names and personal details in this book have been changed to ensure confidentiality. Scenarios have been altered slightly to protect anonymity.**

Chapter 1 – Wednesday evening

"Do you think Derek is cheating on me?" Claire enquired, as she explained the latest sequence of events with the barrister she had been dating. When she'd found out about Derek's job, she was on him like a shot. Claire liked the idea of finding a rich guy and tying him down. Recently she'd been giving it her best attempt at making that goal a reality. In the space of just three months, she'd dated a doctor, a pilot and an architect and now she was on to 'Mr Lawyer' (as we called him!). Wednesday evenings were always the same: a drink and a catch up with the girls, getting the latest gossip about who was doing what (or who) at the large fashion house where we all work.

"He is off to Brussels for the weekend. However, he didn't think to invite me, even though he knew I had booked this weekend off." Claire huffed. It was a little presumptuous if you ask me, but then again, that's Claire in a nutshell.

After three years at the same company, it's fair to say that I had become almost too comfortable. My nice apartment in the city centre was convenient for weekend socialising and the occasional spot of retail therapy. I earned a good living, not great, but enough for me to save a little without having to cut back on my lifestyle – which to be honest, at twenty-eight with no children was something I was not prepared to compromise on just yet.

Wednesdays had become something of a ritual for us. After being forced to sit through an unbearable ninety-minute staff meeting, we headed straight to the bar! We were meant to discuss the week's profits and losses, but it could wait… well, at least until tomorrow morning. Plus, we all work in different departments so it's one of the few opportunities we get to catch up.

It was my best friend Claire, who originally chose the venue for our weekly gathering – a small bar which, although aesthetically pleasing, was never up to much. Claire is very vocal and likes attention, but secretly I think she gets a little insecure when surrounded by other females blessed with ridiculously outstanding looks. In the quiet local, we can all escape the superficial pressures of the fashion industry. Compared to others at work, we're an average-looking group of girls. Sasha is probably the most attractive of us all, and I think she would accept that she is only a seven out of ten, maybe an eight if she was really giving it a go.

Me, I err on the other side, probably a six. At twenty-eight, regular workouts have kept me in good physical shape. I am well aware that most men are attracted to me for my well-rounded figure, which is more eye-catching than my sparkling smile (regardless of the attire that I chose to wear). It's the curse of the curvy girl. I do like my long brown hair though; it runs just past my shoulders. Over the years, I've gained just enough confidence to be content in my own skin. Sasha is the other brunette in the group. Julie and Helen are blonde. Claire recently dyed her hair red.

Our rendezvous are rarely special, but they're ten times better than sitting in those meetings. We talk about the usual crap, the sort of stuff that sounds so much more interesting when you're together, but when you get home you wonder how it took up the entire evening. You know what I mean: shoes, sex, men, clothes, that new b★tch Emma in 'admin' who thinks she owns the place, hair, nails, food, diets… the list goes on and on.

As Claire was complaining about her perceived snub from Mr Lawyer, we were quietly thankful when Julie gave us some real gossip, as Claire would've gone on all night.

"I think Gerry's cheating on his wife," she brought up out of the blue.

Julie always called the president of the company 'Gerry', like we were all friends with him. In such a large company, you hardly ever bumped into your superiors; only Julie had gained exclusive access. At twenty-four she is the youngest of the group; riding a wave of good luck to land the role of PA to the company president. She handles all of his personal and professional business, amassing some pretty good perks along the way. Sasha introduced us. Julie is short and cute with an energetic personality; I think that is why she has risen so quickly to her current position – although there were unconfirmed reports she'd slept with one of the bosses at the same time, which may have hastened her progress. We have to be careful with her though. After one too many drinks she gets a little ***too*** loud. It's ironic how freely information flows out of her mouth after a couple of glasses of wine; especially when discretion is essential in her role as personal assistant.

I had met Gerry's wife Jessica before, at the work Christmas party two years ago. My overall impression – after I had bumped into her in the ladies room and decorated the floor with the contents of her purse – was that she was very modest for such an attractive woman and a very caring mother too. Gerry was incredibly lucky to have her.

Jessica had been calling the office regularly in the past few days as she was booked in for a serious operation. She would be bedridden for over a week. After taking these calls and planning a weekend away for two, Julie had assumed they were pulling a fast one on the company expense. *Fair play*! I thought. If I was the president, I would be doing 'business' in Milan or New York every other week. Naturally, you would assume that her husband was planning a surprise break for her recuperation. So why was his flight only one day after her operation? With an unknown Miss Sarah Johnson, who was half his age?

We were stunned. Men are so disgusting at times. The mother of his children was going under the knife and he was trying to impress another girl who was barely out of school. We couldn't understand it. Sasha and Claire were raging as if somebody had wronged a member of their close family.

We went on for another half an hour speculating over how many more of the executive board deserved to be castrated and invented ways to go about it. After disparaging men and their apparent limitations for the best part of an hour, a phone call from Helen's boyfriend James – who for all intents and purposes is pretty much one of the best guys you could get – distracted us for a moment. Claire tried to bring the conversation back to high-level castration when Sasha cut her off.

"Hey, look at that guy over there!"

We all turned to look…

At the bar stood an attractive man; he wasn't stunning, actually he may have been closer to average but he possessed a distinct rugged touch. He was dressed well in a dark suit and crisp white shirt, which was not common for this bar so it made him stand out.

He wasn't the greatest height but tall enough to make you feel like a woman. He was stood in conversation with a very pretty lady. She was obviously his date because her flirting was far from subtle! Even so, the girl was stunning: your stereotypical size 8, not an inch of fat anywhere, long legs and long hair.

Sasha scoffed. She hates women who make too much of an effort. She sees them as a threat. Sasha gets her fair share of attention, but really needs to let go of the constant comparison complex she has. We all compare ourselves to other women, if we didn't, fashion magazines would go out of business. But she takes it just a little too personally – especially as she has lots going for her! She earns the most of us all, supplemented by the flash convertible her parents bought for her. The two houses she owns in an expensive part of town also make her a tidy profit. Despite this, Sasha likes to give the impression that guys want to roll around with her in the dark, but hesitate to stand up with her in the light.

As we were all fawning over this mysterious man, I suddenly realised that I knew this 'stranger'. I struggled for a minute to remember where from exactly. He looked a little different from our university days. He'd filled out a bit more, and I didn't remember him having that rugged sexiness about him either. I took a deep breath. The girls continued to perv over him, suggesting all kinds of things they would do if he wasn't with 'that woman'. They may talk the talk, but none of them would ever have the guts to approach him. So I stoked the fire a little bit.

"Hey, I know him."

"Who is he?" Claire said. I saw her eyes twinkle. It was as if she'd forgotten about Brussels and Mr Lawyer already.

"We had a fling after we finished university, but he looks much better now."

She looked disappointed, but I know Claire better than she knows herself. She wouldn't let the fact that I dated him first stop her. 'As long as it wasn't serious' was becoming her catchphrase. Twenty years of friendship goes a long way. Our university years were an experience for me but for Claire they were a revelation. She was a little wild to say the least, but she had calmed down a lot since I got her a job at the fashion house.

"What's his name?" Helen asked.

As I attempted to answer her, I flashed a stumped look. *What **is*** *his name?* I thought to myself. After a couple of minutes debating about our mystery guest, we returned to our drinks and the usual Wednesday night chat. He was on a date; it seemed rude of us to keep staring. It was not much longer, however, before Sasha announced:

"Well that's the end of their night then," she gestured with a nod towards the door. Smiling, he kissed her softly on the cheek. She left, seeming content with herself despite her evening apparently ending prematurely. As she disappeared, the man surprisingly sat back down at the bar and ordered another drink.

"Why don't you go and find out his name, before I do?" asked Sasha.

"I dare you," I shot back. She didn't budge.

"I dare ***you***, he's your fling," Sasha responded.

What was I going to say? I couldn't even remember his name! What if he didn't remember me?

"OK, I will," I said.

Chapter 2 – Why men REALLY cheat

“Hey stranger, remember me?” I spoke cautiously, hoping to hold my voice from breaking and add an air of adult confidence; after all, we were twenty-one when we last spoke.

He turned to look at me, “Olivia? Wow, how are you doing?”

As soon I heard him speak, his name came rushing back to me, along with a few flashbacks… Originally from a town just outside of London, he moved to Birmingham to study Psychology at university. He was extremely smart, and there were times when he used to say things that made me feel like we were on different levels of educational existence. Nevertheless, Michael was one of those guys who seemed like they were never studying if you looked at him. It was more than likely, however, that he went home and worked his arse off; how else could you explain him gaining first class honours in his degree, when he was as inebriated as the rest of us each night?

Our brief fling didn’t get out of second gear; it was more out of convenience than attraction. In your final year of university you reach a point where reality sets in. Your dissertation deadline is looming. You couldn’t really rely on your friends for help, because they were feeling the stress too. We realised we had to sacrifice our time together, as procrastination would always defeat our half-hearted group attempts to be responsible. Michael was different, though. He could see that I was struggling and went out of his way to study with me.

The more time we spent working together, the closer we became; more out of familiarity than similarity, as we didn’t have much in common; apart from our appreciation of cheap alcohol. After I submitted my dissertation, the inevitable night came. I wanted to thank him for his help. So after dragging him out for a drink – which was a little unfair considering he still had his impending deadline a week later – we ended up playing sexual twister in his student house. I carried on seeing him for a couple of weeks before I started phasing out his phone calls. There just wasn't much spark. He took it quite well actually, and we parted ways without any awkwardness.

We had a quick catch-up; Michael explained that he had completed his masters and was a psychology lecturer at a redbrick university. He had become an expert in relationships, completing several pieces of research. He was in town to deliver a seminar on his latest study. I noticed the girls glancing over to me every so often. I guessed they were wondering what could be taking so long, but Michael had me enthralled.

A few minutes later, I walked back over and said: "Why do men ***really*** cheat?"

"Because they're bastards!" Sasha bellowed. The rest of the girls laughed.

I smiled as Michael approached. "Do you want to find out?"

I ignored the girls' inquisitive looks as I introduced them all to Michael. I kept it short and sweet – name, age and location, that was it. They didn't need to know too much about him. As the waitress passed, Michael called her over and ordered our favourite drinks. He didn't do it in the flashy, 'I've got cash' type of a way; it was nice of him and really unexpected. I briefly explained to the girls about his role and research before letting him take the lead. For the next hour, Michael captivated us with the details.

"So why do men cheat?" he asked to open discussion on the topic as he settled into a seat beside me. The girls were never shy of giving their opinion; tonight was no exception.

You've heard them all before: 'because they get bored'; 'they think with what's in their pants'; 'they are weak and immature, unlike women'; 'they don't know when they've got a good thing'. All the usual stuff came hurtling at him; you've probably used one or two to answer the same question yourself.

Taking what the girls said in his stride, Michael first of all, highlighted the importance of having a clear definition in any debate. He pointed out that 'cheating' is unique to every individual relationship. What one person classes as cheating, the next person may not. So if the debate gets a little heated, (as this one often does), at the very least, when it goes 'all over the place', everybody is talking about the same thing.

He said, "I am pretty sure that 99% of people consider their partner having sex with another person as cheating. But not everything that has been called cheating is interpreted in the same way."

I can definitely relate to that, I thought to myself. Sasha always gets mad if someone she is seeing flirts with somebody else. She calls it cheating. Whereas things like that don't usually bother me. I tend to view it as a compliment when other women are interested in my man. At the very least, I still have good taste! Sash is a bit more volatile. I wondered if Michael was a flirt? He must have lots of girls interested in him. Claire and Sasha were shamelessly giving him the eye, even though they were both currently attached – evidently their principles altered when the tables were turned.

I thought he had provided a fair and balanced introduction to his argument. At least he didn't just jump to the defence of the caveman. He was a gifted speaker with a clear, deliberate delivery, which was not only attractive, but also compelling.

"The biggest mistake a lot of women make when trying to understand why men cheat is that if it happens to them, they consider their event as an 'isolated incident'. This is understandable because it is such an intrusive and personal topic; however, it's hard to get many coherent answers with such a high level of emotional arousal. At times like these, most women will fail to look at the behaviour objectively and consider ***why*** it happened." Michael continued.

"In short, to discover why men really cheat, you must stop looking at cheating as something that is done to ***you,*** and consider it as a behaviour that occurs everywhere. This will minimise the emotional restrictions.

"You also cannot understand why men cheat today without understanding why men cheated in the past. Everything has a blueprint. The smartphone which has multiple functions from making calls to playing music is one of the most innovative inventions of the 21st century. But it couldn't have been made possible without understanding the progression from analog to digital data; or without understanding the progression from audio cassettes to CD players. This is the same with human beings; today's behaviour is just an updated version of yesterday's blueprint. Remember, 'cheating' is a just a word we created to explain a behaviour. It is a social construction designed to maintain order which needs to be understood.

"Men don't just wake up in the morning and think, 'It might be a great idea to cheat on my wife this afternoon'." Michael quipped.

I had to laugh, although I hated condoning anything relating to cheating. It was funny; or maybe it was just one of those moments when you laugh a little harder at the jokes of somebody you find attractive.

"Yeah, but some men ***always*** cheat. No matter what you do and how good they've got it." Julie retorted cynically to Michael's statement. "They're all the same. Look at all those celebrities and sports stars, they have everything and they still cheat."

"It does seem like that sometimes doesn't it? That some men always cheat. And they appear to be far worse than those men that don't; especially when the details are exposed of what they have allegedly done." Michael seemed to agree.

"Nevertheless, there is another significant factor that is often missed in the infidelity argument. No matter what an individual's personality or situation is – cheating can ***only*** occur with accessibility. For example, celebrities and men with lots of power and money have more opportunities to cheat because their fame and finances attract more female attention. If those everyday men who don't cheat had the same amount of opportunities, would they still be able to resist?"

Michael continued into a brief but intriguing background of evolutionary psychology and how survival of the fittest relates to cheating behaviour today. He suggested that our evolutionary past may be the reason why many women are considered to struggle when forming physical relationships without emotional attachment; and why many men are viewed as being unable to 'keep it in their pants'.

"This is the first brick in the wall of why men cheat today." There were a few puzzled looks from the girls, but they were clearly engrossed. Michael duly continued. "Nowadays, if given the choice, the majority of people will select a partner that has some sort of financial stability. That's now the way of the world. Finances provide the stability we desire in relationships"

Visions of women seeking out men with wallets the size of doorstops flashed into my head. For a second an image of Claire materialised. She's my best friend but I can't deny the obvious.

"But if we look back at our evolutionary history when money wasn't a factor, it could be argued that the most valuable commodity in a time with no buildings, cars, bank accounts or computers, was the ability to produce children.

"By nature, humans will engage in behaviours that will promote our survival and ensure that our genes pass on to the next generation. In terms of having children, a woman's reproductive capacity is relatively low compared to a man's. In theory, if a woman had sex with 100 men in a year, she could only get pregnant, at best, twice in that year. On the other hand, if a man had sex with 100 women, each one of them could give birth during that same year. If children were the main commodity, that made men potentially very 'rich'.

"The more they 'spread their seed' the more likely it is that their genes will survive. This was important as men were never really sure of parentage although women always are. Therefore, it is argued that evolving the 'desire for sexual variety' and seeking out new females to reproduce with was ***necessary*** for males. It increased the chances that their genes would survive to the next generation. They played the percentages and thus, had a beneficial impact on the overall survival of the human species during our evolutionary past."

I didn't want to believe it when he explained there is a biological phenomenon in most mammals, known as '*The Coolidge Effect*' which demonstrates this point. For example, if a male rat is put in a box with five sexually receptive female rats, the male will have sex with all five until physically exhausted. Despite the females' attempts to get the male sexually aroused again he will not respond, as it is probable he has already passed on his genes. However, if you place a new female into the box the male will find the energy to have sex with the new female; therefore illustrating the male's desire for sexual variety, or in other words, the 'desire for new'.

"Now I'm ***not*** saying that the desire for sexual variety is built in to the genetic code of the human male. However, recent research into epigenetics and psychology suggests that non-genetic factors (i.e. environmental experiences) can influence the ***behaviour*** of genes and cause them to 'express' themselves differently.

These environmental changes can also be passed down through generations without changing the underlying DNA code. For example, in relation to human males, the desire for new women to aid survival in our past could have altered the genes to interpret this behaviour as automatic and beneficial. This can affect the characteristics and behaviours that are inherited by children when the genes are passed down. In short, it could be argued that the 'desire for sexual variety' that can be observed in most men today is a non-genetic 'expression' of genes that began millions of years ago.

"In contrast to males, a woman would have very little to gain from having sex with many different partners – except perhaps a few unsavoury nicknames and some infamous anecdotes. Instead, women evolved a different need, an alternative method of making sure their children survived to the next generation: they evolved the need to form a close, emotional bond with one partner and this may have been passed on in their genes as a non-genetic expression to aid survival.

"If a woman could achieve this 'connection', her children were more likely to survive and continue to pass on her genetic material. This is because men would be more likely to stay involved in child rearing due to the strength of this emotional attachment. They would provide resources and protect their family from predators and danger. And with those women who were unsuccessful in their attempts to create this emotional bond dying out, future generations of women would be composed only of the successful woman's offspring.

It is also argued that women create a stronger emotional bond from sex than men do because they had to be 'choosy' about their selection of partner as they allow someone to enter them. This is much more personal. Whereas it could be argued that as men are the ones that enter (and because of their increased sexual variety), it made more sense for them to be emotionally detached. Therefore, through the process of natural selection, all women possessed the adaptive gene to form emotional bonds."

This made me breathe a secret sigh of relief. I always felt aggrieved if a man criticised me for being 'too emotional' quite early into a relationship – although I admit some women can take it too far. Perhaps when I have been called 'clingy' in the past, I was just displaying an evolved behaviour; a trait shared by all women that was essential for our survival. I like this psychology stuff, wait until I can drop that in conversation at my next dinner party!

Michael explained that these evolutionary gender differences were one reason why men had more of a compulsion for sexual variety than women. What we call 'cheating' today, has its origins in a basic, and necessary, 'survival schema' from our adaptation to our evolutionary requirements. Our ancestors were serial cheaters. The genes of men who did not evolve the desire for sexual variety did not survive.

"Remaining with one female limited their chances of passing on their genes. Disease and death during childbirth were both likely outcomes without hospitals, antibiotics and anaesthetics. Many children did not survive the pregnancy never mind the birth." For Michael, the infidelity displayed by men of today is a by-product of millions of years' reliance on this basic schema. Ingrained in male behaviour as a primary function, the 'search for new' that led to successful reproduction and survival of the human species laid the template for male sexual behaviour today.

I began to understand this concept, even though I did not completely agree with all of its suggestions. We had heard this argument before, usually in a bar with a bunch of drunken guys trying to explain their sleazy behaviour, or during the office banter, when one of the genders is trying to get the upper hand over the other. And today we were hearing it again. 'It's natural' just sounded like an excuse, but Michael's explanation did seem more authentic and plausible than the usual nonsense we were subjected to.

However, I could see Helen edging to interject. She was by far the most intelligent of us all and although usually the most stable, she was also a bit of a female activist, especially at work. She would never let any comment of male superiority slide without a fight, or at least a comment. To be fair, she'd never had any personal experience of men cheating on her, that she was aware of, (unlike the rest of us), so I was totally expecting her to challenge Michael from the start.

"Wait! So are you trying to say it's 'normal' for men to cheat?" she questioned forcefully.

"No, that's not what I am saying," was Michael's calm and confident response. "Yes men have an ingrained desire for sexual variety based on millions of years of habitual behaviour; although this is not an excuse for infidelity today. It is the same with aggression. I think you would all agree that we all possess aggressive tendencies. In our evolutionary past, this may have been necessary and aided our survival. However, like infidelity, if we look at it objectively, aggression is simply another behaviour.

"When survival is the only thing that matters, a human will do whatever it takes to live. Have you ever seen the film *Alive* based on the plane crash in the Andes Mountains? When trapped in the mountains with no food or sign of rescue, the remaining passengers made the decision to eat the flesh of the passengers who did not survive the crash. Humans will engage in behaviour that aids their survival, however small or extreme. Your survival schema is in place to facilitate this. You have to appreciate the reason for the actual behaviour at the time of its ***original*** requirements. Most people couldn't imagine this scenario because they use modern social constructions about cannibalism to interpret the situation. However, if you were actually in that position, what would you do?"

As we considered this notion Julie asked, "So what's a schema then?" Obviously soaking up every word that passed Michael's lips.

"Put simply," Michael said, "imagine your mind is a computer and a schema is a programme that you load onto it. Schemas are based on ***your*** unique experience of the world. Each 'programme' will help you understand and interpret situations in the future and how to behave accordingly. You use them to make assumptions and predictions on how to handle any circumstances you find yourself in. For example, you have a schema telling you how to behave in the social situation we find ourselves in right now.

"We have millions of schemas," he continued, before gesturing toward Sasha. I think he found her attractive but then again, a lot of men did. Sasha was the kind of girl that knew men were interested in her sexually, although she hated the fact. Indirectly though, she played up to it because it gave her an ego boost. It was like some soul destroying self-fulfilling prophecy. She smiled at his attention. "Take that dress you are wearing, for instance. You have a schema which influences how you dress, look and act, especially working in the fashion industry. You all do," he said, turning his attention back to the group.

"Your previous knowledge and encounters make you believe that there is an impression you have to make. If you moved to a different job, that programme may not be useful anymore and you may be required to adapt your schema or develop a new one."

We all related to this scenario. How much time in the morning did we spend selecting the right lipstick and matching skirt for our new designer blouse? How long does our hair take? And of course, the right shoes are necessary to set it all off. Was this all a mental programme as Michael had said?

We loved hearing him talk; he definitely understood women. I think I could have sat with him for hours. Although he was clever, he was never this captivating at university. Now, his words painted pictures in my head. I had always been interested in psychology, and who didn't want to know why men cheat? He provided both. Why didn't I have teachers like him at school?

Nevertheless, I couldn't help but think that his argument still didn't sufficiently explain why today's men cheat. Do they not have a brain?

"Actually," Michael began again, "the mechanics of the human brain make one of the biggest contributions to understanding why men cheat today. After all, the survival schema is only one out of the millions that influence us as human beings.

"The development of the human brain began millions of years ago. It has doubled in size compared to that of our ancestors. The reason for this occurrence has been a topic of debate amongst scientists. However, regardless of the answer, the increase in brain size has contributed to humans becoming the intelligent and creative individuals that we are today. Although we have only had 'conscious' thought for a relatively small period in human history, some consider it to be the latest feature of evolution. It may be hard for some of us living today to imagine but, it is estimated that we have only had conscious, reasoned thought capabilities for less than 1% of human existence. That being the case can you really believe that 99% of our historical behaviour would be wiped away via a social construction?

"In pre-historic times, humans were simple beings and 'infidelity' was just a necessary behaviour in order to ensure the survival of the human species. But in our current modern times, men have taken advantage of their developed capabilities. They attained positions of power, and in turn used their intellect to manipulate how infidelity was viewed. It also allowed them to 'have their way' with women with very little complaint.

"Once the schema for infidelity was no longer 'necessary' it was modified throughout the ages by powerful men until it became 'acceptable'. Humans are creatures of habit. Although we proclaim to revel in drastic change, reality suggests the opposite. Therefore, we prefer to 'modify' slightly what we already have.

"Even as far back as the Ancient Greek era, men in power have been adapting the concept of infidelity to their advantage, angering women with their exploits. According to Greek mythology, Zeus fathered multiple children with a plethora of different women. In our own recent history, famous kings were notorious adulterers. In the 16th century, Henry VIII was so powerful that he created his own religion – which remains today – in the pursuit of sexual variety.

"Infidelity was publicly accepted and tolerated. Men kept their power by establishing women as subservient second-class citizens. Cheating wasn't questioned by their partners, peers or society. However, in the 21st century, a time moving closer to gender equality, cheating is no longer necessary for survival nor is it acceptable. Consequently, the current modification of how infidelity is viewed today, explains why cheating behaviour is now mostly kept as a shadowy secret. This is evidenced by the alleged escapades of famous sports, music and television icons nowadays. But why does infidelity still occur today if it is no longer acceptable?"

We all looked at him in silence, waiting for the answer…

Chapter 3 – 'Twenty-seven?'

Michael had us caught in his web. He became more and more appealing with every word he spoke. How things had changed. When we had parted ways after university, I didn't even bat an eyelid – actually I was quite relieved. Now, I couldn't even imagine him walking away.

"The reason why some men still cheat today is because the schema that justifies the desire for sexual variety has become ***automatic***. For those men that cheat, it directs their behaviour by unconsciously selecting an excuse. The schema uses incoming information from his environment to support his decision. The 'justification schema' makes it 'okay' in the mind of the man to ***act*** on his ever-present desire for sexual variety. For example, he wants to have sex with another woman but he is already attached; there is information all around him that he can automatically select from to justify the infidelity. This can come from his peers, his family, his partner, the media or his culture amongst others.

"Any piece of ***information*** that contributes to his use of the justification schema, (no matter how small), makes it easier for him to formulate an excuse" Michael emphasised this point.

"One example could include that his friends cheat and don't get caught. This may occur so frequently that he passively internalises these influences on him. So when they encourage him to do the same, it almost seems like a normal thing to do. Another could be that his girlfriend said she would never leave him, even if he cheated on her. This reminds him that his father cheated on his mother, but they are still married today. Different circumstances and information but both contributing to the same schema and outcome. From a personal view that 'cheating is not as bad as people say' to celebrities, (who are role models), that have a reputation for cheating; there is so much information around us that can make the justification schema become just as automatic as changing gears in a car or texting on a mobile phone.

"In today's Western society people have become heavily reliant on the flow of information, and how quickly we can access it. This has fundamentally changed the way in which we work, communicate and most importantly, form and maintain relationships. We now live in an 'information age'.

"In this age, we are overloaded with sensory information; which for some people can be too much to handle at times. Think about how your computer performs when too many programmes are open. It rarely operates to its full capacity. This is the same with people! So to deal with this information overload, we have learned to repetitively adopt schemas that accept the things that we see and hear automatically – and usually without challenging them. This especially includes the use of excuses for our own behaviour.

"However, many women caught in the crossfire of infidelity try to explain the excuses they hear from men by 'catastrophising' the event: 'he doesn't love me anymore'; 'he has no respect for me'; 'he wants to leave me' etc. and in the small minority of cases this may be true. But for the vast majority it is not. However, thinking patterns of this type imply that the woman has done something wrong. That she in fact did something to 'cause' the event in the first place, therefore, providing the reason for the infidelity. This couldn't be further from the truth. A woman could be stunningly beautiful or appear 'perfect' in every way but a man may still cheat. And no matter what she may believe, she usually has little bearing whatsoever on his decision to do so. She is definitely not the conclusive reason.

"There is a big difference between a 'reason' and an 'excuse'. A 'reason' is a basis or cause for your beliefs and actions or for some fact or event. It is a justification or explanation. An 'excuse' on the other hand, is an attempt to lessen the blame for an action or belief (or to make it forgivable).

"These are very different things! And yet one of our schemas in today's society makes us accept 'excuses' in place of 'reasons', as if the two are interchangeable. This incorrect substitution is so frequent that some people do not even notice, or no longer care.

"This particular schema allows the creativity of the human mind to come into play. Some men, at times unwittingly so, have mastered this knowledge. They understand there is a discrepancy between excuses and reasons and use it to their advantage. As we have already pointed out, the desire to have sex with a variety of different women is argued to always be present in ***every*** modern man; however, the choice to act upon it is down to the decision-making process of the individual.

"Let's take a classic situation. A man cheats on his wife, is caught and he says, 'You've stopped having sex with me, I had no other option'. He has justified his actions by creating a schema using the information around him. Of course there are ***always*** other options to infidelity, but there was also enough supporting information in this man's view to justify his desire for sexual variety. Utilising the information around him formulates the excuse, but does not provide the reason.

"Granted, the wife may have contributed to this information by restricting the sexual contact (whatever her reasons). Society with its current views on relationships may have also contributed too. There is an expectation, in many circles, that a time comes in every romantic relationship when it moves beyond the physical; when companionship and parenting perhaps becomes the epicentre of a relationship and not sexual intimacy. Views such as these (correctly or incorrectly), can provide further information which, can either feed or inhibit the use of the justification schema in some men.

"Those men that do choose to cheat on their partner can justify the desire to do so – whether their reasoning is rational or irrational – from a variety of different information sources including: peers, family, culture, religion, the media, technology, misplaced logic, whatever… and it is spiralling out of control! For example, some men will rationalise infidelity in their male peer groups by processing special occasions like 'lads' holidays' or 'stag parties' as valid justification for a 'one off' indiscretion.

"Such excuses are rampant in our 'tolerant' Western society. No punishments are imposed for infidelity, and numerous high profile personalities adorn front page headlines, being 'caught in the act' with very little reprimand. It's unsurprising that with role models such as these, many men can easily justify their own behaviour.

"Acting on the desire for sexual variety can also be justified by the example set by ***some*** women. Many female actions can give the impression that infidelity is not the 'crime' that others make it out to be. By 'taking back a cheating partner' or knowingly being the 'other party' in an adulterous relationship, these women can indirectly strengthen the justification schema used by many men."

Claire and Julie looked awkwardly in opposite directions. Both are notorious for 'taking back' useless men despite our continuous protests to get rid of them. The amount of times Ben has cheated on Julie and she has 'forgiven' him can be counted on both hands. But how can you have truly forgiven somebody if you argue about it on a regular basis like she does? Her trust must be irreparably damaged, but their relationship is like a boomerang. The incident with her sister was beyond forgivable.

Michael was very observant of the girls' reaction, however. It was as if he was tuned into the same flashbacks we were all having. Clearly not wanting to make them feel uncomfortable, he subtly summarised his point, changed the topic, and made them feel included again. He definitely had a way with words.

"In turn, these excuses have diverted everybody's attention away from objectively considering the 'reason' why men really cheat. Instead we have become a society trying to interpret the varied excuses used by men (and women), which is far from ideal. Psychologically, some people struggle with the reality that a reason can provide. They choose to ignore it as they dislike its connotations or consequences.

"For some men, using an excuse is just another schema; an automatic programme to avoid the reality of dealing with an uneasy situation. Consequently, any woman trying to understand why men really cheat by trying to decipher an excuse is wasting time and energy. Simultaneously, she is probably creating unknown amounts of emotional anxiety for herself too.

Alongside the 'justification schema', we create millions of other schemas for ourselves to navigate successfully through our regular lives. Using excuses may just be one of them. Some schemas are simple. They contribute well to our superfluous daily habits, having no actual purpose aside from what makes us feel comfortable, such as hugging. A hug can always make you feel psychologically better, even if it is just for that moment, despite having no physical benefits in its social guise."

We all have a different 'programme' for hugging, I thought. I like a good hug, but Helen doesn't. I remember this boy in high school;

each day he would ask every girl for a hug, and we all submitted out of guilt or sympathy because none of us fancied him. I think that was his way of maintaining some female attention and it definitely kept his confidence high; he is one of the biggest players around. This, I supposed, was a schema that had influenced his relationships in the future.

Michael was right. Schemas are amazing, the way you interpret things from situation to situation. We even interpret the ***same*** information differently, depending on the schema we use to process it. Men have been asking women to have sex with them since before language was invented; now I realised that some men are more successful in this request than others, not because of what ***they*** do, but depending on the programme individual women use to 'process their request'.

"Some schemas may be easy to decipher, but others are much more complex mental programmes." Michael continued.

"Some schemas have roots deep in childhood and are still used automatically to solve adult relationship issues. For example, some people 'run away' from problems, whilst others get angry and lose control. Some like to argue inexplicably, whilst others like to 'talk their way out' of situations. These responses may create more problems than they solve for the user. Nevertheless these behaviours are influenced by the individual's own defining life experiences and are completely unique – even though they may appear to be the same as those shown by other people.

"With the multitude of different schemas that people possess, it's almost irrational for women to think that men are 'all the same'. Michael stated.

"Unfortunately, many women do believe that all men are the same. This is because they focus more on the similarities in male behaviour and the familiar outcomes in many negative relationships. They look to other women with similarly shared experiences to provide supportive evidence for their beliefs. Research suggests that we are more likely to engage with people who have similar beliefs to us; they provide us with validation that our own experiences and opinions are correct – in this case, that men are all low-life deceitful creatures that cannot be trusted with the heart of a woman. But this is incorrect!

"Bearing this in mind," Michael continued, "how many

different types of men do you think there are?" He asked, breaking stride in his psychological explanation.

"Two or three?" I offered confidently.

"Twenty-seven," Michael responded instantly.

"Twenty-seven?" Sasha queried in sarcastic disbelief. "No way! There is only one type of man: the dirty bastard type." We laughed.

"My research suggests that there are at least twenty-seven types. They are all different; some types are more prone to cheating, regardless of whether their relationship situation is positive or negative. Some are less prone to cheating, regardless of whether their relationship situation is positive or negative. The majority of men, however, are average and may or may not cheat, depending on the dynamics of their relationship situation.

"Just because some men have admitted (or have been caught) cheating and countless others probably have numerous skeletons in their closets, it does not make every man the same. This view is another example of people and their schemas again accepting information far too easily and thus making sweeping generalisations – seeing what they want to see.

"In my research, 27% of men admitted cheating on their current partners, which implies that 73% of men have not. A quite convincing majority that suggests it is unfair to generalise all men in the same way. Even if the behaviour of men you know, their environments and your own experiences are so similar that it is difficult to differentiate, it is still unfair.

"Yet many women still persist; treating all men the same in a negative manner as if they all cheat. What would women actually do if 100% of men admitted infidelity? Would it herald the end of the monogamous relationship as we know it? Or make womankind feel any better about themselves? Probably not; therefore having an objective frame of mind in this discussion seems like the most appropriate option. Especially considering that it is not only women who are seeking the answer to this question… some men are too."

"Well how do you know they are different?" Sasha asked sceptically.

"I was just like you Sasha. I actually stumbled across the difference when interviewing the men in my study. I noticed, as I am sure you all have, that a lot of men ***appear*** to be very similar in the way they behave and their influences. Their hobbies and values are moulded by a society that encourages social norms and predictable behaviour.

"However, when you conduct detailed interviews you pay a little more attention than you do during a regular conversation. And what I noticed (even in men who could have been best friends, who were similar in almost every way) was that there were subtle differences that influenced their behaviour. These differences would normally go unnoticed. I nearly missed them myself! For example, two such men who had both cheated on their partners on one occasion were experiencing severe guilt. They had not repeated their behaviour. One of the men was thinking of every possible eventuality he needed to deal with. He wanted to bury the details in order to protect his partner from his secret. The second man on the other hand, was reliving the events daily and considering how his partner would feel if she knew the truth. He was thinking about telling her and making it up.

"They were both experiencing the guilt but dealing with it in totally different ways. Are these men really the same? One was systematically thinking of a strategy to remove the guilt, bury it and move forward. The other was empathising with his partner's emotions. He was living in the past and contemplating his confession to relieve the guilt. This made me question, for these men whose majority of behaviour patterns were almost identical, what had happened in either their brain, environmental influences or their thought processing that had brought about this subtle difference. And was this a consistent pattern that could be attributed to their specific type?"

"The 'basic' human male from millions of years ago has evolved and developed into these twenty-seven 'unique' types that we meet today. Today's men all experience things and process information with significant differences, and you must look carefully to identify patterns created by these differences. Some of the patterns are extremely subtle. You must understand the 'BET' you make in every relationship; do you really know what type of man you have 'BET' on? This is my theory," Michael said.

According to Michael, B.E.T. theory explains the complex interaction taking place at every moment between each individual man's brain type (B), their individual environments (E) and their preferred method of thought processing (T). Put together, the output of these factors produces their type. Michael stated that having a thorough understanding of how these components interact will help every woman understand the 'BET' she makes when embarking on a new relationship with a man. In turn, it will enable her to make a more informed decision and may minimise the potential for infidelity (see chapter 15 for a full explanation of B.E.T. theory).

We were gobsmacked as Michael ran through the twenty-seven types. There was so much detail, so many behaviours. Some were obvious ('The Manipulator'); some were not ('The Visionary'). Some of the guys were similar ('The Stupid Mistake' and 'Act Now, Think Later'), and some were very different ('The Family Man' and 'The Chameleon'); some were familiar, some resembled urban myths. It had my head racing, and I could see by the bamboozled – but intrigued – looks on the girls' faces that they were too. All but Helen, she was begging to interject again.

"You can't just put men into specific types like that. It's a bit rigid don't you think? Isn't it possible, some men might show behaviours of lots of different types?" She questioned.

"Of course, you are right" Michael answered. "Being a man myself, I am well aware that at times I, and every other man on the planet, will occasionally display behaviours characteristic of other types of men. Even though I have already identified my own type, this is important to be aware of.

"This is one of the fundamental mistakes we all make in assessing another person's behaviour. It is not the uncharacteristic one-off responses or the superficial surface behaviours that are significant. It is the underlying regular patterns of behaviours, (that take much more time to uncover), that are important. And because we always tend to be in a rush, we may not notice the patterns, and as a result, confuse one type with another. We also may miss when a man has encountered circumstances that encouraged him to 'shape shift' (this is when men change into a different type – see chapter 22). So a manipulator ***may*** use charm as part of his game, and a charmer ***may*** on occasion use manipulation as a tool to gain a result, that does not make them the same type.

"When you look at the different types and the patterns of behaviour, you will see that many of them overlap, illustrating why this process of understanding your 'BET' is so challenging".

Helen nodded in considered agreement.

I had listened to Michael intently. To have to deal with the possibility that your man may be a cheat was bad enough, but now you had to work out what ***type*** of cheat he might be. This was too much, but simultaneously it was undeniably the most interesting Wednesday night conversation we had ever had. We had never heard ***anything*** like this before!

I could see the thoughts doing overtime in the girls' heads. *What type is Derek?; What type is Ben?* We had hardly touched our drinks we were so engrossed.

I envisioned Michael's seminar audience giving a rousing round of applause in a few days' time. I wondered what type Michael was. Maybe a 'Charmer' or perhaps a 'Modern Man'! I didn't want to go as far as 'Mr Perfect'; but he was ticking a lot of boxes right now. Every word he spoke seemed to bring me closer to my answer.

Michael quickly realigned my thoughts by suggesting it was highly unlikely that a few weeks (even a few months) would be enough time to determine a man's type. *Even though that's exactly what we all try to do*, I thought.

"Many women, just like men, are inherently insecure. They will continue to use behaviours and schemas, such as trying to 'work men out' to remain in their comfort zone. Nevertheless, attempting to understand what men are thinking can result in you feeling decidedly apprehensive, as you rarely find the answers you were searching for" Michael continued.

"But isn't that what your research is about? To help us know what men are thinking?" Claire asked.

"No. It's impossible to know a person's thought processes for sure. Psychologists cannot read minds, but we can understand and interpret patterns in observable behaviour. This is sometimes easily done, because as I said earlier, most humans are habitual creatures of comfort."

My mind was opened to this new perspective like never before. This was not the average Wednesday night 'b*tch' about sleazy guys. We already thought we were professionals at spotting the wastes of space, who try to monopolise our time with their lies and childish games. We had seen it time and again, and had come to despise them. But twenty-seven different types! Twenty-seven! How could there be so many? I opened my mouth to ask my first meaningful question of the evening but Michael politely cut me off before I could even start.

"I know what you are going to say. I get it at the end of every seminar… how do I find out what type a man is?' He flashed me a sweet smile, which made me blush slightly.

A couple of the girls nodded in agreement but no words passed anybody's lips. We all just waited in anticipation. Every one of us tries to work out a guy with potential the moment we lay eyes on him. I know I do. I start taking a mental record from the second he opens his mouth. Noting the things he said to the little things he did, just in case we ever meet again.

"In the early stages of a relationship, few men will feel comfortable enough to really relax all of their protective barriers around you," Michael continued. "I am aware that some men will unwittingly give themselves away early, but the majority will protect their insecurities. You will have only met his alter-ego, his mouthpiece; the part of his persona that he lets speak on his behalf because he feels it will provide the best impression of him. This means you have to spot the ***real*** signs, but these are so easily misread and will take time. Being patient in an impatient world has become increasingly difficult, and men can use many shrewd schematic smokescreens to throw you off the scent.

"Of course, on other occasions the chances of understanding a man are increased if you start dating somebody who was a friend beforehand. You may already know some of his patterns if you paid attention."

Michael glanced at me quickly… or at least I thought he did.

"But then, this may leave you more susceptible to the error of confusing this man's type" He stated. "Based on your previous platonic experiences, you may want to view him in a positive light; or perhaps he changes his normal patterns as the circumstances altered from associate to romantic interest. All in all, understanding a 'BET' is a difficult task.

"Nevertheless, there are some 'sure fire' signs to identify the different types. Men leave patterns of behaviour, especially those who fear leaving the safety of their mental comfort zone. This betrays them without them realising; they only escape without punishment if nobody is really paying attention. As a woman, if you see too many of the signs associated with a specific type in your man, then you definitely have a decision to make as to whether they are worth the risk or not…" (See chapter 21.)

At that moment, Michael's dialogue was interrupted by the familiar 'ping' of a mobile phone. "Unfortunately ladies, I will have to love you and leave you," he said, rising from his seat after reading the text.

"What?" I said. I for one felt abandoned. I don't know about the others but I'm sure they agreed that we needed to know more! He couldn't tell us that there are twenty-seven different types of men, and then disappear before telling us how to pick them out. He must have sensed my alarm.

"Hmmm…" he muttered, looking as if he was contemplating a huge decision.

"I don't normally do this, but since it was so good seeing Olivia again after all these years, I think I'll make an exception." Michael reached inside the leather laptop case he was carrying and produced a book, titled *Why Men REALLY Cheat: The Psychological Secrets of Male Infidelity*. He handed it to me.

"This is my new book; take care of it ladies! I'm sure all your questions will be answered inside there."

He kissed me on the cheek. "Good to see you again Olivia, we should stay in touch this time; don't be a stranger!" He placed a business card in my hand, with the briefest lingering touch of our fingertips.

"Nice to meet you all," he said, before turning away and strolling towards the door. This time I did more than bat an eyelid when he left.

Chapter 4 – 'You shouldn't be goin' through my stuff, Liv' – Nick

After his figure was no longer visible through the frosted glass entrance, I turned to look at the book. It had a white cover with four images of playing cards on the front, which had been changed to illustrate four of the twenty-seven types. I ran my finger across the title. Helen glanced at me and continued to sip her cocktail. She wasn't really into this sort of thing. Although she did admit later that week she'd found Michael's perspective on this topic and their exchanges intriguing.

The rest of the girls pushed behind me, jostling for position like teenagers around the latest gossip mag. It was like I was holding the Holy Grail in my hands, and to an extent I was; this book could provide an insight into men that none of us had ***ever*** had before. I calmed the girls down before turning straight to the contents page. One section grabbed my attention immediately. Chapter 21 – *'The 'Sure Fire' Signs to identify a man's type – The Quick Guide'*. I turned towards the back of the book.

Ignoring the cacophony behind me, I clasped my eyes on the first description; a man that sounded just like Nick.

I did not realise at the time, but I was blindly in love with him. It must have been painfully obvious to everyone else. I was twenty-two; he was nine years my senior. At such a young age I thought I had a wiser head on my shoulders than my tender years suggested. I was into older men; I was sick of the immaturity of your stereotypical jack the lad. Even though I had never been with anybody of Nick's age, I thought I could handle it. I remember thinking at the time: *he's over thirty!* It's funny that when you're in your early twenties, thirty seems a long, long way away.

Nick was a loveable rogue. We were together for three years after I had finished university, meeting at my first job as a fashion merchandise purchaser. He liked to call me 'smart arse' because of my degree in International Business Management. This is far from the truth. I would have preferred a degree in Economics, however, my A-Level's fell a little short of the AAB grade requirements. Before we started dating he would banter with me and try to illustrate his superiority above me. There was nothing malicious about it. He made me laugh. He would say things like, "It doesn't mean you're clever 'cos you got a degree. I've got life experience. You can't buy that at university."

In fact, ***he*** was the smart arse, always wanting the last word, not letting you leave the conversation until his viewpoint was accepted. He had an answer for everything – even if his argument was fundamentally flawed. He was a master at manoeuvring himself out of sticky situations. To the wrong eyes, his persona bordered on arrogance; I, however, considered this as a misreading of his confident approach and cocky tendencies. But I saw how he could rub some people up the wrong way. That never happened with me, however. He just never crossed that line enough for me to dislike him. And because of that, I found him extremely sexy.

My anecdotes paled in contrast to his life experiences, and yet, in the beginning, he was always considerate, taking care not to belittle me. This was the perfect combination to make me completely fascinated with him and feel appreciated at the same time. But not everybody shared my positive view of Nick; he was quite high up in the company despite leaving school with no qualifications. His manner of speaking to people made them feel unsure about how to respond. This knocked them off balance, which gave him the upper hand in conversation. And that is how he liked it. It was hard to say no to him. Many people thought he was contemptuous and condescending, although with me, he was never like that. Nevertheless, there were so many people warning me against him.

Many people in the company attempted to taint our relationship. Angela had a vendetta against him after he turned her down after a drunken work party. That was the reason behind her dislike for us both he said. Another was Kevin from marketing who was blatantly jealous of him. Nick was better in every way at his job, and this infuriated Kevin. I think this was the catalyst for the malicious rumours he would consistently spread. But I never listened to anything Kevin would say; he was an idiot.

Every other day, Angela or Kevin would have something negative to say about Nick. But their efforts were having the opposite effect to their intentions. They might as well have put me in a gift wrapped box and sent it special delivery to his desk. You know what it's like when you are told you cannot – or should not – have something: it makes it even more alluring. What's more, I was desperate to understand him in a way no one else did. In a situation like this, although it goes against everything you stand for, the rush you get from pursuing the forbidden can (at times) be too much to resist.

It is fair to say I fell into his trap. The first six months of our relationship were a whirlwind. Nick, the intelligent and charismatic gentleman, and me, the naïve university graduate. I became engulfed in his entire professional world, smitten by the nice things he would do for me. The lifts home and the lunch invites were sweet but he would also use his influence to get me assigned to the more favoured projects at work. I felt special as Nick provided the first opportunities to demonstrate my skills, whilst simultaneously placing me on a par with more senior employees.

On our first dates, he would convince the maître d at the busiest of restaurants to move us to a better table. He procured free tickets at the theatre because of 'poor service'. After a head on collision in my car, he managed to get me a courtesy vehicle even though my policy did not cover it. The way he threatened to get the Ombudsman to review their policies had them eating out of his hands.

"Only the best for my babe, I can't have you leaving me for some man who won't appreciate you." Nick used to say. He had a way with people.

In the beginning, I didn't care that Nick seemed to have a lot of female 'friends'. People were drawn to him, so what could I expect? He was so caring and protective when it came to me that I never really minded.

The more time I spent with him, the more I was compelled to pour my heart out. Yes, I thought he was 'the one'. I was young and had only just punctured the protective bubble my parents had created for me. Their constant support was always appreciated. But compared to my friends I still felt smothered, unable to make any decisions – or mistakes – for myself. I was living at home with my mum after finishing university, and it felt like I was still at sixth-form. Nick and I had a serious adult relationship which needed space to grow.

It was nothing like my earlier flings with younger guys; Nick was a man. There is a huge difference between being picked up in a stylish new car and meeting someone at the bus stop. I have never been the materialistic type, but there's just a different air to it. Nick knew I hated living at home and that our relationship didn't have my mother's endorsement, so his unexpected suggestion at the start of our seventh month together seemed like reasoned madness: "Why don't you move in with me?"

He had caught me off balance, like he did to everyone. And it worked. His arguments were compelling, his ideas about marriage and children and saving for a house were beautiful, as if an artist had painted them for me. He seemed serious. Everything was moving so quickly but every step felt so right. I felt like I was floating. Yet in retrospect, I can see how it was just a controlled scheme that suited his needs at the time.

He knew my parents would object. He had seen it coming. His subtle 'warnings' that my mum was intent on separating us were forcing me to choose between them. He said her behaviour was selfish in wanting to control me, and I couldn't argue with him. Why did she want to control me at my age? It was ***my*** life. I would not let a stranger live it for me, so why should my parents have the privilege? Nick astutely pointed out that trying to pick my partners was akin to trying to pick my primary school. She was treating me like a child, incapable of taking my own steps. He was right. I put it down to my mother's jealousy of my happiness after her messy separation from my father. And with that belief, I didn't give one thought to her disapproval.

Once we were living together, my mother's calls stopped. She never saw the apartment. She never met up with Nick and I either. He said that ***she*** should be the one making the effort; "She is ***your*** mother after all." She should have been setting an example, regardless of what she thought of him. Whenever I had a weak moment and was missing my mum and family, Nick would say, "If she was as caring as you said, wouldn't she have put her pride aside by now?"

She never did; again, Nick was right. Her behaviour upset me, but at the same time, it really didn't matter. Nick was being strong for the both of us. And living together with the man I loved was a dream that outweighed any distress that I felt. My mind was distracted by meals together, sleeping in the same bed and sharing our own place. Bliss! I thought I could not have been happier. However, I remember the start of the break-up as if it was yesterday…

Michael's words echoed in my head: *Relationships do not break-up instantly. The process begins a long time before, when you aren't paying attention.*

Nick was in the shower while I ate breakfast on the bed, when I noticed something vibrating on the side table. It was a mobile phone, but it wasn't Nick's; his was a new one, this was an older model. It was slightly covered by his office files, but didn't look deliberately hidden. I managed to see the name 'Natalie' flash on the screen just before it stopped ringing. After a few seconds, curiosity got the better of me. I tried to unlock the phone just as Nick walked into the bedroom.

"What are you doing?" he said, coolly continuing to dry his hair.

Startled, I stumbled over my reasoning. I explained that I had heard a vibrating, and had come across this phone. His suddenly cold tone of voice made it seem like he didn't believe me. His face turned to stone.

He bluntly replied: "It's Dave's."

"It's fine! Somebody called Natalie was ringing him." I said. I felt uncomfortable. For the first time in our relationship, I felt like his inferior. Like one of our work colleagues who he spoke down to, whom he toyed with for amusement. There was no love in his voice. I couldn't figure it out.

He casually strolled over to me. "You really shouldn't be going through my stuff 'Liv, should you? It makes it look like I was hiding something and now we have this awkward situation that I have to explain."

"No, it's fine, I don't need to know why you have Dave's phone. I'm sorry for going through your stuff," I said, feeling slightly guilty. I don't know why I felt that way. I hadn't really been through his stuff and I didn't distrust him at that point. And yet I felt as if I had crossed a line, like I owed him an apology.

"No it's ok, I'll explain," he said with little expression.

He then went into a very detailed story about the problems Dave was having with his ex-girlfriend. Dave was pestering her, so sometimes Nick would take his mobile phone to stop him calling her in the middle of the night. After a few drinks Dave could get abusive and Nick wanted to prevent this. I thought that was nice of him, but could not understand how somebody else's problems had caused such an issue in ***my*** relationship.

The drive to work was silent that morning. Any attempts to start conversation were shot down straight away. I felt like I had violated his trust and abused the fact that he had let me become so close to him. The journey seemed excruciatingly extended. I would have done anything to get back in his good books, anything.

Over the next few months I was not shocked to see Dave's phone lying around every once in a while. Call me naïve, but I had no reason not to believe what Nick was telling me. I was with him most of the time, apart from when he went to the gym. We worked together, we lived together and we still did things together. He could not be cheating on me. "*He wouldn't*", I would tell myself. And yet the thought still tiptoed across my mind.

That was just the start…

Our relationship changed over the next eighteen months. We still went to nice places, but not as freely or spontaneously as before. Phone calls from female friends became suspiciously more frequent. The fact that he 'knew them before he'd met me' meant little to me; such an increase in calls was conspicuous by their absence in the first year. With his continual refusals to introduce them to me, it was becoming an issue. There was no logic behind his reluctance; he could have reassured me in a second. And yet his typical response was, "Do I ask you to introduce me to your friends?"

"No, but that is because you know all my friends, idiot! I am not secretive about them!" I wanted to shout. He still managed to make me feel possessive, paranoid and insecure for questioning the identity of these women. He made me feel like I was constantly overreacting, that I didn't deserve to be in such a relationship. It always ended up with me apologising for my interrogations. The mystery behind their anonymous spectre taunted me and had me in an emotional mess. I prided myself on being independent and secure, but the way I was behaving lent little support to that idea.

Sometimes, I could not bring myself to endure the torture of the drive to work together, so he would leave me to catch the bus. I would be late and had several run-ins with my line managers which he completely ignored, despite his role in the situation. Wednesday evenings with the girls were accompanied by larger drinks receipts. I was spilling all the beans on Nick and his 'friends'. Sasha and Claire advised me to get rid. They had seen this behaviour before. But Nick had convinced me that I was a victim of my own doing. In being neurotic and clingy, I was the one to blame for our conflict. I didn't want to admit it at the time, but he had complete control of my mind and emotions. He could pull my strings like a puppet show, but had an amazing way of laying all blame at my door.

He had one 'friend' who was a little bit cockier than the rest. Naomi would sometimes hang the phone up if she heard my voice. At other times, her rudeness when demanding to speak to Nick resulted in full-scale slanging matches. But he never reprimanded her, or told her to respect me as his girlfriend.

"But why would she hang up, Liv'?" he would say. "Are you being rude to her? I have never heard her say anything out of place. As soon as she does I will put her straight."

But he never did. He wouldn't take my word for it. I felt like they were playing games in order to belittle me for their own amusement. When we would discuss it, his ability to reverse questions was amazing. I felt like I was being cross examined in a trial; a solicitor tearing holes in my story, whilst his alibi remained as tall as a skyscraper.

Arguments after a night out or during dinner with mutual friends were no surprise. On every occasion I would be made to look like the instigator in front of others, portrayed as an insecure and meddling little girl. As I had introduced him to most of our mutual friends, I felt the most uncomfortable. I was always trying to hide our tension, partly to maintain the pretence of happiness, against embarrassment. He was a different person when we argued. He was somebody playing a game with my emotions, and I felt like he enjoyed every moment of it.

My self-confidence was non-existent. The continual stress had led to me gradually gaining a few extra pounds and I was told I had let myself go. I felt repulsive. Nick pointed out that he stayed with me even though no other man would.

"What?" was the only response I could muster!

I was confused whether he still wanted me or not. Our sex life obviously diminished too, the infrequency of it was down to his insensitivity to my figure, more than anything. Not only was I disgusted with his behaviour but it also seemed like a chore on his part. On the rare occasions we did, he was usually too tired from the gym to meaningfully engage.

The end was near. At work, Nick would make comments to our colleagues that would paint me in the worst light without actually bad mouthing me. He was so manipulative. Deep down I knew it was over but chose to ignore it. I was convinced I could salvage what we had in the beginning, even in the final weeks of our relationship. I was willing to disregard everything that had come before in order to instigate the perfect plans that we had once discussed. I picked my moments carefully to raise the topic; days without arguments which were supported with some laughter seemed like the right time. I was hoping that talk of the future, the house and children would bring us together, but instead he would just say:

"I think you are thinking too far ahead. Just appreciate the good moments we have right now."

I had had enough. My eyes were opened.

The moment you realise that you are no longer in love makes you renounce any belief of previous affection. The veil of deception and illusion is removed. After all the games and the systematic dismantling of my spirit, I realised I did not know Nick at all. I could suddenly see the strings he had been pulling from day one.

It turned out that he had been seeing other women throughout our entire relationship. 'Dave's phone' was Nick's 'other' phone; it only required a quick look through the sent items to put the jigsaw together. His female 'friends', who he refused to introduce me to, were being strung along as much as I was, unsurprisingly.

Whilst he was turning my mother against me and 'going to the gym,' he had been entertaining a range of other women – including Angela from work. After three years, her sincere and tearful confession in the staff cafeteria to their affair, illustrated that we had more in common than I had thought. He had convinced her that we had been living in a sexless relationship and that I was emotionally repressed. However, her guilt had got the better of her. A few texts and phone calls confirmed that there were at least three others.

Even when I caught him at a bar with that b*tch Naomi draped all over him, he tried to suggest they were just friends; that I was overreacting. However, the disparaging look on her face convinced me otherwise. It took every ounce of my respectability to not drop to her level and teach her a lesson or two. But I would not rise to her attempts to rile me. His deception and controlling nature had created a great web of situations with many different women. He was the spider in the very centre that had me trapped for over three years.

I was just glad that at twenty-five I had the strength to walk away from him!

DID YOU SPOT THE SIGNS REVEALING HIS TYPE?

Chapter 5 – The *'Common'* Types

"I definitely need my own copy of this book. Ask him if I can get one?" said Sasha. "I'll pay double."

The selfish need to read it alone seemed to encapsulate us all; I wanted to hide it in my bag. I didn't mind the girls finding out its secrets, but I wanted to know them first. As the evening continued our conversations seemed less interesting as my mind wandered to the train journey home. I'd be able to read more into the types of men we had come across rather than the aimless guessing we are used to. The 'sure fire' signs would be a great reference point.

Claire was the 'dater' of the group – although the women who disliked her called her something else. She was more than likely to have had liaisons with the majority of the different types. This being the case her desire to discover 'Mr Lawyer's' type was incessant. She was dying to know. Actually, so was I. It was a less threatening scenario to analyse my friends' partners and pry into their lives rather than my own. It wasn't fun showcasing the fact I had spent three years of my life entertaining a 'manipulator'. But I knew that not all of the guys I'd been with were as bad.

I finished my cocktail quicker than it probably took to make it. The girls and I gave the usual goodbyes but there were a few more 'make sure you call me later' comments than usual. I frantically made my way to the station, found a seat on the train that had just pulled in and began to read.

Even though the title of the next chapter seemed straightforward, it was plainly obvious from Michael's opening sentence that the real psychology had begun.

'Utilisation of the justification schema is more prevalent in some men than others'

I would need to engage my brain just a little bit more than the previous sections; it was time to concentrate. I started reading.

THE FREQUENCY OF COMMON MEN

Women know that they meet some types of men more often than others; especially if they regularly frequent the same environments such as pubs, clubs and social venues. They are usually the men you ***don't*** want to meet. They say the same things and they display similar behaviours; a familiar chat-up line may come to mind. This prompts some women to utter the immortal phrase, 'all men are the same'. When in reality, nothing could be further from the truth. The men that they are referring to by using this statement are simply the 'common' types.

THE COMMON TYPES OF MEN are:

- The Opportunist
- The Rationaliser
- Easily Influenced
- The Charmer
- The Sucker For Love
- Back and Forth

Although it may make many women (and some men) feel better to think that all men are the same, this is merely an illusion. It's actually baffling to conceive such a notion when you consider the statement objectively. How can men all really be the same? They are not robots.

Ironically, many women (that tend to use this statement) still reel off a series of standard questions whenever approached by a potentially dateable man. What do you do? Where do you live? Where do you work? However, aren't these questions irrelevant if all men are the same? If their behaviour is predictable and women are aware of this, then what is the need for this Spanish inquisition?

Yes, these questions are often used for small talk. The reality may be that she holds little interest in what the man actually has to say. But unwittingly, some women use these questions as a protective tool to shield her from the unwanted attention of the common types. She in fact is just searching for confirmation that the man who has approached her fits the 'common' type stereotype. Say the wrong thing (i.e. a grown man still living with parents) and he will lose his 'potential' as an 'option' in her mind straight away. The common types regularly put their foot in it.

HABITUAL BEHAVIOUR

Of course, some men don't help themselves by boring women to death with their habits and repetitive actions. During a night out with friends, most women are constantly interrupted by multiple variations of the phrase, 'Do you want to meet up sometime?' However, all these women want to do is dance, have fun with the girls and explain to their best friend how much of an insensitive idiot her boyfriend is. These male intrusions are not helping; but these types of men can't seem to help it.

However, women need to recognise that most common types of men are simple creatures; tending to form behaviours out of convenience rather than consideration. So this type of behaviour is unlikely to stop any time soon. And despite how annoyingly frequent these monotonous displays of behaviour are, simultaneously they are so powerful that they outweigh and trivialise the sincere attempts made by other types of men. These men are made to suffer because of the common types.

The common types lack the ability to truly think outside the box; sticking to behaviours they ***believe*** work well for them. They provide little variety in the strategies they employ to tackle their daily lives. When painted into a difficult corner, they only seem to have one way of dealing with things. They will continue to gravitate around familiar environments such as men's clubs, sporting venues and gyms. These places are easy to deal with and female influences are usually minimal. Of the female presences around, they rarely challenge any stereotypical behaviour. Think about the stereotypical barmaid who banters with the men; cynically to get tips or to just pass the remaining minutes of her shift.

The common types are rarely challenged in their daily lives. They rely on their habits. So now, their thought processes are laden with such a brash overconfidence of

> *"The chances of my girlfriend catching me were slim. She lives in a different town and as long as I was careful, she was never going to find out. I was being discreet about it." Dan, 'The Rationaliser', aged Twenty-Nine, Leeds.*

their normal existence that most of their behavioural responses are now automatic. And for many common types, the automatic use of the justification schema is just one of these responses. For example, the 'Back and Forth' type may believe that his common sense view of the world is always right. Alternative perspectives are rarely considered; that is until there is a problem after the fact, (usually when it may already be too late and he has some explaining to do).

Predictability is a hallmark of a common type. Most women, with enough experience of them, can see their moves coming from a mile away, (even if they do not want to admit the truth to themselves when they have become emotionally compromised). The common types are too easy to dismantle. But it is important for women to not only recognise their similarities but to also be able to distinguish between their different characteristics. There is much diversity in their patterns of thought and behaviour. Many people miss the significant differences between these types as they appear insignificant in their eyes. This is because these men are easy to deal with until a problem is raised. This is the big mistake!

FIRST IMPRESSIONS

In Western society we speak a lot about first impressions. However, first impressions only count because they form the initial schemas which we know are very difficult to change. Usually, when a woman has had a disappointing experience with a man, there is a high likelihood that he was one of the common types. These men are everywhere, forming over 1/3 of the total types of men who were interviewed in this investigation.

The common types not only paint the landscape for themselves, but they also dig the ditch that every other type of man may fall into. For example, to some women, if a 'non-common' type fails to successfully negotiate past her initial 'introduction or interrogation' process, the same fate as the common types will befall him. Put simply, her schema for dealing with the common types, may have become her default process for ***all*** men that make an approach; and she may later begrudge letting 'a good one' pass her by, because of overuse of this thought processing.

> *"I can't help it that I love women. I just have to please them all. It's just me." Jason, 'The Charmer', aged Thirty-Six, London.*

Based on this schema, some women form restrictive dating 'principles' which they believe will protect themselves from the common types such as, 'I don't date men who approach me in bars or nightclubs' or 'I don't date men from (a certain geographic area/socio-economic group)'. By holding views such as these, women are understandably trying to improve their chances of meeting an appealing type. They hope that by restricting access to men that frequent environments where the common types are numerous, they will be more successful in the game of love. The reality is that they are just restricting their pool of men. Viewpoints such as these seem to inaccurately imply that it is only the common types that reside in nightclubs or certain areas.

However, the development of schemas such as these, are usually based on a woman's experience(s) with a common type. How many women actually believe they ***haven't*** been taken advantage of by an opportunist at some point in their dating history? If falling for the charms of the common types has been a regular occurrence, can you blame a woman for the formation of such automatic dating principles?

Nevertheless, although we can understand her barriers being up as a response to the common types, she shouldn't use this as an excuse for initiating hasty decision-making in the future. If she is passive, her schema will make the decision for her (based on a common type) whether any non-common type will be taking her for a date or not. However, she does not have to erroneously decide that 'Mr Perfect' will not approach a woman in a bar. It is unfair to disregard the individuality shown by new men that make an approach. By doing this, she again indirectly suggests that all men are the same (although the counter claim is that she is just protecting herself).

★★★★

(Note: ★★★★ Signifies a break in the psychological explanation and the start of Olivia's dialogue)

"The lads didn't think I would have the guts to pull another girl even though I was with Jasmine. I didn't really want to but I couldn't have them thinking that about me." Tom, 'Easily Influenced', aged Twenty-Four, Bolton.

My train came to a halt at the second station as I

contemplated this last point. "But it's difficult when we keep coming across these common types of men?" I said out loud, as if Michael was sat next to me. *We must be able to avoid them,* I thought to myself noticing a few inquisitive glances at the book's cover by other passengers. If they all tend to act the same, I want to know the signs. I carried on reading as the train started moving again.

++++

(Note: ++++ Signifies the end Olivia's dialogue and the re-start of the psychological explanation)

COMMON INSECURITIES

Unfortunately, these men are everywhere. There is no getting away from that fact. It will always be hard for women to avoid them as ***they*** will approach you. But it's not difficult for you to recognise their discerning traits. Once understood, women can then decide for themselves whether to continue interacting with them.

Common types usually possess a set of insecurities that drive their behaviours. These insecurities create their patterns of behaviour which are so important to identify. These insecurities can include not feeling loved or appreciated; being overly concerned with the opinion of others; not accepting that they are wrong or feeling like the world owes them something. They hide these insecurities with a series of daily patterns, behaviours and serial habits. They are easy to spot. They can include flirting, displaying machismo, being the loudest person in the room, turning on the charm and being compliant.

These tactics work as a defence mechanism for them, providing sufficient protection for the fragility of their ***true*** character. The common types will regularly 'pop up' and engage women in every day places such as the supermarket, the gym or the local bar. They do this in order to feel comfortable in a surrounding that won't challenge their facade.

> *"Women always present themselves to me. They want to have fun just as much as I do, probably because they are miserable at home. I am just taking advantage of the situation." Simon, 'The Opportunist', aged Twenty-Six, Bristol.*

Their insecurities are predictable.

However, it is easy to understand why so many miss the subtle differences between 'The Opportunist' who sensed that you were struggling with a new piece of gym equipment and offered to help, or 'The Charmer' that cannot help but flirt dangerously with you. You did not pay attention. But these common types of men are so consistent in their predictability, the probability of a woman coming across at least one every day is high. So no doubt, an opportunity to observe their predictability should present itself soon.

SAFTEY NETS

The common types of men do not venture far beyond their safety net. This is the smokescreen created by their 'flirtatious, rationalising or charming' approaches that forms their own personal comfort zone. They aren't prepared to take any risk or use any additional time or energy on dating. Why deal with the real world or be forced to grow emotionally? It's an unnecessary challenge. And what's more, there is very little that any woman can do to prevent a common type from engaging in their comfort zone. They will only leave their safe haven if ***they*** choose to.

The self-worth they show (which is often displayed in their often confident demeanour), is incorrectly amplified even further if they receive ***any*** positive feedback to their behaviour. This encourages them to continue as they are. Women who respond positively to their 'charming' approaches make the common types believe it's desirable, and will justify further behaviour; including infidelity in certain situations. We all know those men who appear to be 'full' of themselves, strutting around the office or the local bar like a peacock displaying its plumage. Nevertheless, they must have got their ego from somewhere.

> *"Sometimes, I just get a connection with a woman and just have to be with her. I know it's bad when I have a girlfriend but I can't fight the feeling. When I get that magnetic connection, I just fall for them and forget everything else around me."*
> *Neil, 'The Sucker for Love', aged Thirty-Nine, Hertfordshire.*

★★★★

That sounds like James, I thought to myself. James is the security guard from our work building. He's tried it on with me every day without fail! I knew he had a woman at home, so I never took him seriously. Although he's not the most attractive of men, his confidence definitely raises the roof. I can see why some women would like him, with that outrageous personality. Some girls just love a funny guy.

He never seemed fazed when I turned him down each day either. I used to think his self-esteem must be so high, but perhaps he was just hiding his insecurity as Michael had suggested. Or perhaps he just did it out of habit; was he a common type?

Would he continue to pursue me with such vigour if I gave him my number? Maybe the thrill of the chase sates his insecurity. In fact, when I come to think of it, he became even more relentless when he found out I had a boyfriend last year. I predicted tomorrow would just be another day of charm, jokes and chat-up lines. I expected nothing less. That was his safety net. I wondered which 'common' type he was.

'The Bastard type!' I heard Sasha's voice shriek in my head. I laughed to myself. I was sure Michael would have a better explanation than that.

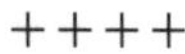

WHY THEY ARE COMMON

'The Opportunist' – Opportunities always present themselves in life, and he will always be willing to take advantage.

'The Rationaliser' – Everybody wants to know the reason for something occurring and more times than not there is a logical explanation. Rationalisation usually works well in solving most dilemmas for him.

'The Charmer' – He gets a huge ego boost from pleasing women. And what man doesn't enjoy being liked by women in return?

'The Sucker for Love' – 'Romance' is a state of mind. Some guys can feel just as romantic as women do and get lost in an unexplainable moment.

'The 'Back and Forth' – Hypocrites are commonplace because contradictions are commonplace in modern society. He is a reflection of the society we live in.

'Easily influenced' – There are only a few true leaders, a few trendsetters. The majority of people are followers and easily influenced in some way, shape or form.

EASILY INFLUENCED ♦

How this type looks / or comes across to women

The Easily Influenced man appears to lack belief and true independence. He is not naturally appealing to most women, although there are many men like this. He comes across as being indecisive and lacking assertiveness. He will rarely take charge of situations and can also be manipulated by his peers amongst others. This gets him into situations which may spin out of control as it is not based on his own decisions. **His insecurity relates to the fact that he is worried about what other people will think of him far too much. This can play havoc with his decision making process. Before he knows it he is in an uncomfortable situation usually not of his own making and he is forced to respond.**

THE CHARMER ♦

How this type looks / or comes across to women

The Charmer loves being the centre of attention especially when women are involved. His confidence is heightened in social situations and he comes alive with a flirtatious environment. He appears to have the gift of the gab. Wordplay comes with ease to him, and this lowers the barriers of females. In the early stages, the Charmer's charisma inhibits the female's ability to acknowledge and gain access to his driving insecurities. **His insecurity relates to him not fully loving himself as a person yet, so he chooses to lavish 'love' and superficial attention on others instead to compensate! Their responses to his behaviour provide him with an ego boosting sense of self-worth, whether it is actually real or not.**

BACK AND FORTH ♦

How this type looks / or comes across to women

This man comes across as very informed, intelligent and powerful. These are traits that a lot of women like – especially in older men. He is used to being correct and not many people question his judgement. But when times take a bad turn, he can appear to be hypocritical because his ideas are not always consistent. This at times makes his decisions seem very strange. It causes problems as he will rarely see (or acknowledge) his own contradictions. **His insecurity relates to rigidity and stubbornness in his thought and behaviour. He finds it difficult to be flexible. He believes what has worked previously should always work in the future, even if the circumstances beg to differ.**

THE RATIONALISER ♦

How this type looks / or comes across to women

The Rationaliser appears to always be thinking. He should not be confused with 'The Thinker', however. The Rationaliser has to understand whether his actions and those of others make sense. He is sometimes accused of being cold, uncaring or lacking emotions in sensitive situations. Women think that these men 'love' with their head rather than their heart, and to an extent this is true, as things that are not logical tend to be dismissed very quickly. **His insecurity relates to his over-appreciation of logic and not wanting to be seen as taking 'reckless irrational' risks. If it doesn't add up, then it doesn't make sense. He is not willing to lose everything on a gamble.**

THE OPPORTUNIST ●

How this type looks / or comes across to women

Opportunists are the type to ask suggestive questions. He will try to 'create' situations rather than allow them to happen naturally; he will have spotted an opening in the current circumstances and is prepared to go to the very end to exploit it. To some women who do not understand or really dislike his nature, he can appear sleazy or slightly pushy. **His insecurity relates to the fact that he feels he is not getting everything he deserves or thinks he is 'missing out on something'. He believes he needs to take every chance that comes his way because it may never come again. He doesn't like living with 'what if's'.**

THE SUCKER FOR LOVE ♦

How this type looks / or comes across to women

The Sucker for Love can seem very romantic and considerate. To a woman he comes across as the ideal first date; the kind of guy you would like to get to know a little bit better. He is the type of man you would like to show off to your friends or introduce to your mother. His initial ideas of relationships and love do not seem corny or made up. He actually sounds sincere and believes what he is saying. And this belief quickly convinces many women of this too. **His insecurity relates to not feeling completely loved or appreciated by others, so he creates idealistic moments to fill these hollow gaps in his armour. He longs to be loved. However, he struggles to express real love and devotion beyond the initial superficial stages of relationship formation. Anything beyond this scares him.**

Chapter 6 – 'An honest woman of you' – Maurice

As the train settled into its next stop, I wondered how many of the common types I'd actually encountered. I flicked quickly through the 'sure fire' signs to identify them. The majority of the men seemed to be more up Claire's path from their descriptions, but also mine, if I was being honest with myself. Was I a magnet for the common types? I knew getting between the sheets was probably high on the priority list of most guys, but do I come across as an easy lay? What was I putting out there that made them think that I should be their next target? I liked to think I was a friendly girl who was able to socialise with anyone, but do men misinterpret this as being 'up for it'? There must be a way to ward them off?

By this point, I was analysing every guy I had ever dated, slept with, or even just interacted with; including those secret rendezvous that not even Claire had any idea about. The flashbacks were swarming through my mind like a bees' nest; some memories made my stomach turn, while others brought a sly smile. Nevertheless, the entire exercise left me in no doubt that almost every guy I knew was full of it in some way or another.

Darren was one of my best friends. Not only was he educated, intelligent and successful, but he was also funny, charming and attractive. Everybody liked him, especially his beautiful girlfriend of six years. But even he cheated on her! I had asked him why on numerous occasions, displaying my disapproval, but simultaneously I sensed I was stepping into a place where I had no right to interfere. It was a moral dilemma; we were still friends regardless, but would Michael say I was indirectly justifying his behaviour because I disregarded it? I felt like the biggest hypocrite, but do you stop being friends with someone just because they'd made a poor decision in their personal lives? I supposed Darren was just another common type. Was this the case for every man that I knew?

No; it wasn't long before I remembered Maurice, and it brought relief to my overworked mind. There was no way on this earth that he was one of the common types.

Maurice had always been the gentleman. He was a couple of years older than me and had lived around the corner when I was growing up. At school he'd hung around with the popular guys, but he'd never really fitted in. They were into sports, sneaking out to concerts and throwing huge parties, and although Maurice was occasionally a participant, he was never the architect. He wasn't exactly the boy next door, but my mum loved him because he was impeccably polite and would call her by her surname, instead of 'Jackie', like the rest of my friends. What's more, he seemed determined to make something of his life; which is more than could be said for most boys at his age. Everybody in the area knew Maurice because he would always do odd jobs in the neighbourhood to make extra money: gardening, car washing, running errands, you name it. He always had the latest bike or computer game from the money he earned. Nobody had a bad word to say about him.

Even with all the girls he came across through the various activities in his life, Maurice always had a crush on ***me***. He would regularly remind me that I was the one he was going to marry; at the time I would nervously laugh this off! He always chose the wrong moment to say these things… like in front of the guys I was dating. I think he thought it was funny to create these awkward moments, but I just wanted to curl up and hide. I didn't like my boyfriend's making fun of him like they did. They called him a 'geek' as he never had any girls of his own. In retrospect, I never really stood up for Maurice as much I should have done. Mum was always confused as to why I would chase around these 'idiots' and in turn, be 'so horrible' to Maurice. I swear she would question me about it daily.

"He's such a nice lad," she would say affectionately.

And it was true; he was nice. He had a complete respect for everybody and was really close to his mum and younger brother. His dad had left the family when he was ten; no warning, no goodbye. It was at that moment that Maurice became the man of the house, long before he was ready for the responsibility. He never really spoke about it, but he was always certain that he would never follow in his dad's footsteps. They struggled financially for a long time after that, and I don't think his mother really recovered. It all seemed so hard, even for the strongest individual.

As he was so close to my family, he seemed to feel a sense of responsibility towards us too. Maurice's mum had always vowed that she would only have children to one man, with one family. He had no sisters, so he treated my little sister as if she were his own, always being protective of her. But he would go especially out of his way for me and this never changed, despite the jeers from my boyfriends.

I concluded in my head that I was not horrible to Maurice. It was more like I took his kindness for granted; he was just always around, so I thought he would never go away. He was the shoulder to cry on when the latest boy had dumped me for somebody else. He would do anything to cheer me up; riding his bike to my house in the pouring rain to tell me I deserved better. Even though I knew he had a crush on me, there seemed to be no obvious ulterior motive, he just had a heart of gold. It was nice that somebody still cared at times when I was feeling really low. In hindsight, Maurice was a really good friend.

After ten years of spurning his advances, I surprised myself when I actually accepted one of his offers of a date.

Time can play funny games with your thoughts; I had never considered Maurice in a romantic way before, but as the word 'yes' left my lips, I remember not being able to think of a reason why I shouldn't. Maurice was really surprised; I think he'd just asked me out of habit and had not anticipated a positive response, but he got himself together quite quickly. He arranged to take me out the following weekend, and as he left he said this was 'phase one of his plan to make an honest woman of me.'

I had no idea of what to expect. One thing that I did know, however, was that Maurice had grown to be everything I had expected him to be. He had bought his own home, and his career as an assistant primary school head teacher provided an above average salary. He drove a nice car and the investments he had made in his younger days had turned into a tidy additional source of income. This was the platform for his multiple holidays and social life which revolved around nice bars and the classiest restaurants. With no children at this stage in his life, he was able to lavish luxuries on himself. Nevertheless, he never did anything too crazy with his money, despite the freedom. He seemed to be really settled and the only thing that was missing was a family. All of this sounded brilliant, so why was I not interested?

Maurice and I dated for about six months, which if I am being honest, was probably about three months longer than it should have been. There were never any arguments, but simultaneously there aren't many significant memories I could recall either. Our conversations very quickly began to centre on Maurice's ideas about settling down, buying a bigger house and a future with kids.

"Not with each other, just hypothetically," he would point out.

I would have freaked out if he had mentioned my name in any of these plans so early. Nevertheless, with three promotions in five years, it wasn't surprising that his thoughts swayed in the direction of further stability and 'taking the next step'.

It was obvious to me quite early on that we were never going to be anything serious, but I didn't have the guts to end it. After all, he was so sweet and had never done anything wrong. Sometimes, people are just not right together, but to him I was perfect. That's what made it so difficult. I used to think there was something wrong with me; I was dating a solid guy with prospects beyond belief. He would be a great dad. Also, the passion he had for me – shown in his visions for the future and engaging recollections of our own childhood – was scorching. Having a man that would go to such lengths to express his emotion is what every girl desires!

Just not from him! His intentions were sweet, but simultaneously they turned me off faster than a light switch.

One night particularly stuck in my head. To mark our third or fourth month of dating, Maurice surprised me with an extravagant evening. I wasn't trying to be heartless, but this 'event' really wasn't significant for me, and I could tell he was unimpressed so I tried hard to disguise my apathy. He had booked a really nice restaurant and had arranged for a private driver to pick me up. On the seat adjacent to me sat four red roses being propped up by a gift-wrapped box. A display card read 'Do not open until midnight'. It killed me not to take a peek!

After a fifteen minute drive, I was escorted to a beautiful candlelit table in the centre of the restaurant. A pianist could be heard playing beautifully in the background. I realised that this part of the restaurant had been sectioned off exclusively. Maurice was waiting in an outstanding tailored suit, and as always, he made me feel like a lady as he pulled my chair out for me; the perfect gentlemen. The three-course meal was supplemented by my favourite bottle of rose champagne.

After leaving the restaurant, further pre-ordered champagne accompanied us at a few swanky bars and then to a five-star hotel suite. The drinking continued at a steady pace throughout the night and by midnight, I was a little more than tipsy. Nevertheless, I still had enough wits about me to appreciate what was inside the box; a stunning set of diamond earrings that seemed to illuminate the room and sober me up immediately! I threw my arms around him to show my gratitude, but at the same time I also had an unerring feeling of guilt. I wanted them badly but I couldn't accept such a gift. Could I? Maurice made the decision for me by pleading with me to put them on. Looking around at the luxurious décor that surrounded me, I complied with his request, mostly not to spoil his evening. And I thought to myself that I was having fun as we kissed on the queen-sized bed.

The next morning I awoke slightly hazy and tried to recall the events of the night before. I had a really good time… but not a ***great*** time, if that makes sense. The spark between Maurice and I was minimal at best, and because of this, I knew he would never be able to show me any more than just 'good'. Helen was the biggest advocate for 'growing to like someone'; she would have frowned at the fact that I wasn't giving it more of a chance, but nothing was happening. I kept the relationship going for about two months after that, and slowly stopped responding as frequently to his messages in order to let him down gently. I would make myself less available by making arrangements with the girls so I had valid excuses.

I wouldn't say he was a rebound, but to be honest, my first date with Maurice was only six months after I had split up with Nick, and I was still hurting. His dismantling of my self-esteem made me question my own self-perception and my confidence was at a massive low. So it was nice to feel wanted again, obtaining an affection that Nick had never really given me. Nevertheless, I wasn't ready for a mature relationship, no matter how badly I craved it. I always believed that I would never let a man break my spirit but I was wrong. I could not share all these emotions with the girls. I guess there are just a few things we keep to ourselves!

I did feel sorry for Maurice though. I had used him like a

comfort blanket, just like when we were kids. I had taken advantage of his kind nature in order to feel wanted, to feel attractive; to feel like a woman again. Perhaps I did give him a false impression and slightly lead him on, but I can see him making another woman very happy. There is a possibility that in a few years' time I'll be jealous. I'll look back and think to myself, *why didn't I stay with Maurice?* Especially if I've not found somebody by then!

Maurice was one of the good guys. He had wanted to build the family that he was deprived of. And he would never have cheated on me. It was obvious his dad running out on them had a profound effect on his beliefs. But I never gave myself a chance to find out, simply because there was no raw magnetic attraction.

Therefore, on the train, I was left to question whether my pickiness with partners was going to leave me as an old spinster. Maybe I needed to be more realistic; I had no real idea of what I was looking for anyway. Maybe I should have realised that unconditional love was not around the next corner and Maurice had actually been everything I needed. Even if he wasn't everything I wanted.

DID YOU SPOT THE SIGNS REVEALING HIS TYPE?

Chapter 7 – The *'Rarer'* Types

The 'rarer' types of men are as scarce as their name implies.

It is unlikely that many women will have dated such a man. So this chapter may appear abstract to some. But for those women that have, every syllable will be meaningful. Nevertheless, no matter who you are it is still important to recognise the rare types as he could be your friend, colleague or relative. There are several types of rare men who unlike their common counterparts do not share similar behaviours.

THE RARER TYPES OF MEN are:

- One Step Ahead
- The Swinger
- The Enigma
- The Woman's Mind

The rare types are far from average. They are unique and rarely conform to the norms. Each rare type of man tends to focus and define his life by one particular personality trait which sets him apart. Their chosen characteristic drives the majority of their thoughts and behaviours, at the particular time in their life when they discover its influence.

Most other types of men do not tend to be so focused in the way they live their lives. They instead have several drivers for their behavioural responses in relationships and everywhere else. Rarer types tend to place all of their eggs in the basket of one personality trait. This energises their motivations as they strive for a true sense of self-identity. The only facet of their characters that groups them together is that they are indeed rare.

THE 'RARE IDEA' OR THE 'RARE PERSON'?

Let's explore the concept of the word 'rare'. To a woman who is used to the approaches of the common types, the rarer ones may not sound so bad. After so many disappointments, any kind of difference can seem positive. In fact, when the word rare is generally used in society, it is implied that it is something fresh and new. That it will provide a break from the mundane life.

So do not expect a rare type to approach a woman in the supermarket, or to use a chat-up line in the club. Although they are not immune to this, it is not really their style. Therefore, without these obvious common behaviours in their interactions with females, it could be argued that our understanding of them in comparison to the common types is fairly limited. Although one distinct trait should be easier to spot, the rare types guard this with their lives.

Not many women have tales to share about a romantic situation with a rarer type. However, for the minority that have, nine times out of ten, the man will have left an undeniably significant mark on the woman's relationship recollections. The memory will live on, even if they go their separate ways. The rarer types will be brought up in conversation for storytelling purposes; comedic value or as a stiff warning for the benefit of friends who have not experienced one.

The females touched by a rarer type hope that other women can empathise with how difficult, confusing and emotionally tempestuous a situation with this kind of man can be. This is especially so if you have confused a rare man with a different type. You may realise that you misread the qualities that attracted you, leaving you in a psychological quandary; while those who haven't experienced one wondered what all the fuss was about.

Most people believe that 'rare' things are (more often than not) 'good' things. Your birthday for instance is a rare, but not always a good day. Rare artefacts discovered by archaeologists are championed as valuable and significant contributions to history; when in reality, they may just be very old, irrelevant objects.

> *"I feel like I understand what women go through. I'm an emotional guy and when you get hurt you wouldn't wish that pain on your worst enemy. I could never cheat and cause that pain to anyone."*
> *Chris, 'The Woman's Mind', aged Twenty-Four, Ipswich.*

For many women the idea of

a rare man is formulated in their minds as something which is desirably special or 'out of their reach'. When asked to describe a rare man, the consensus will conjure varying images of the archetypal 'Mr Perfect'. The value placed behind the word 'rare' misguidedly leads many to hold idealistic views believing that it is always something positive.

In reality, however, the rarer types of men tend to be far removed from this ideal. Instead, they may be the type to shock, upset, surprise or intrigue you; if not leaving you in a state of total disbelief. Take 'The Enigma' for instance, he knows that he causes problems, sometimes he revels in it. He needs the dysfunction caused in order to have normality. He sometimes has no idea that he is doing it, but always leaves a trail of confusion behind him.

The rare types have found that concealing their deepest wishes is a valuable ally to them. In Western society, it is believed that romantic relationships are supposed to have open lines of communication and disclosure; or at least aim to achieve this over time. This should limit shocking and surprising incidences. Partners can have confidence in each other and find comfort in the knowledge that they 'know' their partner. In the eyes of women, open communication may be a sign that the man is ready for commitment, responsibility and a wholly 'adult relationship'. No secrets, no hiding; but this is not always the case with a rare type.

★★★★

Many of us fail to find this openness, I thought disappointedly. I considered the countless number of women I knew, (myself included) who at some point, had found the search for a 'good' man seem comparable to a quest for the Lost Cities of Gold. *But then maybe it's our own fault for setting standards that are unreasonably high,* I contemplated.

A 'good' man is not as rare as many of us believe. Men like Maurice are everywhere, if you look closely enough. But we don't ***just*** want a good man. We want a good man with 'all the trimmings', otherwise dating is like eating dry

> *"I can understand why some men cheat because the emotions that people feel can be overwhelming. You cannot control it sometimes when your body is telling you to do something." Wesley, 'The Swinger', aged Twenty-Eight, London.*

apple pie. Maybe this is why people are sometimes initially attracted to the novel idea of 'rarity', even if it is just another dating illusion.

++++

THE RARE TRAITS

Any prolonged interaction with a rarer type is likely to create a 'flashbulb' memory; a recollection that you can recall in clear descriptive detail; regardless of whether the memory was positive or negative. The man may have been a grown-up mummy's boy; a reclusive introvert of few words; or a man with some personal 'interests' that most would not understand. Women will always remember the time spent with a rare type. Vividly!

Nevertheless, an experience with them starts off 'normally' to the average eye. They come across as either very quiet or extremely outgoing. Nothing too much is out of the ordinary. If you spend enough time with them, however, you will see that these men are definitely individuals in every sense of the word; failing to 'follow the rules' with their distinctive and unforgettable traits. You may stumble across a secret of theirs that is so uncommon, that it becomes ***your*** secret too. Out of confusion, necessity or embarrassment, you try to protect it as well.

During their formative years, the rarer types may appear to struggle with having a clear self-identity. This is something we can all have trouble with, but for these men it can be especially challenging. For example, they may find it difficult to fit in with other people. This can cause him problems in social situations. When everybody else seems to be handling them like a duck to water, rarer types may feel like they are drowning. These struggles are a continuous burden to this type of man and because of it, your relationship situation may become turbulent as many rare types learn to direct their energies inwards.

"The reason why people make mistakes in relationships is because they do not plan properly. When everybody is running around like a headless chicken, I like to stay calm and not panic. " Jonathan, 'One Step Ahead', aged Thirty-One, Southend.

They can become unnecessarily angry, disappointed or upset with themselves, thus, resulting in social isolation and marginalisation –

psychologically if not always physically – from people who have no idea about the inner conflicts within them. They may not recognise that in the information age, people do not always have the energy, or the time, to invest completely in their journey.

THE RARE PERCEPTION

Some rarer types of men hold the perception that other people fail to understand the volcanic emotions stirring beneath their surface; consisting of their desires, needs or feelings. They interpret the empathetic attempts made by others, as superficial and therefore unsustainable. They may feel that any interest shown in them personally will wane over time and therefore, any efforts the man makes in response are futile.

To counteract this, many rare types create diverse, wide-reaching social networks; searching for any person who may understand and invest in them. Befriending people who, based on first impressions, seem to be their polar opposites isn't uncommon. For instance, it wouldn't be peculiar for a rarer type to have a close friend who is more than twice their age during their teenage years. Their unique circumstances can cause them to appear mysterious or bizarre to those with whom they have very little rapport.

Many rarer types possess a strong indifference to being open. Thus, they are introverted; keeping their feelings locked inside because they are unsure how they would harness them again if they were exposed. This is a huge fear that they have. This can be the platform to secretive and aloof behaviour. Although ***appearing*** distant, they remain uncannily aware of their surroundings at all times.

Nevertheless, the rarer types exist on a spectrum and therefore, some may show the complete opposite to this introverted behaviour.

Figure 1. The introvert/extrovert spectrum: the average positioning of the rarer types

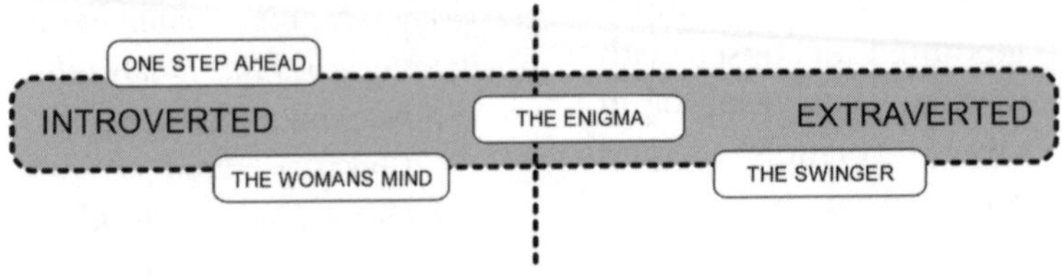

THE OTHER SIDE OF THE COIN

The emotions of the extroverted version of the rarer types are uncomfortably contained. Their bottled energy may be compulsively expressed in erratic displays of exuberance that verge on anti-social. There's no missing the behaviour of a rarer type of man if he's an extrovert. Random, over the top arguments, emotional outbursts and/or inappropriate shows of expression with no clear explanation may be all too familiar.

Many rarer types have not come to terms with their own personality traits, so it is likely their introverted/extraverted responses will continue throughout adult life. For example, 'The Woman's Mind' type may not fully understand why he worries about everybody else and may disregard his own development because of his over-focus on others.

In the case of the extraverted rarer types, this lack of awareness can lead to uncontrolled emotions such as anger, denial or a dislike for oneself. Unlike the introverted version (who turn the emotions on themselves), the extraverted ones project them onto other people. This can make the search for identity seem like an extremely lonely journey – even if they have people trying their hardest to accompany them.

MY DOMINANT TRAIT, MY COMPANION

Whilst this journey is commencing, for any of the rarer types, they find one quality within them that holds a lot of value or personal significance. They can rely on this characteristic to never desert them. They can define themselves by it and shape their personalities around it. No matter what happens, they stick with it. Whether infidelity becomes a part of their make-up, depends on how well the justification schema fits with their defining trait.

> *"Sometimes, I don't even know myself what I am going to do from one minute to the next. It's not like I have a plan. I just end up doing things or not doing them."*
> *David, 'The Enigma',*
> *aged Thirty-Seven, Huddesrfield.*

The trait could be something as simple as 'I am organised,' for the 'One Step Ahead' type or 'I am caring' for 'The

Woman's Mind'. It could also be something more intricate such as 'I'm complicated, nobody can understand me' by 'The Enigma'. Regardless of what the trait is for each type, they believe ***'This is who I am'***. Any incompatible traits in others are quickly disregarded or ignored. If differing traits do not mould well with their dominant characteristic, this can make dealing with a rarer type awkward and uncomfortable, especially in conversation. Many a social gathering has been interrupted by a clash between a rare type and someone with different views.

★★★★

I looked away from the book for a moment and contemplated. I didn't think that I'd ever dated a rarer type of man and because of this, it was difficult to imagine what a relationship would be like with one. But I was sure that I had made the acquaintance of a fair few in my time – at both extremes of the spectrum. Glancing at their characteristics, I decided Simon would definitely be on this list; a 'Swinger' if there ever was one!

Claire and I had known Simon since sixth-form college. Initially, we thought he was a little bit strange, conflicted even. His bright outfits and penchant for attention seeking definitely drew a few curious looks and rubbed some people up the wrong way. Anything he could do to get noticed, he quickly considered. Everybody in the college knew him for playing outrageous pranks such as 'mooning' out of the classroom windows. It was a little immature for sixth-form, but none of the other students took him seriously anyway. They knew what he was about.

We became friends as he sat next to me in A-Level Sociology. He was always making contradictory and controversial statements in class. One minute championing the arguments of Shulasmith Firestone, the next, claiming every home should have a patriarchal head. Even so, I admired his confidence and we soon started chatting.

Simon's trademark shriek would always garner attention. But it wasn't long before we started suspecting why he always needed to be like this. It also struck us why he never gave his 'dates' a real chance or saw a picture of any of them, let alone met them. He could be extremely argumentative when people would question him about his personal life outside of the college. But four years later, Simon asked to go for coffee, admitting that he had been keeping a ***big*** secret for a long time. I remember the serious tone in his voice, the only time the shriek had ever been absent.

"Liv, I've got something to tell you. You'd better sit down, you'll probably be shocked."

It took everything inside me to hold myself together and not burst out laughing. Like everyone in the world didn't know that Simon was gay! He seemed so vulnerable but I loved him even more after that. Nevertheless, I played along and made sure I reassured him by acting really surprised and supportive. Maybe I could be an actress.

++++

WHY THEY ARE RARE – THE TRAITS THEY FOCUS ON

'One Step Ahead' – He needs complete organisation. He never leaves anything to chance. He is always one step ahead because of this focus.

The 'Swinger' – This man just wants to express his individual freedom whenever possible. He may feel extremely trapped without this.

The 'Enigma' – 'Who am I?' His understanding of his own personal identity (or lack of) is his focus. And if he's not sure, how can anybody else be?

The 'Woman's Mind' – He focuses completely on how others feel. Empathy is his dominant trait. He is very rare.

ONE STEP AHEAD ♦

How this type looks / or comes across to women

The 'One Step Ahead' type appears cool, calm and collected at all times. For him, patience is a virtue; he never rushes and always seems to be in control. He definitely comes across as a man in charge as he has understood that self-control is a skill, something to master. He knows that 99% of the population do not possess this and it puts them at risk. He refuses to be part of this group. **His insecurity relates to allowing others to make decisions on his behalf. He does not like this. It has to be on his terms at all times to feel anywhere near comfortable. The only risks being taken will be calculated ones made solely by him, even if he pretends to make the other person feel they were involved in the process.**

THE SWINGER ■

How this type looks / or comes across to women

The 'Swinger' may be hiding something; a secret or a desire. He may not be sure of it himself or maybe he doesn't want to admit it. But on the other hand, it may be as obvious as day and they are struggling to contain their new found psychological liberation. The 'Swinger' is either extremely extravagant and outgoing or heavily closed and reserved. They are rarely in the middle. **His insecurity relates solely to acceptance; he is driven by it. To see who will continue to accept him, extroverts show people the most outrageous sides of their character. For introverts, their personality becomes a 'living secret' and they see which people persevere to 'unlock' this secret. Both of these behaviours are driven by the need for acceptance from others to fulfil their self-identity.**

THE ENIGMA ➔

How this type looks / or comes across to women

The first impression of this type of man may be 'mysterious'; therefore intriguing. He can seem dangerous and will lure women in with his compelling story. He does not seem like your average 'common' type of guy. He may share some characteristics with them but there is... something else; hidden and elusive, under the surface. Magnetic at first, you cannot help but be drawn to him. **His insecurity relates to not fully understanding who he is. So he feels it's hard to believe that anybody else could truly understand him either. He feels that his daily existence is a complicated puzzle. Perhaps with one piece missing being the root cause of his angst and difficulties. He searches for it, sometimes causing destruction on the way.**

THE WOMAN'S MIND ■

How this type looks / or comes across to women

This man is very in touch with his feelings. Initially, he reassures you and makes you feel comfortable with his surprising amount of empathy. Women may connect with him on all of the right levels except the one that counts in these circumstances: as a potential partner. Nevertheless, he is definitely somebody women want to keep around and as a part of their lives (perhaps selfishly). **His insecurity relates to a feeling of inequality. He sincerely dislikes how one collective in society can have more influence, opportunities or rewards than another just because they are part of an 'in-group'. He feels this especially related to women and internalises their experiences on himself, almost sharing their pains and joys.**

Chapter 8 – 'I wish my girl was as understanding as you' – Ramone

I was soon home. The book had to be put on hold as the heavens made a relentless pursuit to drench me after exiting the train. As I entered my apartment, I noticed two missed calls from Claire and a text from Sasha. I wasn't ignoring them. I had just been so engrossed in the book that I hadn't even noticed. I ***would*** reply eventually, but if it was between having a nothing chat with Claire or reading the next chapter, my mind was already made up.

Before delving into the book again, I decided to send Michael a quick text to say thanks; and also to say how nice it had been to see him again. I fished his business card out of the rubble in my bag, but paused before hitting the send button. I didn't want to come across as too eager, but then we were friends. I was sure he wouldn't see it any other way.

I flicked through a few more pages of the 'sure fire' signs whilst my phone confirmed that my text had been sent. *It's done now*. I thought.

My attention was soon recaptured from my momentary distraction, as I realised that Ramone, another man from my past, was described quite accurately in the 'sure fire' signs too. Playing on his father's Spanish heritage and his sultry brooding looks, Ramone already had most girls' attention before he had even spoken a word. He was always going to have more female attention than a sale in a designer store anyway. So the wonderful things that came out of his mouth were just the icing on the cake. It was like he was possessed by the soul of a poet laureate with the way he constructed his sentences. His tongue was dipped in caramel.

"I wish my girl was as understanding as you," he would say. Most women wouldn't admit it in public as it sounds 'bitchy', but we love nothing more than 'winning' against any other female we are compared to. We don't like coming second best to another girl;

it's as simple as that. Secretly, some of us love it when a man puts us on a pedestal and Ramone was an expert at making me feel that way. He hardly had to work to have me in the palm of his hands. I was warned. Everybody said he was a 'player', and to be fair, I knew he had a string of girls after him. But he enticed me. I couldn't explain the hold he had over me. I was always lost for words.

The most confusing thing about our relationship was that even though I should have despised the game he played with me, I just couldn't. Perhaps this was because I didn't think Ramone was maliciously trying to upset me or any of the other women who gagged for his attention. He was genuinely a nice guy, one of the most naturally caring men I had ever met.

I met him a few years ago through a group of mutual friends. Sasha had arranged an evening out one night after work. We noticed Ramone sitting with a couple of our male colleagues as we approached. Although attractive, he didn't seem anything too special to begin with, quietly blending into the background. As soon as we made ourselves known, however, he sparked into life.

Ramone was witty, but at the same time, polite and courteous. He was soon grabbing the attention of everyone around him, and as more friends joined during the course of the evening, he grew in stature. Everybody was gravitating toward him, and the more women that were present, the more his confidence seemed to flourish. There was no flirting or any sexual charge that first night, but he had definitely made a positive impression on me.

Ever since that first evening, Ramone had always looked out for me. We went clubbing a lot at that time. Whenever he saw my friends and I waiting for a taxi at the end of the night, he would always offer us all a lift home. "Hey 'livia! Where are you going?" He would say, rolling down his window, with that accent that always made my ears melt. It was one of those rhetorical questions that loosely translated to 'get in the car'. If it was any other guy, it would have seemed sleazy, but not Ramone; I guess my initial schema for him had been a positive one. I was always secretly hoping that my house was the last stop (but so were each of my friends!). He had an amazing knack of interacting with us all without singling anybody out. It kept every one of us captivated and wondering whether he could possibly find us as attractive as we found him.

I became better friends with Ramone after a chance meeting at a hotel in Manchester. I was on a training course with my line manager whilst he was on an overnight stay with work too. One evening, after my training had finished, I was more than happy to accept his invitation for a few drinks in the hotel bar. On a one-to-one basis, I discovered that Ramone was a very interesting man; deep and spiritual. He had a fond appreciation of novels and was well travelled, visiting so many different countries, on every continent. He had a great passion for discovering new places and cultures after living in Spain, Thailand and the UK all before the age of fourteen.

As he recounted his unique experiences, I quickly realised that I could listen to him for hours. But it was the fact that Ramone himself was an excellent listener that allowed our friendship to blossom. Most other guys I knew loved the sound of their own voice. He looked directly at me as I explained about my struggles with my career and whether or not it was the right time to move on to another job. As I spoke, I knew that I was moaning, which wasn't attractive at all but Ramone genuinely took an interest in everything that I had to say. The cynical side of me would believe that he was trying to entice me to his hotel room. However, that appeared to be the furthest thing from Ramone's mind and I lowered my guard immediately.

We began to speak regularly after Manchester. I had become intoxicated by his presence. His voice was always reassuringly competent when he provided answers to my dilemmas; so much so, that I used to wonder why I had worried about them in the first place. Who needed the problem page in the glossy magazines when Ramone was handling my problems with the skill of a craftsman? Occasionally, we would meet up for coffee or lunch, but it wasn't a regular thing so I always looked forward to it. He would make our meetings sound like the highlight of his day. He made me feel like my actions had a purpose, like the fact I had even turned up was doing something important for him. It made me feel like I was number one. So I would try that little bit harder for him.

And it wasn't just me; Ramone was a hit with all the ladies, old and young. One Saturday evening we were chatting on the phone as usual and I was telling him about my hell of a day. I had taken my youngest sister Jessica shopping with me and after hours of trawling around the city centre, the day ended in tears. She had lost her favourite teddy on the bus journey home. She was absolutely distraught. The next afternoon, Ramone showed up at my house.

He had driven several miles across town especially to present Jessica with a brand new, gift-wrapped, custom-made teddy bear. It was one of those that you build in the shop. You should have seen the look on her face when he pulled it out the bag; it was a beautiful moment. I couldn't believe anyone would be so wonderful and unexpectedly kind. He even played with Jessica for about twenty minutes before going through an elaborate naming ceremony. To this day, Jessica still asks how Ramone is.

He was always full of surprises, going that extra mile to leave you grinning like a Cheshire cat. I decided that this guy was in the higher echelons of manhood. It was his aura that captured you, not his looks. He made you breathe him in. I felt like the chosen one.

Unfortunately, I wasn't the only girl who felt that way, which was understandable. Could you really believe Ramone was single? Alongside his other female friends, Melissa was his long-term girlfriend. Our relationship grew to the point where he felt comfortable enough to talk to me about their problems. Normally, I would feel uncomfortable about this. If the shoe was on the other foot I would hit the roof if my man was confiding in another woman. But I rationalised it in my own mind that I wasn't overstepping the boundary because we were just friends. It's funny how hypocritical we can all be when it suits us.

In his usual composed and considered manner, Ramone chose his words carefully when speaking about Melissa. He made sure he didn't badmouth her or shift the blame for any situations; nevertheless, he did explain how things hadn't been great between them for a while. He felt unfulfilled; sexually, intellectually and emotionally. In a strangled tone (that betrayed his usual fluency), he told me that he'd tried to reach Melissa on every level, but she'd always remained… beyond him.

I couldn't believe that any woman would take Ramone for granted. It made me despise her at times. But that may have been envy more than anything. He'd told me he longed to one day meet a woman with qualities like mine who would help him become whole. I felt fifty feet tall. We never crossed the physical line, even after he and Melissa had been separated for three months. At first, he seemed like he just wanted somebody to listen. So for the millions of times he had heard my tales of heartbreak, I returned the favour. With no girlfriend on the scene, we were able to meet up more frequently for our discussions. I was now the one who he confided in, and as time progressed, inevitably, who he also shared a bed with.

But as I said before, I wasn't the only female magnetised by Ramone. They swarmed to him like bees to pollen. For a short period of time, I revelled in being his 'number one', but I hated the attention that he garnered. On evenings out at the local bar, I felt the piercing stares of women who detested our connection. But Ramone was just as delightful as ever. Not dissimilar to Nick, we were all flies caught in this different type of web, him being the spider at the centre, but taking his time before devouring us all.

What's more, his 'women' never vented their frustrations towards him; we directed our hostilities onto each other. I couldn't have told Ramone not to talk to women that he knew before me just because of my insecurity. I wasn't suspicious of him, I just didn't like it. And as I said, he wasn't doing it maliciously; he just naturally charmed any woman he came into contact with. Secretly though, I think he loved it.

He'd still devote loads of time to me, much more than any other partners had done in the past. But he'd completely blurred the lines of what was cheating and what wasn't. I was unsure as to whether his behaviour could be categorised as such because he'd never hide anything. He was the same with everybody, and because of his alluring demeanour and appearance of sincerity, I never really challenged him on it.

For all his qualities, I could never have been truly happy with Ramone. Deep down, I knew I wouldn't have ever been completely number one. When I was 'the friend' he was the greatest, always being there for me. When I was 'the girlfriend', his behaviour made me feel so insecure. And he wouldn't have changed; it was in his nature. He was an expert at filling the gaps where women felt they were missing something. Doing the 'little things' that no-one else would do or could be bothered too. That's what made him stand out. He just had to do it; he couldn't help himself. We still stay in touch.

DID YOU SPOT THE SIGNS REVEALING HIS TYPE?

Chapter 9 – The *'Appealing'* Types

Let's deal with the myths. The 'appealing' types aren't immune to problems, insecurities or disagreements. Nor are they immune to cheating; this isn't a fairy tale. Of course, that doesn't make them sound any different to those men that constantly try to orchestrate a new sexual situation, even though they are already attached to another woman. Fairy tales seldom occur in a world where realism – from time to time – likes to slap you in the face just for giggles. But there is a light at the end of the tunnel…

THE APPEALING TYPES are:

- The Secure Man
- The Modern Man
- The Family Man
- The Appreciator
- The Thinker
- The Visionary

****

What made these men appealing then? I pondered as the different names darted across my line of vision. The fact that they were susceptible to the same problems as every other guy sounded completely disheartening. Could it be that there really weren't any good men in the world? I felt like throwing the book at the wall, but continued to read. I was instantly reassured for my slight overreaction to these types.

++++

FUTURE-ORIENTED TIME PERSPECTIVE

The appealing types of men are not held back by the problems identified earlier, that seem to ail other types of men. They are equipped through their perspectives on life to deal effectively with most challenges that come their way. By using effective assessment of their experiences and willingness to consider those had by others, they are more accomplished. Even though the appealing types are surrounded by the same issues as other men, they are not ***afflicted*** by them as such. Instead, one of their traits buffers them from many of the hazards that trip up other types of men; they have a unique 'perspective of time'.

This is based on a concept developed by the famous social psychologist Philip Zimbardo. The way that an appealing type of man views 'time' is central to understanding the way he behaves.

The appealing types possess what Zimbardo would call a 'future-oriented' time perspective. This is characterised by traits such as patience and considering the consequences of his actions. He is able to defer his gratification. This is the ability to put off immediate satisfaction of his desires, in the belief that he will be rewarded later for demonstrating self-control now. Out of the six time perspectives that Zimbardo categorised, this is the most beneficial for forming long-lasting, 'fully grown' relationships that move forward. Being future-oriented also contributes to the appealing types being less prone to cheating than their counterparts.

There is a famous illustration of this time perspective in the Mischel 'Marshmallow' experiment. Children as young as four years old were given the choice to either eat a marshmallow immediately or to control their urges for immediate gratification, (a future-oriented time perspective), and be rewarded with two after a short period of time. Mischel found those children who were able to control their need for immediate gratification, were more likely to be trustworthy, self-reliant and do better in school several years later. The children who couldn't control their urges, (a present-hedonistic time perspective), grew up to be impulsive and stubborn.

MATURITY AND APPEALING CHARACTERISTICS

In addition to this trait, appealing types also possess other fundamental qualities that most women crave, including:

- Security and commitment

- Physical and mental strength
- Determination and effective communication
- The ability to trust and be trusted

Although an abdominal region with more bumps than a roller coaster; or a profile picture that would not look out of place in GQ magazine may be incredibly desirable, it is the above characteristics that really single these men out. Put simply, these men are appealing because they achieve a fundamental characteristic of ***'maturity by assessment.'***

This may seem like an obvious statement but most people claim to 'recognise' maturity when they see it, but struggle to 'explain' what it is with any certain clarity. However, one thing is for sure, maturity does ***not*** come with just age; nor does it come with just experience. Regardless of what the generational myths may suggest, maturity comes from ***effective*** assessment of one's experiences.

We all have insecurities, even the appealing men and women on the planet. But with this attribute, appealing men are more capable at dealing with their own insecurities efficiently. They objectively assess their own influences and decisions instead of being pre-occupied with psychological defence mechanisms. Therefore they are less likely to impose their own issues onto others. They do not automatically seek to protect themselves from ridicule, 'the obvious' or the judgement of others. They do not search for information around them to instantly justify their desires and beliefs. This implies that men who possess these traits will be less likely to justify infidelity.

Appealing types are the men who can 'get over their own egos' and are not driven by their sexual bravado and/or inadequacies. They are not intimidated by independent women and they find more efficient ways of dealing with conflict than immediately resorting to confrontation or domination.

★★★★

This is what I wanted to know! I thought, sitting upright on my sofa. I was prone to meeting the type of guy who had turned lying into an Olympic sport. Or worse, those inflicted with 'Peter Pan Syndrome', refusing to ever grow up. They wanted me to be a mother to them, not an equal. But I didn't want to iron his clothes, make his lunch or tidy up after him, unless I chose to do so myself. I didn't plan on having children for a few more years yet, so why would I have wanted an adult version? Thinking about the number of guys like that, polluting the planet, frustrated me. But finally we were getting to the bottom of which types women really need. These were the guys in the rom-coms and novels; the guys who until now had elusively been out of my grasp!

I felt determined that I hadn't met any of these guys yet, but Michael suggested otherwise. According to him, I had met lots of appealing types, but whether I had paid ***attention*** to them was a different story.

++++

PATIENCE IS THEIR VIRTUE

Although beauty is in the eye of the beholder, some appealing types are immediately obvious to everybody. They are attractive with a kind heart, a good personality and a self-actualising nature. And usually, they are already taken! Most women know a good thing when they see it and don't waste time hanging around. On the other hand, some appealing types are not as easy to pick out of the crowd.

These men don't tend to go scouting at the local bar or gym looking for you. They ***will*** have a range of priorities in their life i.e. work or family commitments and finding the correct woman may not be the only one. They tend to use patience well in most areas of their lives. Therefore, the appealing types don't go fishing, casting a wide net, trying to catch something whenever they see water. They choose the right moments and the right oceans. This is a quality they possess that separates them from the general masses. They are the men that women find themselves uncontrollably drawn to. They almost always make an impression!

Appealing types also possess the following characteristics to complement their patience:

- Confidence,
- Assertiveness,
- Ambition,

- Decisiveness
- Unique charisma.

Meeting men with an outstanding combination of these traits can cause many women to miss a heartbeat. But be careful, as engaging with men with an exciting combination of these traits can lower your defences. You may be seduced into not paying attention and as a result, frequent errors in identification occur.

Confusing a man's type is an easy slip-up to make.

This is because the above qualities are not only characteristic in the potentially appealing 'good' partners, but can also be found in ***abundance*** in the 'get rid' and the 'common' types. This is why most women have also had experiences of a 'bad' partner. One who was confident and stunning to look at, but had as much depth as a bar of soap. Or a charismatic charmer, who had you eating out of the palm of his hand; before you realised that you were not the only lady lapping up those sugar cubes.

As the above examples illustrate, these characteristics are not the 'be all and end all' in the quest for a fulfilling union between two people. But in the early honeymoon stage for a couple, a combination of these traits is usually what provides the quintessential 'spark' that most people believe a relationship requires to 'get off the ground'. We have all disposed of a potential relationship situation citing 'no spark' as the reason.

WOMEN AND THE APPEALING TYPES

When a potentially good relationship doesn't work out, people habitually search for blame. This is usually laid at the other person's door. Of course, there could be a justifiable reason to do this. However, more often than not, individuals need to take a closer look at the role they played themselves. For example, there is no such thing as 'the right guy at the wrong time'. He was just the wrong guy – full stop. Phrases like this are

> *"I trust my fiancé with my life, without a second thought. She gives me everything I need that I cannot get alone. And I give her everything back in equal measure. I no longer need anything else." Andrew, 'The Secure Man', aged Thirty, Leicester.*

commonly used to give a bruised ego a boost. It maintains the belief that we are still a viable option to the opposite sex.

If the guy didn't fully satisfy her needs, perhaps she needs to reassess what her needs actually are. If she hasn't really thought about this, her search for an appealing type may be futile. Even if every one of the appealing characteristics sounds ideal, that doesn't make them right. In recognising what traits she ***requires*** rather than ***desires***, she will not only be able to attract him, but effectively interact with him and keep him when he presents himself.

As well as recognising him, it is essential that a woman recognise ***herself*** too. Many women do not. In the search for an appealing man, many women mistakenly assume that they are already (and always have been) the pristine image of a perfect partner; regardless of their age, experiences or attributes. This being the case, men should just hop on board and enjoy the ride. The woman possesses the map to the perfect destination. If that boat capsizes at any point, it is of course the men that caused the ripples in the ocean. This scenario may sound sarcastic, but it is in fact a well hidden truth that sometimes women need to mature too. That is, of course, if they want to effectively interact with him and bring out the best in each other.

Could you really recognise yourself in a personality mirror?

KNOWING YOUR OWN TIME PERSPECTIVE

Although a positive self-concept is essential for both partners in any solid relationship, sometimes we all (men and women alike) need to look at ourselves from a different point of view. For a woman, identifying the patterns of an appealing type may include recognising her own perspective of time. Just like some of her male counterparts, many women can be 'present-hedonistic' too. A time perspective dominated by impatience and the 'here and now', aimed at maximising pleasure and avoiding pain.

This can be observed in many women who are childless around the age of thirty-plus. It may appear silent to the rest of us, but many women hear their 'biological clock' ticking like a time-bomb. If they see having children as a 'now or never' situation, then a present hedonistic perspective may be adopted. Their romantic relationship may be affected as a consequence. Men and women embalmed in a present hedonistic time perspective are more prone to using the information around them to justify their actions; infidelity may be a consequence.

This desire for immediate gratification in the 21st century is found in as many young women as men. With the persuasive messages in celebrity magazines and reality TV, it is no surprise that immediate gratification is the norm. The desire to be with a man of high social status and financial power above all else is trending for many. It is no longer the exception, it is fast becoming the rule; a by-product of the information age. As a result, these present hedonistic traits are unlikely to produce long lasting relationships, (illustrated by the increasing rates of divorce) and many appealing types are simply being overlooked.

In these 'manufactured' relationships characteristic of the information age, the chances of the justification schema being used increases.

Relationships are never straightforward; and even more notoriously difficult to maintain. Nevertheless, women play an enormously positive role in assisting the appealing types to become the men they are. No man fulfils his appealing potential on his own, because a relationship is a ***reciprocal*** process. When women look at the situation objectively, they will see the real contributions she makes towards this. But for any potential to be achieved, a woman has to first free herself from the shackles of ***presumptive schemas***, so she can connect with appealing types without prejudice and misinterpretation based on any prior negative experiences with men.

For present hedonistic women, this can be harder to do. But it is evident that the automatic questions asked by some women, such as "Why can't I find a good man?" need to be rephrased. Perhaps replacing them with something along the lines of, "Why don't I connect with the appealing types that I meet?" would be more appropriate.

"I have two young girls, Hannah and Rebecca from a previous relationship. They are my world and I am the main example of a man in their life. I want to be a positive example. Any woman I meet has to share the same values to help bring my daughters up correctly."
Mark, 'The Family Man',
aged Thirty-Six, Birmingham.

THE ALLURE OF THE RISK-TAKER

As mentioned earlier, the appealing types are attractive to women because they show clear signs of emotional and psychological growth in their patterns of behaviour. When this is coupled with calculated risk-taking (a trait that has been fundamental and beneficial to human advancement for millions of years; including everything from technology to human rights), these men become extremely alluring. Many accomplishments of man have been achieved by those risk-takers prepared to go the extra mile for what they believe in. As a woman, you have to be ready to ***see*** this and ***support*** this to make it easier for an appealing type to fulfil his potential.

Evolutionary psychologists have argued that risk-taking men in the past were more successful in attracting females, finding new land and acquiring food resources. Risk-taking held huge survival and social opportunities for our male ancestors. Research in 2010, found that risk-taking behaviour still occurs in men today. And it actually ***increases*** in the presence of an attractive woman (Ronay and van Hippel 2010). Nevertheless, there is a thin line between ***risk-taking*** and ***recklessness***. When the risks taken are more foolhardy than intelligent, both survival and social benefits for the man decline (Pawlowski et al 2008).

In modern society, this risk-taking is sometimes interpreted by women as either showing off or arrogance. But simultaneously may also explain why women are drawn to the archetypal 'bad boy' (The Stupid Mistake or The Lads' Lad for example), as they mistake him for the attractive risk-taker. Maybe when women are younger, some feel the need to experience this type of man. However, men who manage to get the balance correct are appealing to ***all*** women.

Never sitting around and waiting for things to happen, the appealing types display the potential for ***loyalty*** and ***determination***, financial ***stability*** and good parenting material. He is ***resilient*** and protective in times of crisis. He is well equipped to deal with her insecurities and he simultaneously brings out the best in her. In times when a woman is distressed, his

> *"Life is all about choices; I pride myself on doing my best at making the correct ones in my life." Jason, 'The Thinker', aged Thirty-Eight, Manchester.*

resiliency encourages you to regain your strength. He is the type of man who is ***proud*** for you to walk by his side as his equal; he learns from his mistakes and deals ***responsibly*** with the consequences of his actions. All in all, these attributes are signposts directing women down the road to happiness. He does not look for the easy way out. These are patterns of behaviour you should look for in his character.

But what is preventing women making a connection in a relationship with these men?

RECIPROCITY AND THE THREE RELATIONSHIP STRANDS

The biggest barrier preventing any woman from having a loving and reciprocal relationship with an appealing type is simple – they are just not ready to. True mutual leaps of relationship faith contain ***reciprocal respect and belief in the other person***. Just because ***she*** will walk barefoot around the world for her partner doesn't make it a good relationship, most notably if he wouldn't do the same for her (or vice versa).

Appealing types are not intimidated by your past whether it is positive, negative or overbearing. Nor is he threatened by the potential of your future; he supports it. He wants to enhance his own happiness by building a life together and experiencing your individual development alongside you. This means he ***will not play games with emotions*** to keep you under control. He won't hold things against you (like throwing the past in your face) just to get the upper-hand. In this, he understands the simple 'Three Strands' theory that forms the basis of any healthy relationship.

The Three Strands theory states that every successful relationship must have three essential aspects within the foundation. In relation to intimate heterosexual relationships, these strands are 'His Life', 'Her Life' and 'The Life Together'. If any of these strands do not exist, the relationship becomes over-dependent on the other two (or even worse – one strand). For example, one partner giving up every feature of their individual life to cocoon themselves in the life together or immerse themselves in their partners lives, friends and activities. This may include cutting communication with their own friends and family and giving up regular activities to spend the majority of their time with their partner.

This makes it almost impossible to carry the entire weight of the relationship, precipitating problems. This outcome may significantly increase the risk of breakdown and perhaps for some men, utilisation of the justification schema that can lead to infidelity. As separate entities that bind together to create a successful relationship, the three strands must ***all*** co-exist, working both exclusively and inter-dependently.

Figure 2 – Depicting a healthy relationship with all three strands working exclusively and inter-dependently

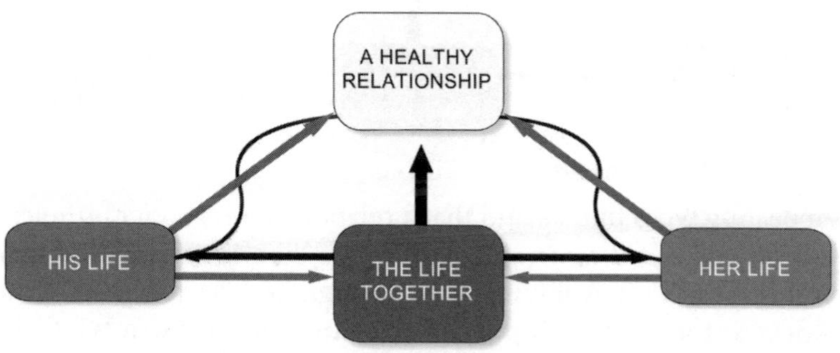

It's inevitable that the two individuals will have to alter their personal lives in some way. But both partners ***must*** retain their individual identity – while initiating compromise – in order for the relationship to survive. A common and fundamental mistake made in many relationships, is that one partner tries to eliminate the other partner's individual life or someone voluntarily gives theirs up (an 'Under the Thumb' or 'Easily Influenced' type perhaps).

Some people may incorrectly consider that doing this is a necessary and beneficial sacrifice for the 'life together'. However, it is a mistake, for example, to give up going out with your ***own*** friends; although we are aware that it happens frequently. If this occurs, it is likely that the relationship will live permanently in the stages of relationship breakdown. This is something that only some mature men (like the appealing types) can understand.

The appealing types of men are unlikely to allow their life to be taken away. Nor will they do this to you, as it is selfishly unfair. He may put up with some unreasonable matters on occasion – in the usual relationship ups and downs – but in the end he sees the bigger picture.

Figure 3 – Depicting an unhealthy relationship with one strand missing and the remaining strands not working inter-dependently

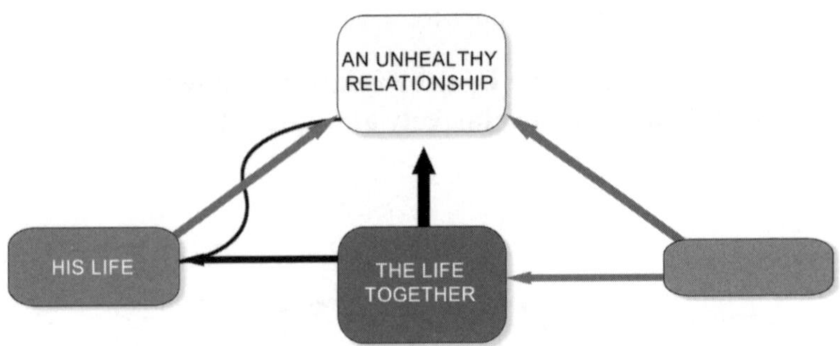

Appealing types understand that a relationship is about ***continuous growth and maintenance***. He realises the 'honeymoon period' will end and cannot possibly see him through decades together. So he works at the relationship. Human nature dictates that we feel a greater sense of achievement at the things that we have worked for, rather than those handed to us on a plate. Appealing types work to consider his partner's perspective; ***involving*** her in his decision making and ***appreciating*** the things that she finds important. He understands that ***supporting his partner mentally*** is a major part of emotional growth, but he will also be ***accountable*** for his independent decisions. These are all further patterns of his behaviour that you can identify.

HOWEVER…THE APPEALING TYPES ARE NOT PERFECT

Despite these plus points, as highlighted earlier, the appealing types aren't angels free from arguments, disagreements nor infidelity. They aren't perfect. Women cannot make the mistake or believe that the appealing men are immune to cheating; just as no woman is immune to cheating either. It is assumed in an adult relationship that superficial things such as looks, excitement, selfishness and public status are overruled by personality, stability, altruism and self-assurance. But this is not always the case. Women shouldn't be surprised if an appealing man cannot sacrifice all of these things.

Each person lives an individual life, and although you may not like or agree with it, you have to respect the right for men to choose how they live their own life. Many appealing types, as mentioned before, are often overlooked in the formation of relationships. Many women do not consciously consider the appealing types in their ***immediate*** environment. They prefer to look far and wide searching for the ideal and missing those good men right under her nose. Consequently, some appealing types try alternative methods in order to catch the attention of females. Some may prioritise their public status over their personality; their accomplishments over their potential. This should not be considered a sign of arrogance, however, ***unless*** it is a consistent pattern with a condescending tone in most areas of his life.

Some women need to take more time interacting with men of potential; taking the time to understand her 'BET'. The appealing types are prepared and equipped to do this, so she must ensure she is too. If not, it might not be the right time for a relationship, regardless of how much it is desired.

LESS PRONE TO CHEAT

The appealing types, (although susceptible like every other man) are less prone to cheating behaviour because they ***choose*** to behave in this way. Not because they possess some idealistic quality which makes them more evolved. They take conscious responsibility for their own decisions. They see the easy excuses, but know that they are not good enough.

Nevertheless, for some of the types, even though they make the correct decision in the end, it is hard for them to do so. For example, the 'Modern Man' understands the ease of infidelity more than most. The advances in communication and social networking have completely transformed the accessibility of finding sexual liaisons. The 'Modern Man' has to kerb the desire to fall into this easy pattern of behaviour almost every day. The 'Thinker', on the other hand, knows that everybody on the planet experiences ups and downs. When people are emotionally low, they are more susceptible to behaviours that they normally wouldn't contemplate. The 'Thinker' knows he could take advantage of this at any time. As a result, he has to choose to disregard becoming the 'Opportunist' type on a regular basis.

Again this is not a defence for men.

Millions of women worldwide turn down opportunities to cheat, probably more often than men do. So those men that do the same are not knights in shining armour by any stretch of the imagination. However, one must take into consideration the qualitatively different psychological nature of male and female socialisation in terms of sexual behaviour. For example, males often receive praise in certain subcultures for having several partners; whereas the reputation for women doing the same is usually derogatory. Bearing this in mind, it would be naïve to assume that it is more difficult for women to turn their back on the opportunity to cheat. It could be argued that they have more to gain socially from not cheating.

Although this isn't excusing men from responsibility, those men who don't cheat and conform to stereotypes, may deserve some credit for displaying independent behaviour. Even if they aren't shining knights, their decision-making comes from mature assessment of the situations they find themselves in. This alone deserves some recognition. Not all appealing types are the most attractive, wealthy or the best physical specimen but opportunities to cheat still present themselves. However, they understand their own qualities and how to make best use of them. This makes them less likely to cheat in their own individual ways. They disregard the seductive information that surrounds them and turn away from the ***easy*** option of using the justification schema.

Things will not always be perfect in a relationship with an appealing type; remember this isn't a fairy tale. But if both individuals are prepared to work at it, recognising the benefits of deferred gratification, using compromises, growing together at a concurrent rate and understanding each other's 'BETs', the relationship has every chance.

"Why would I want to stress myself out chasing a hamburger in a nightclub when I can get a cooked steak at home?" Chris, 'The Visionary', aged Thirty-One, London.

This creates an existence that far

outweighs the trappings and quick 'prizes' on offer in the information age. As long as she can spot him first!

SPOTTING THE CHARACTERISTICS

How to spot some of the characteristics he should possess:

- If he can show ***patience.***
- If his 'time perspective' is mostly ***future-oriented.***
- If he shows ***'maturity by assessment'***, not by age or experience.
- If he possesses a ***combination*** of alluring characteristics (i.e. confidence, assertiveness).
- If he participates in ***calculated risk-taking***.
- He takes ***responsibility*** for his own actions and decisions. He doesn't ***look*** for blame.
- He understands the importance of ***continual maintenance*** in a relationship. He doesn't rest on what he has got.
- If he ***actively*** seeks to have three co-existing strands in his relationships.

WHY THEY ARE APPEALING

The 'Family Man' – He has a great sense of tradition and kinfolk. He will put family stability at the front of his aims, above any other desires.

The 'Secure Man' – He is the closest thing to Mr Perfect, whatever you like in a man he will possess those traits and in every appealing way. You are a lucky lady if you find this guy who is right for you.

The 'Appreciator' – He has a complete respect for women. He will treat you like a queen (and not just a princess).

The 'Visionary' – He sees above and beyond (which is more than most men); being with this man will be a life experience.

The 'Modern Man' – He is the epitome of 21st century expectations. He tries to be the poster boy for all that is good about today's man.

The 'Thinker' – He considers the consequences before he acts. He is cautious and because of this he usually makes the right decisions.

MR SECURE ■

How this type looks / or comes across to women

This guy has everything: charisma, maturity, an edge, power, principles and responsibility. He has a good heart, being sensitive but strong, ambitious and willing to grow. He knows what he wants from his life. He is clear in his goals but flexible enough to adapt if things do not go to plan. He learns from his mistakes and comes back stronger. Everything you could want. **His insecurities are well managed. He doesn't hide from them or hide them from others. He understands that slowly improving these issues and minimising their impact on himself and others is the key to him living a happy and care-free life.**

THE APPRECIATOR ■

How this type looks / or comes across to women

This type appears to be very grateful for everything he receives. He is the type of man to stand up for women if they are being belittled, ridiculed or marginalised. He will not engage in 'banter' involving sexist jokes or discrimination. He seems to take a gentleman's approach to women. **His insecurity relates to not wanting to be perceived as insincere or ungrateful for anything he is given. He understands that many people take things for granted; so he may go out of his way to make it really clear to others that he does not, especially in relation to women.**

THE VISIONARY ■

How this type looks / or comes across to women

This type can sometimes be misunderstood because he isn't your typical man. It can take a while for you to understand his distinctive line of thinking. He looks at things from a very different point of view which is very intriguing, even though it can be confusing at first. You may not always understand his meaning until a long time afterwards. **His insecurity relates solely to thinking on a level that not many can reach or understand. It's like he sees the world in slow motion and without boundaries; this can sometimes make him feel alienated or marginalised as he rarely meets people who think as he does.**

THE MODERN MAN ◆

How this type looks / or comes across to women

This guy is confident and assured. He may not be overly knowledgeable in depth, but he knows a lot of things well in breadth. He may appear to switch interests with societal trends, i.e. music, clothing, occupation etc. However, he always knows what's going on and what's the 'in thing' relating to many areas of life. He never wants to feel or appear redundant. **His insecurity relates to being left behind. He doesn't want to be considered out of touch, so he move with the times, in order to feel that he always has a purpose and he belongs. This can work positively or negatively for him depending on the social group influences he is trying to keep up with.**

THE THINKER ■

How this type looks / or comes across to women

This type sees the world as a place where negative things will always occur if you don't think and prepare. He may come across as very cautious, being very deliberate in his actions. He may like to plan things down to the very last detail and may worry if things are left to happen spontaneously. **His insecurity relates to his overactive thinking processes and strategies, but this is simultaneously his greatest strength. He tends to make more good decisions than poor ones.**

THE FAMILY MAN ■

How this type looks / or comes across to women

This type looks like the kind of guy who always has a plan. From an early age he has known what he wants for his life and what's more, he actually sticks to it. He comes across as very traditional and is prepared to take responsibility when others in his position would not do so. He is understated and just gets on with things; a very decent kind of guy. **His personal insecurities are minimised by the strength of his views on family unity and values. He will altruistically put others, (usually, but not exclusively, close members of his family), before himself because he feels that family happiness is worth more than his own selfish desires. This may lead to his personal dreams not being fulfilled so that somebody else may have the chance.**

Chapter 10 – 'What other people do doesn't bother me' – Cameron

I'd always suspected that Cameron was cheating on me, but I could never prove it. The worst thing was he never gave me any reason to think he was cheating… he was just too cool for me. It was crazy! This was the relationship that sent me mental. I was almost driven crazy by my unfounded suspicions. It was ridiculous. Even though I had disparaged any woman who checked their boyfriend's messages and went through his pockets, I found myself being a total hypocrite. I was questioning who he'd been with and where he was going. And I used to drive myself wild, wondering why he was the only person in the ***world*** who didn't use social media. I tried everything to squeeze an illicit secret out of him, and when I couldn't, I got even more frustrated and persistent.

Despite my alarming behaviour, Cameron never got angry. It was astonishing, but it made me want to pull my hair out. At times, I was dying for an argument. Often, I would instigate them, even over something trivial, like not texting me straight back. I was definitely paranoid, even if it seemed to everybody outside of our relationship that we were a perfect match. Cameron was loving, with a great sense of humour. He didn't shy away from intimacy but he wasn't clingy either. He was a man with seemingly the right amount of emotional depth; what more could any girl want? And believe me; a lot of girls wanted him.

It might sound vain on my part when I say that several women were after my man, but I know for a fact that it was true; we all used to talk about him before I started dating him. They would try everything they could think of to get his attention, but Cameron would just bat their attempts away. He was clearly flattered, but had a very kind way of letting them know he wasn't interested; without leaving any of them feeling disrespected. He was sincerity personified, so you can imagine how I felt when ***he*** asked ***me*** out for a drink.

The first date came and went without the slightest hiccup and things moved swiftly and smoothly after that. Four months in and it still felt like a honeymoon period. Cameron was above average in every way; well out of my league! He was extremely self-assured, and although that made him all the more attractive, it made me more suspicious too but not in the way you would expect.

All men want to be more powerful, don't they? So why was Cameron content as he was? When he was offered a promotion with a huge pay rise, he declined. When we were buying a new car, he refused the latest coupe even though it was well within his budget and went for a much more conservative four-door saloon. "I don't like being on the radar," he explained, but I just couldn't understand it. That's when I started assuming there was something he was keeping from me. Everyone has secrets and memories that shape the person they are, so why wasn't I discovering more about him as our relationship continued? There wasn't anything to distrust about him, but deep inside me, I felt there must be more.

I didn't turn into a paranoid wreck overnight; it started off innocently and slowly as it always does. He always seemed to be on the phone to the same friend: Danny. There was nothing wrong with that, but I was always thinking, *Why doesn't he talk to anybody else?* I never met Danny because he lived down south, but he was obviously a big part of Cameron's life. His work was important to him too, and he knew what he wanted out of it. Being an executive of a fancy banking company, he didn't have much free time. Nevertheless, when we could go out together, we noticed everyone moaning about their bosses or their workloads. I admired the fact that Cameron never complained about his work. "What other people do doesn't bother me," he used to say.

He tended to drink with his work colleagues on a Friday evening; I met them all once at a celebratory work function after a successful merger had been completed. That evening, I discovered that Cameron worked with a lot of attractive women that he had never mentioned. I know it seems irrational; why would I expect him to tell me about ***these*** women? Would I expect him to tell me about a group of unattractive women? Nevertheless, I asked him who they were. "They're all colleagues or acquaintances, nobody close," he reassured me. I think he detected quite quickly that I felt a little insecure, even though I was never usually like this.

The few female friends that he did have seemed to be really nice! Usually, you see some brimming sexual tension from a previous tryst in many mixed gender friendships; at other times, one half of the friendship is absolutely besotted with the other, who blindly (or tactically) doesn't see it. None of this was a facet in any of Cameron's world. None of these girls seemed to be fazed, intimidated or remotely interested that he had a new girlfriend; the complete opposite of Nick and Ramone's lives. For some reason, I found this quite uncomfortable, when in reality, it should have been a dream! I suppose that tells me more about my own insecurities that I hadn't managed to deal with at the time.

I remember one occasion, when I called round to his apartment. He greeted me at the door and told me to take a seat as he just needed to quickly send some work emails. "Sending messages to your girlfriends on the internet are we?" I responded in jest, but also in an attempt to get a reaction from him.

"I don't use social networking. That sort of thing takes up too much time and doesn't fit into my schedule," he replied without even glancing up from the laptop.

A man not using social media shouldn't be a problem, I said to myself. But I couldn't help convincing myself that it meant that he didn't want me to see what he was up to when I wasn't around. Crazy I know, and I had been acting like this for about two months straight. Looking back, I can laugh at how silly it was, but at the time, I thought his behaviour was dodgy to say the least. On top of that, he had passwords on everything; his mobile phone, his tablet and his computer. *Nothing strange there, I do that myself.* I thought. However, his office phone never went straight through to him. It always diverted and he would call me back shortly afterwards. Sometimes, he would have work dinner dates and ask me to meet him afterwards. We would then have a terrible time wherever we were as I would grill him about who he was at dinner with. All throughout this period of time, Cameron remained dignified and unflustered as usual.

I guess it came as no surprise that Cameron ended the relationship with me after the eighth month. The final straw was when I decided to 'surprise' him at his office for lunch. To be honest, I may have also been trying to catch him off guard to see whether he would still remain collected when he wasn't in control.

I marched to his office with a purpose. His secretary directed me towards his open door. I stood in the doorway and watched as Cameron sat at his desk, deep in conversation about a business deal with a stunning brunette. She was sat on the edge of the table, leaning towards him and flicking her hair back every now and again. By the way she was giggling like a schoolgirl, it was obvious that she fancied him. Cameron was being his normal cool self. I stood there for about thirty seconds, which seemed ten times as long before he realised I was standing there.

"Hey Liv, what are you doing here?" he asked, not at all flustered. The brunette turned her head sharply, obviously frustrated that somebody had interrupted her conversation. I shot her a dark look and composed myself to answer Cameron's question.

"I came to surprise you, I thought we could have lunch together," I responded.

Cameron had a quick flick through his appointments for the day.

"That's a great idea! We were just finishing off here. Liv, this is Danielle, Danielle this is my girlfriend, Olivia."

It didn't register with me until the shiny name tag on her chest came into my line of vision as she agitatedly came to shake my hand; Danielle-Danny. Could Danielle really be Danny, the person that he spoke to for hours? Whether it made sense or not, I lost it. This was the ***one*** occasion where I ***didn't*** think another woman finding my man attractive was a compliment. I won't go into detail of the scene I created; it's embarrassing enough just thinking about it. But needless to say Cameron finished with me that night.

We had a long heart to heart. He explained that he couldn't continue with a relationship so lacking in trust, even though he had found no fault with me anywhere else. I begged for another chance because I realised I had been so irrational, creating all of our problems myself. Only now did I see it from his point of view. I understood that my behaviour had been smothering; if the roles had been reversed, we wouldn't have even made it to three months never mind eight. How had he put up with me for so long?

Unfortunately, he was clear in his decision. He was moving on and didn't give me any lingering hope that there might be another chance in the future; just like the other girls, he didn't string me along. I was hysterical, and in my confusion I asked him one last question. "Were you cheating on me? I need to know." He had been straight with me about everything up to this point, so I figured he would be now as well. With an expression on his face that didn't give anything away he replied, "What do you think?" and walked out of the door. That didn't help me in the slightest!

DID YOU SPOT THE SIGNS REVEALING HIS TYPE?

Chapter 11 – The *'Do Not Notice'* Types

★★★★

Cameron still frustrated me at times. He was a puzzle that I just couldn't solve. The soul-searching journey that the book was navigating was taking its toll. Balancing what I wanted with what I actually needed had made me so confused. I needed a rush! So in stereotypical fashion, I hastily reached into the cupboard and grabbed the sweetest thing I could place my hands on to give myself a boost. I hadn't realised how diverse my dating experience had ***actually*** been; evidently, it was not only Claire who went through a multitude of different guys. I thought I had a 'type', but Michael was quickly showing me that I had been mistaken.

I was obviously missing something. Even though there are over three billion men on the planet, I felt like I had seen them all. Therefore, I wasn't surprised when Michael revealed I was wrong again. There was a bunch of 'do not notice' types too. It's obvious that not every guy would catch my eye, but the book seemed to suggest that I was limiting my male experiences more than I was actually aware.

++++

Human beings thrive on visual stimuli. We always spot new things that we didn't see previously. So if women were asked to take a good look round their workplaces, and spot at least one guy that they've never seen before, they could probably do it. If they're brave enough to ask him how long he's worked there, they will probably be surprised! Excluding the ones that you call friends; think back to your first job or one of your school classes where there were males. Years later, you can still recall how they looked, acted and even some of the things they said to you. The chances are that the ones you remember remind you of the prototype of 'a man' that you hold in your head. There are likely to be only a few of their names that you remember.

The ones that stood out!

Across every culture there is a stereotype of what a man is 'expected' to be and how he should behave. Whatever the philosophy of how a man should act, there will ***always*** be those men who fall outside of the bracket. The do not notice types are those kinds of guys.

They get along in life doing what they personally feel they are 'supposed' to do. What ***they*** are interested in and what feels right. This may differ to what others 'expect' them to do. For example, this can relate to his interests or career choice. A man may like an abstract hobby like stamp collecting or have a natural inclination towards caring careers such as nursing or childcare. This may contradict what others may expect of him; i.e. to engage in a more typical career or hobby.

These men do not fit the stereotype.

It could be argued that they are 'bucking the trend'. Not in a trendsetting manner, which garners support and followers but quite the opposite. They are being individual in that they do not conform when everybody else does. Although this may be a commendable trait if used correctly, most people will not see it this way. These men put simply would be deemed as boring.

THE DO NOT NOTICE TYPES OF MEN are:

- The Guilty Conscience
- Mr Adaptable
- Under the Thumb
- The Girlfriend

FLYING UNDER THE RADAR

Generally, in Western society, we don't ***expect*** men to be any of the types above. Our stereotypes push us in an alternative direction. We don't expect men to be overly worried and neurotic because they spent 'too long' with their friends (the 'Guilty Conscience') or to be able to empathise perfectly with the hormone-influenced emotional changes that some females experience (the 'Girlfriend');

Nor do we expect them to be totally under the control of a woman, like a Chihuahua imprisoned in a designer handbag ('Under the Thumb'); but we all know they do exist.

Although they may feel that they are acting on what they want to do, the behaviour patterns of these men are ***indirectly dictated by others***. They all have their individual characteristics but their buttons are pushed in different ways. However, the one defining feature that groups them together, is that the do not notice types don't tend to ***crave*** attention.

Sometimes they actually make a conscious decision to not be noticed and fly under the radar.

We know general male stereotypes exist in every culture. In the west, an example of this is that we expect men to stand up and have their opinion heard. The do not notice types however, do not tend to be as vocal or assertive as this stereotype would suggest. Sometimes, they are considered quiet or weird and some people don't consider them 'a real man' because of it.

On occasion, the quieter do not notice types display a little 'blip' in their regular behaviour! They act loud, assertive or stand up for themselves. This is out of character. They are applauded for it. However, inside, they feel this is crazy for them. It is not a true reflection of their identity and consequently, it is rarely a long-lasting phenomenon. They revert back to being inconspicuous. And it is because of this, women never pay them much attention for too long either.

TAKING ADVANTAGE

The majority of women like excitement with the hint of a challenge. A little bit of danger to distract them from their norms. There are common denominators as to why some women chase the wrong men; why they lust after the men who hurt them or try to tame the stereotypical 'bad boy'. The first thing is that they ***notice*** them.

> *"Whenever I have messed about on my 'missus' I get really guilty; then I go for weeks and weeks trying to make it up to her. She always wonders why I am being extra nice. But I can never tell her." Kevin, 'The Guilty Conscience' aged Twenty-Five, London.*

The men that women notice also possess the characteristics that women are drawn to: confidence, power and assertiveness. But where does this leave the do not notice types if they don't possess these qualities and, as a result, aren't going to be chased or lusted after in the same capacity?

Being overlooked by women in this way may be a throwback to their teenage years. Not being as socially adept as their counterparts, they would have been encouraged to focus on their future rather than fruitlessly chasing female attention. However, although they are considered typically dull by nature, the do not notice types do possess characteristics such as ***organisation, above average IQ and tend to be financially stable.*** As an adult, these types discover that they are able to take advantage of the fact that some women are enamoured with their intelligence and stability. This usually occurs unwittingly and over a sustained period of time on a platonic level. And it brings them 'success' in the form of a girlfriend.

Many of the do not notice types seize this window of opportunity for a chance at romance with both hands. They limit their female experiences to this one relationship. As a result, they may continue to struggle or feel awkward with other females in everyday settings. They just do not possess the appropriate social skills to interact with them on different levels. On the whole, however, they feel that they have 'won', as they have achieved the relationship they never thought was possible.

In another effort to take advantage of the few romantic situations that comes their way, some of the do not notice types access women they know, ***only*** hold a superficial interest in their financial proficiency.

In Western societies, many couples are judged on how they look together. This may seem rather shallow, but '*The Matching Hypothesis*' in psychology suggests that people of similar attractiveness will be drawn to each other. Of course, there are exceptions to this theory but it tends to be generally correct. So if a couple appear to be aesthetically 'out of place', we assume there must be some other motive.

"I'm sensitive and in touch with my feelings. I may not be sporty and hard but this is me. My friends understand me and love me for who I am." Chris, 'The Girlfriend' aged Thirty, Nottingham

Many people are surprised when a man not considered to be

physically attractive, manages to get with a really attractive female. Cynics may argue there is some financial motivation in place. However, some do not notice types find that money can produce a large enough loophole for getting female attention. Their partner may notice their bank balance more than their personality. This enables them to develop relationships with women; but it may also create a tendency to use the justification schema (from time to time) as they know that the relationship may not be completely equal.

★★★★

That sounds like the majority of guys that Claire finds herself with, I thought to myself. But then I guiltily admitted that I too have fallen victim to this line of thinking once or twice.

Nathan, the not so good-looking investment banker came to mind. I couldn't remember the colour of his eyes, but I couldn't forget the gleam of his silver sports car. I remembered one time when he was picking me up after a night on the town. I was on the phone to him as he was manoeuvring his way through the street, full of cars and clubbers.

"Where are you?" Nathan asked.

"I'm right outside the club. Can you see me?" I responded, slightly under the influence of a few white wine spritzers.

"***I'm*** outside the club, can you see ***me***?" His response was slightly frustrated.

"No… oh wait, I can! I can see your wheels!"

I wasn't purposely being superficial, it was the truth! That was all that seemed to stand out about Nathan. Needless to say, he didn't last longer than a few weeks.

++++

WHO WEARS THE PANTS?

> *"I only go out with my friends when my wife goes out with her friends. She says that is best. And I agree." Andrew, 'Under the Thumb' aged Thirty-Seven, Manchester.*

Being with a do not notice type of man, some women will probably get bored of them or recognise that he doesn't possess many other qualities besides the one she was initially smitten with. These men, however, are not stupid. They recognise this and know they may have to make a sacrifice or two in order to keep her around. However, these sacrifices might make them the butt of many jokes in his male subcultures. The commonly used phrase '***whipped***' may come to mind.

****

"Absolutely," I giggled, thinking about how much Helen had James under control like a trained puppy. We all agreed he was 'Under the Thumb'. James couldn't do ***anything*** without Helen's permission. The only time he could go out with his friends was when she was out with hers. And even then, he had to run it by her first! Sports channels were banned in their house. Everything about him was dictated by Helen, from his meals, to his dress sense, to the holidays they went on. He had to 'clock in' regularly by phone and by text. If he was ever somewhere he wasn't supposed to be, trouble wouldn't be far away; and female friends? Forget about it. Helen definitely wore the pants for both of them in that relationship.

But maybe I wasn't giving James enough credit. Maybe he wasn't an 'Under the Thumb' type, but actually a 'Mr Adaptable'. Flipping back to the sure fire signs, I noticed they both seemed to have similar qualities. However, 'Mr Adaptable' ***acts*** 'whipped' for the sake of avoiding conflict. Perhaps James is intelligent enough to let Helen have her own way in order for an easy life. In reality, the things that she wanted to control didn't make much difference to him and so it wasn't worth the fuss. Maybe he ***really*** gave up football on Fridays because he was no longer interested in it, in comparison to his new life at home.

++++

Some do not notice types incorrectly accept defeat that they aren't what women want, in comparison to other men. Therefore, they consider themselves lucky if they manage to

> *"My mates complain that they do not see me as much anymore. It's not always great, but I choose to live this lifestyle now." Mike, 'Mr Adaptable' aged Forty-One, Devon.*

obtain a serious relationship. Regardless of any negative aspects that may come with it. For example, they may choose to accept a marriage where the price of regular female company is the sacrifice of true intimacy. The 'Under the Thumb' type is one such man who may accept living in a relationship that appears to be hollow, affectionless and without respect to others. Their partners may take them for granted (the word doormat may surface), but they put up with these things for the opportunity to raise children, purchase a house or obtain something else that they place much more value on.

But be careful, although some of the do not notice types may be less prone to cheat, not all of them will always take not being noticed lying down (i.e. the Guilty Conscience or Mr Adaptable). Too much pushing can tip anybody over the edge. But nowadays, finding a reason to jump is so much easier to justify in the information age.

★★★★

That was quick, I thought. The chapter was finished before I knew it. But I supposed if women didn't notice them, there wasn't much that could really be said. I touched the redial button on my mobile and called Claire before going to bed.

"Hi Claire," I tried to sound enthusiastic, but she wasn't falling for it.

"How come you've only just called me back? Are you ignoring me?" She demanded to know.

In public, Claire projected a confident aura, but on the inside she was really quite a fragile thing. She was the type of girl who needed constant text message reassurance from both her friends and partners. "Don't be silly," I said. *Being distracted isn't the same as ignoring somebody*, I thought.

"So, how is it?" she queried. I mulled over everything I had just taken in.

"I think it's brilliant. I haven't put it down all night. It makes you look at things in a completely different way. It's not even about slagging guys off; but it isn't defending them either. It just seems like the truth. I'm just getting to the section about the guys you need to avoid and get rid of."

"I'm jealous," Claire purred enviously. "But I'm not sure I could read that part if it's as good as you say." Her tone changed slightly. "There might be too many home truths in there for me…" I could feel her angst as she spoke. "So what are you going to do about that Michael guy?" She changed the conversation. "Are you going to call him?"

"I sent him a text before to say thanks for the book; he hasn't responded yet," I said, slightly disappointed as I glanced at the time. Considering it was 2am, I thought he'd had more than enough time to respond. Nevertheless, I had work the next day, engrossed in the book or not. I said goodnight to Claire.

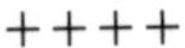

WHY YOU DON'T NOTICE THEM

'Mr Adaptable' – You do not notice him because he consciously makes the attempt to stay off the radar, out of people's way and avoids trouble.

The 'Guilty Conscience' – He is the type that is always sorry or worrying about something; you don't want to hear that all of the time, so you ignore it.

The 'Girlfriend' – This type comes across as a female friend in a male body. You just don't see them as a sexual being.

Under the Thumb – This type of man may get pushed around. It's difficult to respect somebody who doesn't respect themselves.

THE GUILTY CONSCIENCE ◆

How this type looks / or comes across to women

The 'Guilty Conscience' comes across as an average kind of a guy, simple and not very flashy. He goes about his daily activities minding his own business. He can sometimes have peer group members who seem to be complete opposites, and on occasion has moments which are out of his every day character. However, when you speak to him a on a regular basis, you will understand that he is conservative at heart and can even have a few anxious moments and worries. **His insecurity relates to a strong moral conviction to doing the right thing; whatever he thinks that is! If he feels that he has broken the rules in any way, he will feel highly anxious about it and will want to correct it as soon as possible. This can have him going 'over the top' to express remorse.**

MR ADAPTABLE ◆

How this type looks / or comes across to women

This type of man wants to keep stress, drama and complications to an absolute minimum in his immediate environment. He will do anything to avoid it, so he has learnt to adapt his own behaviour to whatever gives him an easy life. You could call him a 'yes' man; likeable but not memorable, efficient but not outstanding. He just does the job asked of him without any fuss, which can be quite boring! **His insecurity relates to not being able to cope effectively with uncertainty, spontaneity, chaos or unreasonable people. He dislikes confrontation as he feels it is never truly resolved, so he chooses to be agreeable, avoiding differences of opinion and the inevitable chaos it will bring.**

UNDER THE THUMB ■

How this type looks / or comes across to women

This type of man is one who will never say no to his partner (or the woman he is interested in). To many women, they may see him as their 'back up' or their 'emergency fix-it'. If a woman is stuck in a jam that nobody else can (or wants) to resolve, this is who they will call. Sometimes you may think it's cruel but he reaffirms your every demand without question or complaint. Like a lapdog. **His insecurity relates to not wanting to be alone; he possesses a subservient personality. He may have a lot of respect for authority figures and hierarchal positions. He understands his role very quickly and learns to play it well. To him, any place is better than no place.**

THE GIRLFRIEND ■

How this type looks / or comes across to women

Women don't notice this man because his primary aim does not seem to be attracting females for sexual purposes. He sticks around in stereotypical female conversation a little longer than usual and his interests may match those of women a little more than other men in the locality. His career aspirations may be aimed at occupations where the consumers are primarily female because he seems to get along with women much more than men. **His insecurities are related to a sense of not belonging. He is driven by his emotions but male subcultures can be quite unforgiving to any such ideas or expressive displays in behaviour. Therefore, he seeks comfort in female company where these views are stereotypically tolerated. He keeps quiet and supportive; careful not to take sides (until he is comfortable). He wants to remain there and feel a part of something. He will always say what you want to hear.**

Chapter 12 – 'Why do girls always want to stop a guy having fun?' – Ben

The next morning, I awoke to a text from Michael asking whether I'd like to meet him that afternoon for a coffee. He was staying at the five-star hotel in town where his seminar was being delivered and had a break in his scheduled appointments. Naturally, my response was an emphatic 'yes', but I struck a more conservative tone in my text back. I didn't want to seem too keen… even though I was. As I selected my outfit for work, I thought about Michael's explanations of schema and the fashion industry. Maybe I should break the mould. I decided to read one chapter before getting ready.

Ben was never going to change. The description in the book cast my mind back to the time I was sitting in Julie's living room, trying not to listen to their argument, but hearing every word. Ben had come home excited after being invited on a last minute boy's holiday to Ibiza. It was only the week before that Julie had told us their plans to go away as a couple – for the first time in their three-year relationship. So you can imagine how well that went down. Especially after his previous trips with the lads to Miami, Vegas and Marbella in the same period!

"Jules, it's really cheap. Somebody dropped out and they need me to fill the gap or they'll lose the money," he protested passionately.

"I thought ***we*** were going away in the summer." The implication behind her words was: 'You are ***not*** going, so don't even try to make it happen.'

"We can still do that!" Ben insisted. I wasn't completely sure whether he had read in-between Julie's lines.

"How exactly, when you'll be off spending all of your money in Ibiza?" Julie fumed, taking a more blatant approach.

Before walking through the door, Ben knew exactly what Julie's response was going to be. But still he came at it from this angle.

Was he stupid? It quickly turned into a full scale screaming match lasting about ten minutes. I just sat there, trying to camouflage myself. Julie and I had decided to open a bottle of wine after our meal – that was before Ben arrived. The two pre-poured glasses were now getting warm, looking desolate on the side table. The mood of the evening had taken an unexpected U-turn. All I had wanted was to have a tipsy, girly Friday night with *Bridget Jones* on in the background. I knew now that I was going to be putting out fires all night. It wasn't long before Ben stormed out, and Julie flopped onto the sofa next to me in a flood of tears.

Ben and Julie's relationship had always been on and off. She had first met him during her teenage clubbing days. He'd always seemed to be sniffing around the girls like a stray dog, but despite several warnings, she couldn't help but be attracted to him. He wasn't a 'looker' by any stretch of the imagination, but he oozed cockiness and she'd had the hots for him immediately. She couldn't explain it, but then, every girl has that one man who casts a magician's spell over them that seems to last forever. They finally got together.

Julie knew that he had cheated on his previous girlfriend because she was the girl he was cheating ***with***. But when he left his ex, he vowed that he would give up his 'bad boy' ways. That was over two years ago.

"He always does this to me. He never cares about how I feel. He just does whatever he wants." I could just about make out her words amongst the strangled wailing. What do you say, as a friend in this situation?

Well, it depends solely on how strong your relationship is and whether you are allowed to speak your mind:

- Scenario 1: You are just a colleague, more than anything else to the person in question. Your truthful opinion is usually not appreciated, especially if it isn't asked for. So shut your mouth, change the subject and try to distract yourself with the most entertaining thing in the immediate environment.

- Scenario 2: You are a good friend, but you are the type who isn't very good with advice. Although your friend would clearly like support, your contribution will probably tip them further over the edge, making them delve into a further state of despair. So maybe shut your mouth, change the subject and try to distract yourself with the most entertaining thing in the immediate environment.

- Scenario 3: You are a good friend. You can say exactly what you want because they know you're not trying to hurt them and have their best interests at heart. They have respect for your views and opinions. And even though they may not want to hear it, they will reflect on your words later and understand what you were getting at.

"He's an absolute pr★ck," I said with disdain. I couldn't help myself. I was in the latter category. "I don't know why you're still with him. He acts like he's single and treats your house like a hotel. He borrows your money and never pays it back. He eats all of your food, and goes out drinking almost every day. He never makes any time for you and always makes you cry. I hate to see you like this, Jules."

After listening to Julie's feeble defence of "if you knew him like I know him…" and 'he's not always that bad', I decided to stop wasting my breath. She obviously wasn't listening, which frustrated me as usual. As I was telling myself to calm down and to not take it personally, there was the sound of a notification on her mobile phone.

Six people had already liked Ben's status: 'Why do girls always want to stop a guy having fun?' Julie was tagged in it.

She saw red and began on one of what we called her 'mental rages'; phoning and texting him whilst barely taking moments to breathe. She was running off raw, heated emotion that lacked any conscious thought. The fact that he was ignoring her calls aggravated her even more. "Why does he do that? He knows it drives me mad!" She screamed. "It's obvious what he's doing. He just updated his status using his mobile, for God's sake!" I thought she was going to smash her phone at one point. She'd fallen right into his trap.

We started on the wine after that. Julie's large gulps were only separated by her desperate attempts to get hold of Ben. From his side of things, eighteen missed calls and numerous texts must look slightly unhinged. But he had to be used to that by now; their relationship was clearly on a destructive path.

We could only speculate as to where Ben was at this point. The safest bet was that he was sat in some pub with his immature friends encouraging him. Whenever he didn't answer his phone, nine times out of ten he would be drinking his sorrows away. Not that he had any sorrows; he knew all too well that Julie would bow to his demands. He was like a spoilt child, never taking any responsibility.

Once Julie realised that she would not be getting hold of Ben, she calmed down slightly. I tried my best to distract her with stories of the office and Claire's usual dating shenanigans, but I could tell that she was still distraught. During their time together, Ben had slowly broken down Julie's self-esteem. It was never direct. It probably wasn't even intentional. Ben wasn't smart enough for that. Regardless, Julie knew that she wouldn't be able to stop him from going, and by allowing him to go, she knew that the possibility of her romantic holiday for two was diminishing by the second.

I decided to let Julie just get her frustrations out whilst I was there. I felt that diffusing the situation a little was the best I could do. We finished the bottle of wine and for about fifteen minutes we even managed to have a 'Ben-free' chat, with a few laughs thrown in before I went home around 12.30am.

The next morning I received a text from Julie. 'Really upset, can you meet me for lunch?' it read solemnly.

I knew what she was going to say, but I was still nosey for the details. On Saturday mornings we both worked at the fashion house. I held a quiet corner in the cafeteria, in order to avoid eavesdroppers. I was having a coffee as Julie walked over. She looked terrible. You could tell that she hadn't had any sleep and at some point today she'd been crying. There was just no way she'd put her make-up on like that! She sat down in front of me, keeping her back turned away from everyone else.

Ben had crawled into bed two hours after I'd left. Drunk and stumbling, he'd passed out as soon as his head hit the pillow. Normally, Julie would have been waiting for him, ready to continue the argument, but today was different. Something was wrong about this Ibiza trip. Maybe he had it planned all along and had not told her until the last minute so she couldn't do anything about it.

Insecurity had got the better of her. Or perhaps it was female intuition. Whilst he was sleeping, she had grabbed his mobile phone out of the crumpled jeans that lay on the floor. After pointlessly debating as to whether she should, she quickly accessed his messages. Unsurprisingly, her investigations revealed some questionable messages from girls she didn't know. She had suspected this for a while, but there's still nothing more excruciating than finding evidence you cannot deny. This was what she was scared of. Although there was nothing absolutely incriminating on his part, (it seemed some messages in the threads had been deleted), there was definitely some flirting from the girls. This discovery was made alongside some raucous messages from his friends about how much drinking and partying was in store for them once they hit the sands of Ibiza.

I hadn't seen Julie this upset for a long time. She couldn't even face him in the morning, so she'd left for work before he'd woken up. He had been texting her all morning, with no concept of what he had done wrong…yet he was still apologising profusely.

"What should I do? Should I ask him who these girls are?"

"No way!" I said firmly. She didn't have any real evidence. Looking through his phone only showed a severe lack of trust on her behalf. Invading his privacy could quickly turn against her. Emotionally, she was in pieces with indecision. Julie knew Ben was a complete let down. She just couldn't face the obvious. He didn't really want to be in a relationship judging by his behaviour. But he had it cushy. Julie wanted to share everything with him. And whether he was aware of it or not, he was taking advantage of her.

That evening Julie and Ben sat down for a chat. Despite yesterday's events, he still didn't understand why she was so upset. The lack of real affection in his vague apologies made the whole conversation seem 'forced' on his part. Julie decided to keep quiet about the girls on his mobile, instead raising her concerns about him going away with boys who were known for taking things too far on their nights out. Ben protested. He felt as if Julie was questioning his manhood. He believed he was his own man and wasn't easily influenced by others. He was just having a break and a good time. She wasn't convinced. But he still got his own way as usual.

After Julie caved in, Ben then decided to charm her into complete submission now he had got his own way. They went for a nice dinner, two days before the flight (Julie had to organise this, of course). The three course meal was filled with Ben making half-hearted reassurances that he would behave in Ibiza and that their summer holiday was still of paramount importance. She was sceptical at the start of the evening, but by the time they left he'd convinced her completely.

The next time I saw Julie, she was in much better spirits and began telling me non-stop about their plans to go to Egypt in June. Ben had told her to start looking at flights and holiday packages whilst he was away. The promise of acting like a real couple had sent Julie practically floating around the office.

I didn't want to be cynical but I ***knew*** Ben. He had let her down ***so*** many times. And he wasn't mature enough to ***plan*** for a holiday; Julie would probably end up paying his half for him. I didn't want to burst her bubble though. In the end, I began to feel excited myself, looking at the pictures of sun, sand and sea in the holiday brochures. I really wanted them to have a great time.

For the remainder of the week, Julie's life and thoughts were plastered all over her social media pages:

'Going on holiday with my Ben in June, can't wait!' Six likes, three comments.

'Missing my Ben! Only four days until he comes back from Ibiza!' Four likes.

'Deposit paid for Egypt. Excited! June hurry up!' Three likes, one comment.

'Love my Ben! I have the best man in the world!' Four likes.

To the people of the world that make their decisions based on this form of electronic communication, Ben and Julie must have seemed like soul mates. But for those who pay a little bit more attention, there was one significant element missing. There was no input from Ben on any of these statuses. No likes, no comments. This was surprising because Ben was usually as active on these sites as Julie was. Of course, it could have meant that he was distracted from everyday life and having a great time on holiday. However, other activity would imply that something wasn't right.

The internet allows rumours to spread at lightning speed. Soon Julie was being bombarded with texts and inbox messages alerting to her boyfriend's activities on Bora Bora beach. None of the evidence appeared on Ben's personal walls, but pictures went around between mutual friends. Information that they thought Julie should see. Ben was never captured without a beverage in his hand. Or a girl draped on his arm.

In the days following these revelations, Julie's emotional state quickly deteriorated. But she still created excuse after excuse to defend Ben's actions. He was only taking a picture. They're only having a bit of fun and it's the girls that are going after him, not the other way around. I wasn't convinced. Having known Ben for a while, there was no way on earth that I could believe this. I wouldn't trust him on home ground, let alone abroad. Not that it mattered what I thought; Julie just wouldn't listen to ***any*** of us. However, on the day before Ben came home, she no longer needed to hear the views of her friends. The video of him dancing and kissing a tall, leggy blonde in some random nightclub said it all.

There was no way she could deny it this time. She was in pieces, not only because the betrayal was so blatant, but because everyone on the internet could see her humiliation. The irony of it was that Julie was renowned for exposing her life through social media; I was pretty sure that this was one of the times she'd wished that it wasn't.

I really did feel for her. But we all expected this was going to happen. Julie stayed with Sasha and I that night, whilst Ben refused to answer her calls or respond to her texts. He knew what was going on after the far from subtle text saying: 'Who the f★★k is that b★tch you're kissing in Kevin's pictures? We're over.' I doubt he was giving that threat any serious thought though. He knew as well as she did that she was only putting on a front; trying her hardest to be convincing. There was very little of her self-esteem left. And Ben had no empathy or consideration for others. He just lived for his own moments.

He came home the next day. Julie said that they had argued well into the night. Ben had defended his corner bravely; protesting that she'd gotten worked up for nothing. That it wasn't what it looked like. "***She*** kissed ***me*** for a laugh." He seemed pretty insistent, but he still slept on the settee.

Julie had plans to find out the truth for herself. When women think the wool is being pulled over their eyes, they need to convince themselves that they aren't just being paranoid lunatics. The belief that someone is trying to deceive us can rile even the sanest of women. So with Julie not being the most 'balanced' of ladies, she went straight for the jugular – hacking into one of Ben's social networking profiles. Reading the inbox messages confirmed what she'd suspected all along. After discussing his dirty little secrets with Sasha and I, she planned to give him one more opportunity to confess before she confronted him.

"I wouldn't bother, Jules," Sasha reasoned. "He's done it before and he'll do it again. He just keeps hurting you. Get rid of him before he gets some other girl pregnant or gives you something nasty."

Julie knew everything that she ***should*** do in order to start repairing her damaged self-esteem. But that was a far cry from what we knew she was ***going to do.*** She may have denied it but she just couldn't give him up now she'd given him her heart. She wasn't going to let him go without trying everything to maintain what she believed she had.

After a few days when things had calmed down, Julie cooked dinner for the two of them and approached the subject again. This time she was armed.

"Do you promise that nothing happened on holiday?" Julie asked meekly.

Ben gave a look, suggesting he was tired of this conversation, before he replied with the straightest of faces:

"I swear. Nothing like that happened."

"Honestly, I do trust you. I just want to go to Egypt and have a great time with no complications." Julie played along.

"Yeah babe, I wouldn't do that to you."

Ben must have been thinking that he'd pulled a fast one when Julie's persona suddenly switched. "So who's Charley then? And what do you mean that 'you're ready for round two when you're home from Ibiza'?" Julie raged, showering Ben with printouts of the conversation thread, moving on to throw in a few other names she remembered from his phone.

His predictable 'defence' to deflect away from the actual evidence naturally ensued. Julie shouldn't have hacked into his private messages; she was crazy; a psycho, anything he could think of that would allow him to avoid taking responsibility. But arguing from this point just made him look worse. Some men are just foolish. Dragging the debate on for a further fifteen minutes was not only pointless, but infuriating. He was caught red-handed, and finally had to confess.

"I'm sorry Jules, I was drunk. I didn't even like her. I don't know why I did it." How pathetic.

As she kicked him out, he was begging for forgiveness (or was he just begging for the roof over his head and food in his stomach?) He grabbed her hands and pleaded with her – he almost sounded sincere. But that night, Julie stood tall. She felt a moment of redemption as the door slammed on his umpteenth apology. Even so, she fell to her knees. Her life as she knew it was crumbling before her eyes. Ben had meant everything to her, but he had treated her as if she was worthless.

Despite Ben's daily, grovelling phone calls, Julie didn't budge as long as one of us was nearby. But we couldn't babysit her, even though we knew she would be vulnerable the minute she was alone. That's why none of us were surprised when she announced a week later that she and Ben had talked. Sasha made no attempt to hide her disgust.

"He's not going to do it again." Julie explained, in a rather subdued tone of voice.

He must have convinced her that she'd been the one in the wrong. The girls flashed looks at each other; we were all thinking the same thing, but there was just no point in saying anything. Thankfully Julie changed the subject. She hadn't been asking for our permission or our opinions. She was simply making her friends aware that she had made a decision, whether we liked it or not.

Is ignorance bliss? The whole situation reminded me of a holiday 'fling' of my own a few years ago. He was an average looking guy, up for a laugh and making the most of the time away with his friends. After blatantly flirting with me all week by the pool and in the clubs, one thing had led to another. Afterwards, he didn't seem too keen on staying in touch with me or taking my number. With this in mind, you can imagine my surprise two months later when Julie introduced me to her new boyfriend. Standing by her side was my holiday fling. He didn't even recognise me. Of course I couldn't say anything, but I always knew Ben was never going to change from the start.

DID YOU SPOT THE SIGNS REVEALING HIS TYPE?

Chapter 13 – The 'Get Rid' Types

****

Ben was a lads', lad. It was easy to see that he was a 'get rid' type. But when I got to the next chapter, I knew he wouldn't be the only type of guy I should avoid. Maybe it wouldn't be as easy as I thought to read this section as Claire had said the night before. It would probably be the most challenging to face up to, especially if it reflected my most glaring relationship errors in stark and descriptive clarity. I was in limbo. I didn't really want to go there again but simultaneously there was no going back now. I was invested.

I knew once I'd finished this section, Claire would be desperate to get her hands on it too. As she was the only one who knew of my little secret related to Ben, I couldn't wait to disparage him further in discussion with her. Armed with the theoretical ammunition supplied in Michael's book, it would be all too easy to dismantle his painfully obvious limitations.

I'll admit the controversy surrounding male infidelity has always been an intriguing topic for the girls and I. As much as we attempt to hold the moral high ground, when it raises its ugly head, we cannot help but syphon out the dirty details; as long as it was outside our immediate circle of course! Maybe we have an unconscious desire to experience the pain of others; opting to hear stories about distress. Perhaps it makes us feel better knowing that there are people in worse positions than one's self. At times, hearing too much about other people's joy can be sickening. It can make us feel as if we have a long way to go to be fulfilled. Where does that kind of thinking come from? It wasn't long before I was reading again.

++++

Male infidelity, when mentioned among women, pushes the right buttons to frustrate, annoy and disgust them. However, the anecdotes of cheating that we regularly hear about are usually incomplete and incorrect. The stories are full of holes because of the numerous tellings, retellings and Chinese whispers. Yet regardless of this, a person's judgement may easily be clouded into thinking that all men are cheaters (or on the verge of doing so) based on such stories. Men are often seen as the antithesis of a good relationship. Women are completely pure whilst men always f*ck it up. This is obviously nonsense.

As previously mentioned, only a minority of people will look at the purpose of this book with an open mind and ask the ***objective*** question: 'Why do men ***really*** cheat?' Are they born to cheat or do they choose to? And what is the catalyst that triggers the behaviour?

THE GET RID TYPES OF MEN are:

- The Lads' Lad,
- The Manipulator
- The Metrosexual
- The Disdainer
- The Stupid Mistake
- Act First, Think Later
- The Chameleon

Some people may insinuate that identifying types of men that women need to 'get rid' of is prejudiced. It suggests that men are being pigeon-holed in a harmful manner. However, it isn't the ***person*** that is the identifiable trait to get rid of; it's the ***behaviours*** that they show. This book is about identifying the differences between men in terms of their behaviour, not who they are.

It is the ***consistent*** patterns of behaviour, highlighted throughout that are important. Obviously, the information and knowledge in this book can be used both positively and negatively depending on how the individual perceives it. However, the aim of this book is to create awareness for ***both*** men and women. Its objective is to improve social and relationship situations between the sexes, not hinder them.

CARRYING BRICKS

Some individuals possess a large number of get rid characteristics, that ***every*** man and woman wants to eliminate from their lives. If the individuals in question are aware of this and do not make any attempt to change, (despite ample opportunity to do so), then they may not only bring dysfunction to their own lives, but to those of others. This is what is unfair.

Everyone has their own personal issues to deal with. But carrying the issues of other people can be a toxic burden. Our emotional battles place psychological weight on our shoulders. You shouldn't carry other people's 'bricks' in the form of ***their*** issues and insecurities. You have your own bricks to carry and they are heavy enough.

If a woman, (or a man if roles were reversed), decided to part ways with a partner because they can no longer bear the brunt of carrying too many emotional bricks, then she isn't wishing him any ill will. She just wants to improve her own future by removing his negative patterns of behaviour from her life.

In relationships, these bricks can be easily observed in actions such as unnecessary arguments, manipulation, psychological dependence, displacement of emotion, (i.e. directing anger onto somebody who is not the intended recipient), and the misuse of coercion amongst many other examples.

The get rid types will make you carry their bricks. Permanently!

INFIDELITY THE INFURIATOR

Everyone knows that the pain caused by infidelity cuts deeply. Male infidelity has stretched female emotions so far, that almost every woman who has been cheated on would be able to relate to a least one of the following responses:

- Public embarrassment
- Not understanding his motive
- The want of revenge
- Not understanding why her trust was so easily broken
- Not understanding why her sacrifices for the relationship were unrequited

- Feeling isolated while he appears to be carefree
- Feeling the damage to her self-esteem
- Not knowing how to move on and pick up the pieces
- Being unable to justify the time wasted with him
- Feeling trapped by her decisions/commitments, i.e. kids or a mortgage and now wanting an escape
- Feeling the need to be reassured that it wasn't her fault

You are not the first, and will definitely not be the last, to feel any of these emotions. Yet, for some, these experiences will be a blessing in disguise as the only ***real*** way to learn is through making errors. 'Errors' – in the context of making good relationship BETs – have to be seen as an essential part of the learning process and should be differentiated in this line of thinking from making a 'mistake'.

Although similar, a mistake can be viewed in situations such as these as final. An acceptance that there is nothing more you can do; giving up if you like. Whereas errors are miscalculations which can still guide you towards your learning goal.

Women must embrace the errors that they have made. As long as you continue to learn and move forward, they will not become mistakes that hinder you or define your relationship history. What's more, by taking this pro-active manner, it will allow women to recognise the behaviour patterns of the get rid types of men much more easily.

THE SYSTEM THAT CREATES CHEATING BEHAVIOUR

There are a lot of get rid types of men. But it is important to be aware that men are not ***born*** into types; the types are ***created*** by a system which encourages the use of automatic schemas. This system surrounds their every environmental interaction. It penetrates their thinking and the engagement within it by the get rid types is usually passive. They find it difficult to change their behaviour because they feel they are doing nothing wrong. They think they are 'normal'. They think the system that they see around them is 'normal'; and as it evolves over the years, these men adapt with it. The system is now the 21st century information age that we live in. But ***what*** drives these men towards negative cheating behaviour?

THE WHAT: THE PRESENT HEDONISTIC TRAIT

The get rid types (i.e. 'Act First, Think Later') are prone to cheat because they are controlled by a ***present-hedonistic time perspective***. This means that their physical, emotional and psychological well-being is mostly made up of decisions which acquire immediate pleasure and gratification; whilst simultaneously avoiding direct and uncomfortable circumstances. If their desires are met, they are content. If their desires are not met, their mind and behaviour is encapsulated by an overwhelming drive to do whatever it takes to get there. This dominates the majority of their actions.

Put simply, this is the opposite of the appealing types of men. The behaviour of the get rid types is prone to damage other people, situations or objects (directly or inadvertently). This is all for their own physical or mental gain. Driven by the compulsive desire to 'have it now', it is unnecessary whether the behaviour they show is appropriate or not. On occasion, this occurs at a conscious level, but more often than not, it's an automatic response provoked by situation and circumstance. If you understand this pattern, it is obvious to see why these men may feel the obligation to cheat. But where do these types learn this behaviour? How does it come about?

THE WHERE: EARLY SOCIALISATION

According to psychologists such as Freud and Zimbardo, we ***all*** begin life with a hedonistic approach; an unrelenting pursuit of immediate pleasure to get the things that we want. Impatience is the norm.

For young girls, many are brought up reading fairy tales such as *Sleeping Beauty, Cinderella, and Snow White*, whilst, young boys usually are not. These stories illuminate ideas of romance, idealism and true love 'beating all the odds'. Whether conscious or not, most girls are heavily influenced to desire such a happy ending for themselves. Every little girl has dreamed of being a princess. In the information age, this message is more powerful than ever before. With the aid of

> *"I hate how women think they are equal to men and can do what we can do. They can't." Eric, 'The Disdainer' aged Forty-Five, London.*

high definition TV, 3D images and ultra-re-mastered DVDs there is no escaping the message. The hedonistic pursuit begins.

For young boys, this hedonism typically manifests in the desire for action and adventure through physical and visual stimulation. Statistics suggest that boys are now playing more video games than ever in search of stimulation. It is also noted, however, that playing such games may be a factor in the decrease of their social and communicative skills; skills that boys lacked compared to their female counterparts in the first place. These differences between boys and girls in their early socialisation are the start of the differences in adult male thought processes. These are essential to identifying their behaviour patterns and types.

In opposition to these present-hedonistic desires, Zimbardo says that children are supposed to learn to become future-oriented. They should acquire the morals, values, attitudes and behaviours necessary to function in society. This is acquired through supportive environmental experiences. Parents are the first teachers, who later entrust the school, the peers and the local community to show their children how to behave appropriately. The need for young boys to have positive male role models to ensure their transformation from hedonism to maturity, is well documented. These men should then be capable of manoeuvring efficiently throughout life in a 'sophisticated' society, becoming good fathers, husbands and citizens themselves.

However, it is evident that not everybody's environment is supportive, nor the role models positive.

Over the last forty years (in the UK and America especially) there has been a significant change in family values, dynamics and structure. This combined with the lack of the aforementioned male role model in a boy's life (whether a parent, teacher or other) may be a significant factor in them not making the transition into a future-oriented individual. Of course, this is not the only contributor. The behaviour displayed by the get rid types of men is a complex interaction of their biological and socio-cultural influences. Nevertheless, it simply highlights the changing nature of today's early socialisation and environments. The environment being one key component of the 'BET' that everybody needs to understand.

Without the correct guidance, the get rid types unwittingly allow the information age to become the dominant teacher.

A large number of men no longer acquire the social and practical skills, traditionally found at home or at school. The individual presences and boundaries that should buffer them from being trapped in a present-hedonistic lifestyle are absent. Times have well and truly changed, and men have adapted with them. It is clear to see ***when*** many of these changes occurred.

THE WHEN: THE CHANGING TIMES

In a culture that is barely recognisable from the one that existed in the late 1940s, some types of men are also no longer recognisable. The notion of a traditional 'gentleman' is not completely extinct, but the norms and values of today's contemporary man do not lend well to this concept. Schools and family structures have altered irrevocably as society has been caught in the 21st century grip of the Internet and technological advances; changing the calibre of environmental experiences of today's man.

Young people no longer gather the majority of their knowledge from parents, schools and libraries. Computers, music, TV and social networking have replaced traditional methods as the dominant sources of influence, information and learning. The declining number of books being borrowed from libraries and the rise of internet search engines support this. For many young people, the life lessons taught by these traditional institutions are old and take 'too long to bear fruit'. Nowadays, most people want their information instantly; and most websites provide just that. The focus on the 'online world' has dramatically changed every aspect of people's lives, from shopping to socialising, and consequently the adults that they become.

Many of us have passively accepted this change and alongside its positive contributions, we have passively accepted its negative consequences as well.

Research by Backstrom (2012), in the largest study of Facebook involving 721 million users, found that with the development of mobile technology, there are now only 'four degrees of separation' between every person in this world. This means, that in just over four 'steps' you can be linked or connected to any other person on the planet. With this in mind, it is obvious why connecting with people and furthermore, infidelity, are a lot more accessible and popular than ever before. Remember, cheating can only occur with ***accessibility***.

Anybody born before 1975 should remember a time before this internet explosion. A time without mass mobile phone usage and social media led interactions. You would arrange to meet a date at 8pm and you would just trust that they would be there. But anybody born just a few years after this will probably not remember such a time as clearly. The arrangement of a date is now likely to be accompanied by a glut of texts and status updates. Oh yes, the world and relationships within them have definitely changed.

For many young men (not just the get rid types), five minutes ago is not quick enough! Impatience is normal; nobody writes handwritten letters anymore when there is email and instant messaging. Why wait for an album or film's actual release date when you can download a leaked internet copy? Computers can be switched on within seconds but that can still be long enough to frustrate many. This new world has changed men, resulting in a systematic upheaval in their environments and thought processing. And this unforeseen and unprecedented acceleration in technological advances, has had a damaging impact on the overall ***social skills*** and ***emotional intelligence*** of males.

The impact on social skills and emotional intelligence can be observed in relationships forming between the people ***most*** affected by the information age; Generation X and Generation Y individuals.

In the last century or so, writers such as Strauss and Howe (1991) have argued that there have been several distinctive generations of people. Two of the latter generations known as Generation X (people born approximately between 1964 – 1981) and Generation Y (people born approximately between 1982 – 1995), have witnessed many cultural boundaries be broken and the world become smaller through technological innovation.

Relationships are now forming between the last of the Generation X individuals, (born in the late 1970s/early 1980s), who are adjusting from a pre-internet technological era and those people born in the middle of Generation Y, (born in the late 1980s). Generation Y individuals are

> *"Things only 'happen' to you if you allow them to happen to you. If you offer people the chance to take advantage of you, they will." James, 'The Manipulator' aged Forty, Manchester.*

immersed immediately into the globalised internet dominated world of today. Their experiences are qualitatively different to Generation X individuals in relation to their environmental influences, childhood, role models and socialisation. Based on the impact of the information age, the social and emotional responses of people born in these generations appear to be significantly altered. But why?

THE WHY: THE EMERGENCE OF NEW MEN

Some men are easily seduced by the information age. Its lack of real external punishments and constraints are appealing. The temptations are almost inescapable. The dominating use of social media and mobile technology indulgently feeds the justification schema. Despite being told it is wrong in one ear, contradictory information encourages them to act upon their desire for sexual variety in the other. It is easy to find excuses to do so from the masses of information around them. The feeble attempts they make to fight it are easily overpowered by their present-hedonistic ways. ***Thus, the get rid types could be considered the poster child for this new age.***

Societal attitudes have changed. This modern information age now encourages individuals to be more 'self-centred' than 'altruistic and person-centred'. For some, this continues the infantile drive of immediate gratification. If they are unhappy with something, they are told to walk away from it without a care and find something else: jobs, entertainment, friends and partners. Perseverance seems to be a dying viewpoint. Alongside this, attitudes towards dating, sex and relationships have changed dramatically as well. This is portrayed through the 'sex sells" marketing industry, the influx of 'liberated' sexual experiences and the documented cases of alleged infidelity in the media. With such information in our midst, it is not surprising a new man has emerged.

> *"Women cheat as much as us nowadays, so I really don't care whether I cheat or not. I just do whatever I want to have a good time." Joe, 'The Metrosexual' aged Twenty-Four, Liverpool.*

Not to say these things didn't exist before, but the ease of finding extra partners via social networking, anonymous internet identities, instant messaging and smartphone apps has definitely influenced its increase. A man raised in the information age, is a very different creature to those who grew up before it became dominant.

Our society is built on ease. Its aim is to satiate selfish needs amongst its occupants with minimal effort. How many people search for the television remote without leaving the sofa, when it may have been easier to walk to the TV and press the button? Although we are ***all*** susceptible; with twenty-seven different types of men, it is obvious that some will be more vulnerable than others to using the justification schema.

The modern get rid types maintain their dominant hedonistic trait after discovering 'life and interaction' on a range of computer screens (TVs, laptops, mobiles and computer games consoles). Now young boys are no longer forced to participate in face to face interaction. One consequence of this, is they are less likely to experience rejection, anticipation, excitement or confrontation with other people in the same ***social*** capacity as their predecessors. A status update will handle all of these emotions for them, with an appropriately selected 'smiley'! These missing experiences are a vital learning curve in acquiring empathy and emotional intelligence.

Subsequently, many get rid types don't acquire the skills to handle ***different*** people, when they are unexpectedly thrust into ***new*** social situations. These men struggle to cope with emotions and circumstances outside of their experiences. Thus, it's easy to see why they could struggle with the complex experience of a relationship. More confident and comfortable on some form of computer screen than anywhere else, some men cannot hold an engaging conversation for longer than five minutes; even if an hour-long dialogue on instant messenger might not be a problem. ***However, the most important aspects of relationships do not take place on computer screens.***

There is no denying that technology has both positive and negative impacts on human communication and relationships. And of course it is not the sole determinant as to why these men are more prone to cheat. However, technology has become so important to modern adults, that the numbers of people developing ***'Nomophobia',*** (the fear of being separated from your mobile device), are increasing. Present-hedonistic males are a high risk of becoming psychologically dependent on their mobile phones and similar computer related devices. They will have strong needs to contact others or to be contactable, (although they may claim that this is not true). How many men do you know that will consciously leave their mobile phone at home?

And alongside Nomophobia comes another psychological phenomenon enhanced by the information age known as ***F.O.M.O.*** or the 'Fear of Missing Out'. How many times have you been out with a group of friends and one person is glued to their mobile phone? Some people see this as just being rude but more likely F.O.M.O. has probably struck. It is a negative psychological state of mind, which induces fear or anxiety that they are missing something important. They cannot wait to find out. The information stalks their mind; they cannot concentrate. The texts and messages will torment them until they check.

This is the type of thinking of many young men today. And although it may seem like a senseless and irrational thought process, it keeps them fully connected to the information age. It's clear to see why this fear can influence possible opportunities for infidelity. ***Research shows that F.O.M.O. is most common amongst younger Generation X individuals, (thirty to thirty-three years), and Generation Y individuals, (eighteen to twenty-nine years), than any other group.*** They just do what everybody else is doing, which creates another passive cycle; the 'copycat' culture.

THE HOW: THE 'COPYCAT' CULTURE

The onset of F.O.M.O. and Nomophobia is spreading fast. The more people created by society that are snared by these mental traps, the more likely they will encourage, and maintain, these thinking patterns in ***others***. It becomes the 'zeitgeist' or 'the spirit of the times' snowballing out of control. Following the crowd is the norm. We have seen these trends in music, fashion and sub-cultural behaviour. Individual identity is rare. Therefore, by extension, those get rid types that maintain cheating behaviours create blueprints within their families and peer groups, for the other 21st

> *"I don't even go out to pull girls, but next thing you know I end up getting off with some random bird. I don't even know how it happens." Daniel, 'The Stupid Mistake' aged Thirty-One, Birmingham.*

century men who come after them. The information is there. The justification is easy.

Some of the get rid types ***don't even know what they are doing wrong*** (i.e. 'The Stupid Mistake'). They just think their behaviour is correct because everybody else is doing the same. Solomon Asch in 1956 found that 75% of people will knowingly agree to an obvious wrong answer at least once; just to be liked by or to fit into a group. This is an alarming statistic, considering how important public perception is to people nowadays, especially young men in search of their identity. The desire to be accepted in modern society is corrupting male minds, making them partake in inappropriate behaviour, just to 'fit in'.

However, not all present-hedonistic men who display this 'copycat' behaviour, lack the awareness to understand the impact of their actions, (i.e. 'The Manipulator' or 'Act First, Think Later'). Some of the get rid types are conscious of the possible negative consequences for their future. The problem is they do not consider this information to be immediately beneficial enough to their life, to filter through their automatic thoughts. Thus, the 'correct' decisions are often ignored, and the get rid types become slaves to their desires.

For example, this can be seen in the lack of patience some men have in new relationship situations. Many men know that waiting to begin a sexual relationship, with a new partner, will probably bring more emotional, self-worth and holistic fulfilment. However, some get rid types, (i.e. The Lads' Lad or The Disdainer), may be unwilling to wait with their girlfriends; and will instead 'take what they can get', even if that means being sexual with someone else. They want quick and easy satisfaction of their physical needs, regardless of how this decision might jeopardise their chances of developing a serious relationship with their original partner.

"I cheat on my girlfriend, but it's only for sex. I would never leave my girlfriend for any of these girls. They are not worth it, I just tell them what they want to hear to get what I want." Dave, 'The Chameleon', aged Twenty-Four, Chester.

Whether we like it or not, Nomophobia, F.O.M.O. and the copycat culture are all now well established features of our current societal system. Consequently, a large percentage of people are now products of that system; we may be included ourselves. We may proclaim that this isn't true, but if the current system was taken away, (no mobile phones, social networking or other technology that eases our peer group conformity), would we quickly become disillusioned; stumbling around like headless chickens?

Findings from the State of Social Media study shows that nearly 40% of people would rather do an arduous mundane task or spend a night in jail than give up their social networking account. This over-reliance can automatically control our behaviour, massively contributing to use of the justification schema and subsequently infidelity. And the chances are that if the system remains as it is, it will continue to create these get rid types of men. Would you spend a week in jail just to keep your mobile phone?

However, ***you*** don't have to be a 'product' of the information age. This is where your happiness begins. It is an idealistic possibility that the system that solidifies the justification schema may be completely eradicated in the future; eliminating the negative influence it has on the population, and allowing everybody to live in harmony… but until then, you will have to rely on yourself. Men who cheat prey on women with low self-esteem and a poor self-concept, so take action on yourself – men and women. Men, try and recognise your own patterns.

WHAT CAN YOU DO: MINIMISE JUSTIFICATION

Women are less likely to be targeted, or influenced, by the get rid types if they break the system's influence in their own world. This can be done by adopting a few simple behaviours:

1. **Understanding your 'BET'** and avoiding the behaviours shown by the get rid types. Most people who are dependent on this system do not understand their relationship 'BETs' (see B.E.T. theory – chapter 15). Every man is a complex amalgamation of their brain type, environmental influences and their thought processing of information. You need to understand this before you will ever know what type of man he is. But if he shows regular present-hedonistic behaviours from day one, more often than not, he is not desirable. If you aren't

quite sure when deciding which type he really is – take your time! It will ***always*** take a while to truly understand the patterns in someone's actions anyway. Don't rush.

2. **Take a good look at <u>yourself</u>.** People dependent on the system do not look at themselves, they look at others. Men do cause problems but, rest assured, not all women are perfect either. Every problem in a relationship is not caused solely by the male species.
   i. Many women are present-hedonistic too. People who share this time perspective will attract each other, as they will both seem exciting and spontaneous. However, there will be problems because ***they won't be able to satisfy each other's desires fast enough***. They are unlikely to be able to grow together.
   ii. Times have changed, and ***women*** have also changed with them. It is argued, that people are spending more time on computers than in real social situations. Many even prefer to do this. Research from Muise et al (2009) shows that women spend more time on Facebook than men, checking statuses and other peoples' pages, (40.57 minutes per day compared to 29.83 minutes for men). The study suggests that increased use of Facebook predicts higher rates of jealousy, especially in women. Is this something you need to look at? If so take action to minimise this.
   iii. Are you a victim of Nomophobia, F.O.M.O. or the copycat era? Women are just as susceptible as men. For example, Jordan (2011) suggested that Facebook users consistently engage in more Facebook use, (perhaps via mobile devices), because of a ***distorted perception of missing out*** on the better life experiences they ***think*** others are having. Limiting the impact of these influences, will see any power the get rid types have over you wane.

3. **Make a choice.** People dependent on the system wait for things to happen. They don't ***make*** things happen. If you come across a get rid type, and infidelity occurs, you have three simple choices. Don't wait too long to make up your mind. Be decisive and stick with it.

i. Accept him as he is and don't complain. This is an option, but you must take responsibility. Remember, by doing this, you may be indirectly accepting the system as it is, (including the justification of cheating), and severely damaging your own self-esteem simultaneously. Is this what you really want?
ii. Try to change him or wait for him to 'shape-shift', (see chapter 22). Either way, this is an unrealistic proposition as most men will ***not*** be easily manipulated. Any change is simply out of your control, no matter how much you want it to happen.
iii. Show ***independent behaviour*** and take positive action. You may be able to forgive one incident of indiscretion, but if you are on the receiving end of multiple betrayals, then somebody is clearly having a laugh at your emotional expense. If recurring infidelity is a feature of your relationship, carefully consider the circumstances, and get rid of the undesirable traits from your life. We know in a serious relationship it isn't that simple, with factors such as mortgages and children to be handled. However, that doesn't mean it cannot, or should not, be considered for the best.

SPOTTING THE CHARACTERISTICS

It isn't hard to spot a present hedonistic individual, if you pay attention. The get rid types of men are easily characterised by:

1. **Consistent displays of selfish behaviour**. These are often used, by many men, as an easy route out of situations they perceive as difficult.

2. **Concentrating on the here and now.** When consumed by emotion, they reveal their insecurity; they cannot see more than five minutes in front of their face. You must identify this insecurity quickly to understand his patterns. Immediate gratification is an obvious indicator.

3. **Avoidance of taking decisive action**. In 'real' difficult situations, most get rid types will avoid challenges that involve psychological, physical or emotional pain. This avoidance may manifest itself in habitual lying, evasion tactics, creating smokescreens or pretence.

4. **Understand his fear responses, (as well as your own)**. Everyone is afraid of something. Is it change, loss, knowledge, the unknown, the obvious or rejection? What does he fear that makes him react negatively?

5. **Searches for blame**. He automatically looks for someone, or something, to blame rather than taking true responsibility for his actions and decisions.

However, not to end this chapter on a negative tone, the get rid types are not completely lost causes. Everybody can change. If ***they*** decide to make a conscious choice, they can become independent and break free of the copycat era. They can 'shape-shift' into future-oriented men, (see appealing types in chapter 9 and shape-shifters in chapter 22). This is not an easy process for any man, ***but it isn't a woman's responsibility to make this happen.***

WHY YOU SHOULD GET RID

The 'Lads' Lad' – He has traits of deep insecurity and immaturity; a combination definitely to avoid. He doesn't want to grow up.

The 'Manipulator' – He is psychologically damaging to your confidence and self-esteem. You may look good and be able to hide on the outside, but he will leave you broken on the inside.

The 'Metrosexual' – He is over-focused on his narcissistic trait. It may mean he has little quality time for you, which is a relationship 'no-no'. He thinks some people are just not good enough.

The 'Disdainer' – This man has no respect for women; you are a second class citizen in his eyes. Stay with him at your own risk.

The 'Stupid Mistake' – He makes stupid mistakes. Your stupid mistake is continuing with him after you're aware of this.

The 'Act First, Think Later' – He thinks 'sorry' is always good enough. It isn't.

The 'Chameleon' – He is only interested in himself, what he needs and he wants, even though at first it doesn't seem like that. He is a master of disguise.

THE LADS' LAD ●

How this type looks / or comes across to women

His outward façade is that of arrogance, cockiness or machismo which protects him from a deep rooted insecurity and immaturity. He tends to be driven by immediate gratification. At times he appears loveable and fun; this is his appeal. A lot of women are attracted to him superficially and this indirectly reinforces his current worldview and behaviour. **His insecurity relates to a complete rejection of responsibility for his decisions. He wants somebody to make all the hard decisions for him, or to pick up the pieces when he inevitably messes up. He is like a big kid; the living Peter Pan, refusing to grow up.**

THE MANIPULATOR ●

How this type looks / or comes across to women

He comes across as intelligent and powerful. He likes to dominate social situations, often, psychologically fighting his way out of corners if he is in trouble. He's the type to go up against the odds and win most of the time. He uses his confidence to put people in uncomfortable circumstances in order to get his own way. He always has to have the last word. You wouldn't automatically think to question him because he is always so self-assured. **His insecurity relates to an inherent inferiority complex of not being 'good enough'. So he goes out of his way to manipulate situations and others to show how good he is; or to pull the wool over his own eyes, avoiding the pain, embarrassment or disappointment of his own shortcomings.**

THE METROSEXUAL ◆

How this type looks / or comes across to women

This type of man is on the increase; they might look like they're everywhere, but they're still a minority. He can appear to be self-indulgent and overly concerned with his physical appearance. He stands out because it's obvious that he has made a serious attempt to look just as, if not prettier than, you! He has always been the 'pretty boy'; or perhaps being considered attractive is new in his adult life and persona. Nevertheless he realises that looks are about style and he has to maintain that image above all else. Maybe even you. **His insecurities relate to being superficial and shallow. He may have always been or recently has, (maybe out of the blue), become self-absorbed, lacking true empathy and being primarily concerned with life's aesthetics.**

THE STUPID MISTAKE ●

How this type looks / or comes across to women

He might not be a particularly likeable person, but there's something about him. He seems reckless, but this is exciting. Every girl likes a bad boy. He's the kind of guy you'd play with, but not one you'd want to take home to mum. And even if you are intrigued by what she would say, is he really what you want? **His insecurities are linked to looking for 'love' in all the wrong places, just like the women he attracts! In this scenario, 'love' could mean attention, affection or reassurance of his desirability. It could mean being 'looked after' or being excused from responsibility. He is constantly seeking recognition that he is 'somebody' and will make stupid decisions in order to obtain this.**

THE CHAMELEON ◆

How this type looks / or comes across to women

This type of man seems to be 'normal' and safe. He fits in well to the environment where you first meet him i.e. work or a social gathering. He isn't over the top with his behaviour and yet he isn't too understated. He appears to have a typical everyday existence, trying to get a good balance between his responsibilities. Nothing seems to be amiss... at first. **His insecurities relate to not being ready to settle down. He may have a life that includes commitment and responsibility already, but he may do this just to keep up appearances. In reality, 'he just wants to do him'. He may feel slightly trapped, just wanting to be free, so he adapts to every situation that allows him to do both. He is 'playing the game' expertly, whilst simultaneously being whatever he wants to be, whenever he wants to be.**

THE DISDAINER ●

How this type looks / or comes across to women

This type of man appears to be really arrogant, sneering and condescending in regards to women. It can almost seem hateful. He disregards their contributions, opinions and feelings. He typecasts their strengths. He views any shortcomings a female may display as a fatal weakness in any comparison to their male counterparts. The impression you gain from him is not positive and he is well aware of it. **His insecurity is related to the loss of patriarchal-led homes, male dominated societies and women being inferior to men. Times have changed and he doesn't like it one bit. In a world where women are considered equal, he likes to display that they are not. In many ways he feels men are still superior – physically, intellectually and emotionally.**

THE ACT FIRST, THINK LATER ◆

How this type looks / or comes across to women

On first impression, this type comes across as very similar to 'The Stupid Mistake'. The difference is that this man has a reflective period, ***after*** his decision making. He thinks about what he's done afterwards, but this is where you may make an error in judgement; just because they've thought about it doesn't mean he won't do it again. **His insecurity is a fear of missing out. Compulsive drives and immediate gratification are his enemies because, deep down, he knows he can be much better than this. As soon as his desire has been satisfied, he has an immediate 'rebound effect' in the opposite direction. He will be full of remorse and reflection, until the compulsion builds up again; and he just can't help satisfying his craving.**

Chapter 14 – 'I've never met anyone like you before' – Richard

Claire has probably dated every type of guy there is; a few get rid types for sure. But there's always that one ex that will continue to mystify each of us; mine was Cameron, Claire's was Richard. They are the men that we could never understand, the ones who left us with no real explanation for how things turned out.

Richard was attractive, successful and charming. He and Claire met through a mutual friend, who felt that they would be an excellent match for a blind date. Claire wasn't having it; blind dating is such a bad idea. First of all, you could be paired with the most unappealing man of the decade. But it's even worse, if he says he isn't interested before ***you*** get the chance to say it first. Regardless, we all convinced her to go. After all, it was about time she met someone who wasn't just a rich, superficial loser.

The friend, who set the date up, was actually a well-off financial advisor, and because he was so convinced they would hit it off, he paid for the meal at an exclusive uptown restaurant. Claire dressed to impress. Richard was already there when she arrived. He was tall, dark and handsome; a stereotype, a cliché, call it what you will, but it was true! The closer she got to him, the more in shock she was. She couldn't believe that this guy was single. Claire was glad she took that little bit longer to get ready.

Richard was articulate and funny. He could hold a conversation and he really was gorgeous. He seemed to be genuinely interested in what she had to say too. During our hour-long phone conversation after the date, Claire said she'd felt herself melting every time she looked into his eyes. But the most amazing thing was that he seemed to be just as into her.

Apparently, the evening flew past. The conversation went from childhood fantasies, to adult passions, to teenage mistakes and lifelong dreams. And every topic seemed natural to have. There was no awkwardness at all. At the end of the night he dropped her off, giving her a kiss on the cheek, and asking to exchange numbers. What a perfect date. I was so jealous when she told me!

The icing on the cake was the text she received just as she got into bed:

'What a pleasure to meet such a wonderful person. Thank you for a great night'.

Claire dissolved into her pillow.

She was beaming the next morning when she came into work. Having woken up to a text asking for a second date the following weekend, she had wasted no time with her response.

The following month would seem like a dream to a lot of women, including Claire. They had a range of different dates, moving from the usual bar, restaurant and cinema scenarios; to picnics in beautifully scenic parks, art galleries and theatres. They shared tender moments and opened their minds to the world outside of their normal environments. They even went skydiving! Claire had finally discovered what dating was all about. It was fair to say Richard had swept her off her feet, and completely enticed her with his ideas for the future.

Richard's 'ideal' was no different to anybody else's. He wanted to be financially successful and stable. He wanted a big house, where his children could play and he could have close friends round for dinner. He wanted to minimise stress in his life and see everything that the world had to offer. This was all compelling, and he seemed to believe it was realistic. However, what really sealed the deal for Claire, was when he described the woman he wanted to share it with. He never said her name, but she seemed to possess every quality that Claire believed she had. He wouldn't be insincere; why would this man, beautiful inside and out, not be genuine?

Claire had never met a man so intensely involved with his feelings before. His 'liking' turned into 'loving' during the second month. It all seemed a little bit fast, but it didn't seem wrong at all, so Claire lapped it up. Richard's place in her affections was cemented one afternoon. The office was quiet and work was slow, so when a bunch of twelve beautifully cut roses turned up in a ribbon-tied box, we all got very excited. In anticipation, each of us wondered if they could possibly be for us.

As I've mentioned before, Claire is very insecure, especially around women who she perceives to be more attractive. She wouldn't in her wildest dreams have believed they were for her, but the delivery man headed in her direction to sign for the flowers! Of course, I was disappointed that no-one had thought of sending me roses; however, I was over the moon for Claire. She was absolutely glowing.

The card read: 'To the girl, who has given my dreams a new direction!'

She decided there and then that he was going to be rewarded. There had been no pressure or hurry to have sex on Richard's part, but after at least six dates and now ***this,*** she believed that he was more than worthy. For their next date, Claire would be wearing her sexiest lingerie underneath her most revealing but elegant outfit. She planned to make Richard want her from the moment he arrived.

The evening didn't disappoint. He was just as affectionate in his love-making as he was in everything else. She told us that it was ***more*** than just sex. Their connection was strengthened with every caress. Not only had there been 'electricity' between their bodies; afterwards Richard had whispered, "I've never met anyone like you before Claire. I think I'm falling for you." Claire was blissful.

This may seem too good to be true; unbelievable, even. But in that bed, considering Claire's insecurity, you can understand why she embraced every syllable.

"I think I am falling for you too." Was her reply.

When she told me all of this, Claire was like a can of cola that had been shaken up and opened. She had never really experienced love before. Of course, she'd heard the words, but she believed it had always been a ploy to remove her under-garments. This time she felt Richard was genuinely on the verge. And she didn't mind reminding me of it every five seconds.

The next couple of weeks followed suit. Every time Richard left, he gave Claire the impression that he couldn't wait to see her again, bombarding her with sweet texts and picture messages. He once drew hundreds of love hearts on a piece of paper using a highlighter pen from his work desk. The words 'I think I love Claire' were written underneath. She received the picture as she was in the waiting room for the dentist. He had remembered, since their first date, that she had been scared of the dentist ever since she was a little girl.

The dating ecstasy continued. Richard thought it was time that they went away for a weekend. He wanted some alone time with her, where he didn't have to 'give her straight back'. Claire made a preference for Paris, and a fortnight later they were jetting off to the romance capital of the world. I waited patiently for Claire to get home on the following Tuesday; I needed all of the gossip.

Her account was so detailed I thought she may have morphed into a tour guide! It started with a few drinks in the airport. Being tipsy on the plane was fun, behaving like touchy-feely teenagers and pretending to be sober to the stewardess. The hotel was more beautiful than the brochure gave it credit for, and they were given a room that was definitely designed with a new couple in mind. The amount of pictures of Claire and Richard together, gave the impression that they had stopped every tourist in the city in order to document their weekend.

Being away from the UK with Richard showed Claire that she could be happy with him anywhere on the planet. And the feeling was mutual. One evening, they went to the top of the Eiffel tower. In the style of a Hollywood movie, Richard looked meaningfully into Claire's eyes, cupped her face, and uttered the immortal words: "I love you Claire."

After almost collapsing from heart-pounding excitement, Claire responded mutually, and they kissed in possibly the most romantic place on the earth. I thought it was all quite clichéd, but my cynicism was dismantled with the joy that I could see in Claire's face. At last, my best friend had found a decent man. I was so happy for her.

What happened next was far from clichéd. I'll get to the point quickly.

There must have been something wrong with Richard's head.

After three months of emotionally intense perfection, he changed overnight. And I literally mean ***overnight***. Claire and I were late night shopping on Thursday. She had spilled the beans to the girls on Wednesday, and now she was revelling in a little retail indulgence. I bet after the boutiques of Paris, the UK high street was a severe comedown, but nothing could spoil Claire's mood. We headed towards a shop at the end of the road, discussing whether we should get something to eat, when Claire pointed into the distance.

"There's Richard!"

She suddenly had an added spring in her step; we were next to him in no time. As usual, he was dressed remarkably well in his business jacket and scarf. She called out to him and as he turned, she went to hug him. Richard was taken aback; his response was cold as ice.

"Hey, how are you?" he spoke in a monotone voice, looking wholly disappointed to see her. I wasn't the only one to notice this; Claire sensed it too.

"What's the matter?"

"Nothing; why? What's wrong with you?"

"Oh, nothing, I was just glad to see you. You remember my friend, Olivia?" Claire was obviously embarrassed by this aloof exchange. He gave a nod, which barely acknowledged my existence, before mumbling excuses about some office work and scuttling off in the opposite direction. I looked at Claire; she was lost for words. His behaviour was completely out of sync with the anecdotes she had been sharing about their trip away. It just didn't make any sense. A few days ago they were lovers in Paris, and now they were behaving like strangers.

Claire was a little shaken as we continued to shop, and I must admit the tone of the evening had become quite awkward. She sent a text to Richard but got no response until later that night: 'Sorry, I have a lot of work on'. It was clear that he didn't want to talk to her, but why? What had happened? Claire was at her wit's end trying to figure out what she'd done wrong. Was it something she'd said, or done, on the holiday that he had kept to himself? She was insistent that they'd had a wonderful time, and were still communicating fine on the way home. It must be something else. But it didn't seem as if Richard would be giving her any answers.

He then began to ignore her phone calls, texts and visits to his home. Any responses were pitiful: 'Sorry, working late', 'Will call you soon', and so on. Not one of his responses asked how she was. Claire quickly moved from confused and upset to p★★sed off. What was he playing at? Did he already have a girlfriend, or wife, and Claire was a bit on the side? Did he get cold feet? It was weird that Richard was suddenly so busy; when a few weeks ago he had all the time in the world.

Claire knew that if she gave up her efforts, all communication would grind to a halt. "He's fobbing me off," she said, during one emotional conversation. "I don't want to pester him but he needs to explain why he's changed."

A week later, Richard paid Claire a little bit more attention, mentioning that he was going away for work and that it would be lovely to have some company. This may not have been an invite, but she hurried to book time off work anyway. He ended up going alone, and afterwards his communication faltered again.

I could feel Claire's frustration building; I knew she would soon take decisive action. If Claire is anything, she's persistent. She wasn't going to take this lying down. Richard was finally nailed down, in a coffee shop that she knew he went to in his lunch hour. This time, he couldn't keep avoiding her. And now in this 'chance' meeting, he would have to explain himself. On seeing her face Richard knew he had no other option. He duly followed her to a corner booth, with his head down like a naughty schoolboy.

"Are you seeing somebody else?" Claire blurted out as soon as they were seated. She didn't want to give him any opportunity to conjure up a cover story. If he was playing around, then she wanted him to man up and admit it face-to-face.

"No Claire, I promise. I just thought things were moving too quickly and didn't know how to tell you." He sounded so immature; Claire's disdain for him was growing by the second. What a pathetic excuse. He went on to tell her that they weren't as good together as he'd originally thought. Even though she was 'amazing', he couldn't risk 'ruining it all', so he suggested that they went their separate ways.

Through his entire monologue, Claire stared at him in bewilderment. Although she may be insecure, Claire isn't desperate. She wasn't going to beg on her knees for another chance when he looked like a pathetic shell of the man who she had spent her time with. He went from seeming so genuine, to ducking and diving around what he'd 'claimed' he wanted. His aura was fast becoming a distant memory.

Claire agreed to break up with him. As much as she wanted to find Mr Right, she wasn't going to act like a crazy fool in a cafe. She had got her answers, although she was still mystified as to what had happened. She walked out, feeling sorry for the next woman who would fall for his stories.

DID YOU SPOT THE SIGNS REVEALING HIS TYPE?

★★★★

Whilst reminiscing about Claire's experiences with Richard, I was coincidently sitting in a coffee shop, waiting for Michael. When he arrived, I described Claire's situation and asked Michael to explain what type of man he was.

"Of course, there is no way for me to say for sure without knowing the man. However, if I had to make an educated guess, based on that ***detailed*** information you have given me, I would say Richard is a 'Sucker for Love' type. The majority of relationships with this type of man will be over after a short period (for example, three months). It is not possible for them to sustain the amount of emotional intensity they exude for any longer than that. Because they are usually attractive, and have a decent personality, people like Richard don't usually have trouble finding a girlfriend. Women are drawn by his striking looks, and they think that his personality and behaviour will inevitably be just as good. In psychology this is known as the 'halo' effect.

"At heart, they aren't bad guys either. They just go about everything the wrong way. They have idealistic dreams of relationships, but aren't used to working to maintain one. When attracted to a woman, he quickly begins to revel in her, bombarding her with texts, calls and gifts. He surrounds her with attention and may profess love or strong feelings a lot earlier than anybody would anticipate. However, in the blink of an eye, the relationship is boring! He 'realises' that she is the same as previous girls, and her physical blemishes suddenly become very apparent. This provides him, psychologically, with an easy explanation as to why the woman has lost her allure. He has become desensitised to normal, everyday relationships and requires new challenges to 'ensnare' his heart. This happens over and over again; it's a disappointing cycle of dependence for him.

"In terms of maturity, the 'Sucker for Love' is underdeveloped. He understands that things aren't supposed to happen in this way. Even when the women he dates are shocked and distressed, he understands how they feel. Nevertheless because his experiences haven't taught him to behave any differently, he just carries on as it's easier for him. To 'deal' with the consequences, he avoids any attempts of communication. Sometimes, the girls disappear without a trace. Sometimes, he is confronted, (like with Claire), but their persistence only disgusts him more. That is, until they're forgotten about and he falls hard and fast for another girl."

I liked Michael's confident explanation of Richard; and for the most part I agreed. It was the perfect ice-breaker too. I went on to ask about his goals for the book. Did he think he was onto a winner? He explained that he obviously wanted it to be a success, but he seemed much prouder about the achievement of finishing his book. He had completed an ambition, something I hadn't known anything about when we were studying together.

Of course, throughout this conversation I really only had one question on my mind: "So, which type are you?"

He laughed.

"Now, that would be telling. To be perfectly honest, I was shocked when I discovered my own type. It's definitely a harsh eye-opener." He continued by giving a brief outline of his dating history since university. Nothing too detailed, so the anecdotes I shared of my own were just as superficial. I tried hard to portray myself in a positive light. After all, he might have been trying to analyse ***me*** for his next book. You know what psychologists are like; they can't stop, can they? My cagey responses must have signalled like a traffic light; Michael assured me that he doesn't make a habit of studying or analysing people when he is in social situations. Psychology does not run his life.

"So how are you finding the book?" he enquired.

For a split second I thought about teasing him with an awkward silence, but in the end I went with honesty. "It's great! I'm really enjoying your descriptions and analysis. I can really relate to what you are saying. I think lots of women will buy it"

He looked pleased at my answer. Pointing to a couple on the table next to us, he decided to put my skills to the test. "Look at that man. What type of guy do you think he is?" he asked.

I glanced over, trying to be inconspicuous. Whether the couple were just friends or currently dating was unclear. What was plain as day however, was her positive body language; she was leaning in, suggesting that she was receptive to him. Her slightly flirtatious touching, and pushing, insinuated that she was comfortable in his company. The man was responding in kind.

I remembered reading earlier about the 'BET' that women have to consider – the combination of brain type, environmental impact and type of thought processes. These put together create the type of man. I answered with what I hoped was a confident tone.

"He looks nice; well-presented and clean shaven. They seem to be having a good conversation. I see a briefcase at his feet and a tablet on the table, professional. So I would say a 'Modern Man'." I tried to demonstrate that I had read the book thoroughly so far and had understood the theories he had introduced but nevertheless, he stopped me in my tracks.

"How could you possibly know after such a short period of time? Being so quick to judge is not really understanding your 'BET'"

Michael had snubbed me. He hadn't really wanted an answer. He was just showing me the misconception that we all hold, believing that you can tell someone's type from first impressions. As you can believe, I felt a little bit stupid!

"Don't worry." He reassured me "We have ***all*** done this at some point. This is part of the learning." Michael explained with a smile. *A difficult lesson*, I thought to myself. After we parted, I was left wondering who Michael really was. I was creating an image of him in my head, which despite my bruised ego in the café, I couldn't help but like…

++++

Chapter 15 – The psychology behind male excuses: What is the man made of?

★★★★

It was fair to say that after my meeting with Michael, I was slightly distracted back at work, but surprisingly the rest of the day flew by. On the train journey home, I delved into my new companion again; it was time for the technical part.

Since starting the book, I had begun to look more closely at the men around me. It had made me think so much more about all the things that can potentially influence us; that we take for granted.

At the station, I scanned the man standing next to me. He'd seemed average enough, probably in his early thirties; wearing a nicely tailored suit and overcoat. I assumed, by the way he tapped away on his tablet, that he may have some kind of office job. I noticed the wedding ring on his finger. Could he be a 'Modern Man'? But then his over-confident stance reminded me of Nick. Maybe he was just another 'Manipulator'?

I had gotten carried away again with my guesswork. So to kerb my assumptive behaviour, I decided to read Michael's psychological explanation, rather than rely on my own conjecture. I hoped it might shed some more light on the technique of identifying and exposing of the right types.

But, as I started reading I had a terrible thought: *He's going to spoil the book with a glut of big words, jargon and 'psychology-speak' that I can't understand*. I recognised that the book ***needed*** psychological evidence to authenticate his theory, but I was going to be so bored… I looked at my watch as the train pulled out of the station.

"I'll give it five minutes…" I said, knowing that secretly I was lying to myself. I wouldn't be putting this book down for a second! If I had to try a little harder to understand certain points or read paragraphs more than once then so be it.

Fortunately, I had no problem getting my head around it. Michael was obviously aware that the general public are interested in Psychology, but probably have little knowledge of it. Yes, I had a degree and a good job, but I still wasn't the sharpest knife in the drawer compared to all those PHD types. Michael's 'B.E.T. theory' is a simple way to understand a man's pattern of thoughts and behaviour, which may influence whether he will cheat or not.

++++

If we can understand the 'BETs' we make ***beforehand***, we may be able to prevent the emotion-driven behaviour, that some people, resort to ***after*** finding out they have been cheated on. B.E.T. theory considers the foundations and circumstances which influenced the infidelity, in relation to the man's brain (B), environment (E) and thought processes (T). This concept can help to enlighten, ***both*** men and women, to potentially overcome confusion in situations and enhance their relationship future.

The theory draws from the data collected from interviews and questionnaires with 547 men. It is suggested, that the previously mentioned 'justification schema', was identifiable in over 91% of the men that admitted to cheating on their partners. This schema – that allows men to legitimise infidelity in their own mind – can be shown through a number of behaviours. These include: their ***language,*** the frequency of their use of ***excuses***, their ***explanations of infidelity*** in other men, and if they generally hold ***unequal gender related attitudes*** about relationships and cheating; amongst many others.

We all know these aren't always easy to spot. Most of us attempt to hide our flaws. However, patterns will start to emerge after a significant amount of time; when habitual behaviour takes over. And this is where B.E.T. theory comes in. The ***patterns,*** displayed by a man, can highlight what type he is, and what kind of 'BET' you are making in being with him.

AN INTRODUCTION TO B.E.T. THEORY

Your 'BET' is a ***metaphor*** for entering into a relationship. Obviously, there are different types of both men and women; and ***both*** sexes need to be aware of their 'BETs'. However, based on the research and for the purpose of this book, the 'BET' has been applied solely to a woman's choice when entering into a relationship with a man. Understanding the 'BET' means being as aware as possible to what the commitment with a particular individual may involve.

This is done by considering the dominant components that underlie and dictate the man's behaviour. For example, a strong academic home background could have a powerful influence on a man's level of motivation; whereas a lenient background in regards to education could lead to a man having issues with authority. Both examples are a demonstration of a strong ***environment*** in understanding a 'BET'. These environmental influences may have a significant impact on his thoughts. You must take the time to understand this.

Like gambling as a whole some 'BETs' are well-calculated, whilst others are nothing short of recklessly 'putting the house on red'.

Underestimating the interaction of a man's environment and thought processes, is probably, the most significant aspect in making poor 'BETs'. We have all experienced how some men can shift from the suave, considerate specimen from the first date to someone quite the opposite, within a few short weeks. It is important to not rush into anything. Making poor 'BETs', (whatever the reason), may be a key factor as to why it is estimated that 90% of all relationships don't reach the two-year mark. Successful couples, on the other hand, are based on continual awareness and ***maintenance*** from day one. Understanding B.E.T. theory may just help you clear that two-year hurdle.

★★★★

I could see a little more clearly how both women and men can make poor relationship 'BETs'. For example, some women feel the pressure of their biological clock or go for finances over compatibility. Some women simply feel unhappy compared to other couples, unless they are part of a relationship too. Men also make poor choices, selecting the youthful 'trophy' girlfriend who becomes an extension of his male ego; or seeking someone he can control, who will not challenge his ideas or decisions. Perhaps, in a dysfunctional relationship, both people might have rushed into it.

Maybe men are just as vulnerable as we are, I thought to myself. *After all, some of us girls can be a real nightmare, once the make-up comes off!*

++++

'WORKING HIM OUT'

Many conversations women have about men will reveal that a common desire, amongst a lot of women, is to know ***exactly*** how men think; to be able to 'work him out'. This would make life a whole lot easier. But this is impossible. No-one can take a holiday into the mind of their partner, with a tour guide explaining the way to his inner-most thoughts. So it's important that you stop attempting to do this. All you can do is understand the ***outward behaviour patterns*** that he displays.

Now, being aware of your 'BET' firstly means understanding that there are twenty-seven different types of men to choose from. It is obvious that a large number of people rush into making reckless 'BET's ***not*** knowing this. You now have the upper hand! However, most people base their relationship expectations on optimism. They have an early feeling that things 'might' work out, only to find that the world that they envisioned comes crashing down like a pack of cards.

This is probably because they didn't know which of the twenty-seven types they were with. Knowing the different types will put a more realistic spin on your expectations, assumptions and perceptions.

The following chapters describe the dynamic interaction between the three main components of B.E.T. theory, in great detail, so that you are able to identify different types of men. Together, the nature of his brain, his environmental influences and his thought processing strategies create one of the twenty-seven types. In each man, one of the three components will ***dominate***, having the biggest influence on his behaviour.

Examples of the three B.E.T. theory components will be portrayed through his behaviours and conversation. At times the patterns will be easily identifiable. At others, they will be more subtle. So it is up to you to pay attention to the man in question.

This does not mean you have to study them.

It simply suggests that when you do spend time together, engage with them meaningfully to understand who they are first of all. This is ***before*** considering what they will mean to your life. Remember, you are supposed to be finding out who ***they*** are in the early stages of a relationship, not what they can do for you.

The Three B.E.T. Theory components

- **The brain (B)** is hardwired into a man's individual system. It will dictate the things he is naturally drawn to. For example: the tasks, environments, situations and people he is enticed by. There are three different types of brains, which are 'systemising' (s), 'empathising' (e), and 'balanced' (b) – (Baron Cohen 2003).
- **The environment (E)** that a man was both raised in, and regularly interacts with, is the second component. This will dictate the passive, and interactive, influences that he has automatically accepted into his outward behaviour, from birth to adulthood. The types of potential environments that a man is generally exposed to are 'male' (m), 'female' (f) and 'combination' (c) environments.
- **The thought processing (T)** that a man commonly uses completes the triad. The way he thinks will dictate the conscious and automatic strategies that he uses to handle situations, interpret new encounters and to solve problems. The types of thought processing are classed as 'logical' (l), 'intuitive' (i), and 'amalgamated' (x).

These combined together give you the 'type' of man: so for example **B**-f-l would be the 'Back and Forth' type while the b-m-**X** would be the 'Metrosexual' (see chapter 21).

Figure 4 – The B.E.T. Theory diagram – illustrating the dynamic synergy between the three key components.

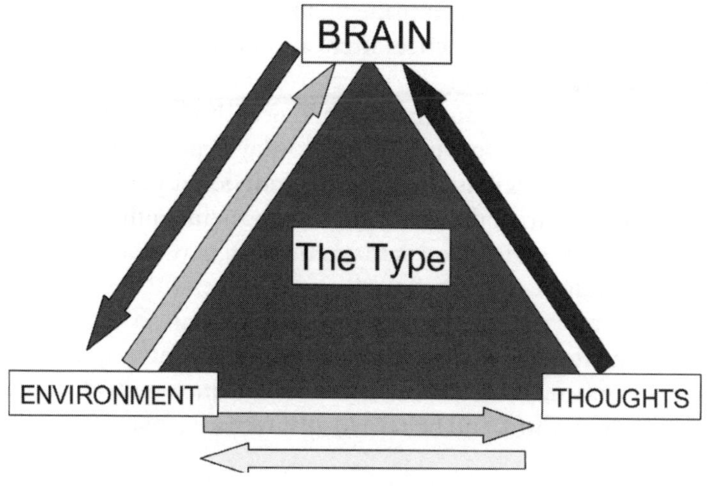

★★★★

That's pretty straightforward, I thought. *We've established that we have many different influences. Tell me something I don't know, Mike.* And he did.

++++

UNDERSTANDING THE COMPONENTS

As simple as it sounds, using B.E.T. theory can make a real difference between minimising and maximising infidelity in your relationship. It really is the ***interaction*** between the three components that creates a 'type' and explains so much.

The brain (B) type dictates the things in our environment (E) that we are stimulated by. For example, if a man possesses a 'systemising' brain, he may be attracted to machines and mechanics. Thus, he may seek out similar environments where he can explore how parts work together. These may include Design Technology classes at school, fixing machines or working with scientific technology as a career. In these environments, a man can feel further stimulated by meeting like-minded people who enhance his desires, such as peers, teachers, colleagues and family members. Simultaneously, he may also meet people who do the opposite, (i.e. try to hinder his systemising yearnings), which ***actually*** pushes him faster towards his desires.

How a man with a systemising brain (B) responds to the people and environments (E) he encounters also depends on his thought processing strategies (T). In the above scenario, his brain and environment appear to suggest that a logical thinking strategy may be best for him to cope with his day-to-day experiences. If so, he will then create schemas based on his individual perception. For example, men who are drawn to and are successful with systemising experiences, (i.e. being good at mathematics), may create a schema which only values people who are just as successful and disregard those who are not. This cognitive interpretation may create challenging interpersonal situations for him with non-systemising people. For example, creative or artistically inclined individuals may pressure him to think and behave in an alternative manner; or they could force him to become more rigid with his own style of thinking.

However, this clearly illustrates that the environment and thought processes working together can either reinforce, or contradict, what is hardwired into his brain type.

Over time, any learned behaviours from his environments may become 'automatic responses'; teaching him how to handle future similar situations, with little conscious awareness. If the three components create a positive outcome in his mind, he will believe that this is how he can, and should, act. For example, if a man is influenced by his components to cheat on his girlfriend, and he believes he will get away with it, he may very well do it… and then do it again.

As simple as it sounds, you must understand that ***nothing*** can be taken for granted, if B.E.T. theory is to be completely mastered.

Consider this example of one man who was interviewed:

The man had been in a relationship with his partner for three years. After a great start, problems began arising around two years into it. He was unhappy in the relationship and for the last year, he had been seeking an exit strategy.

The Man: The Guilty Conscience (Eml)

	Brain	Environment	Thought	B.E.T. code	Type
MAN 1	**EMPATHISING (e) (dominant)**	MALE (m)	LOGICAL (l)	Eml	The 'Guilty Conscience'

He was aware that his partner depended on him, emotionally and financially. She came from a difficult background and he provided the first real stability in her life. He regularly felt sorry for her. He didn't want to hurt her feelings or revisit memories of her past; especially when she brought up his level of success compared to her lack thereof. ***His feelings in these situations could be driven by his 'empathising' (e) brain.*** This was dominant within him, and he was hardwired to understanding what other people may be going through. He wanted to end things with her; however he lacked the 'guts' to go through with it.

He didn't really talk much about his own emotions. Although he felt that he possessed good social skills, he didn't feel he could express his viewpoints effectively to her. He had two older brothers and lots of male friends. He socialised regularly with them in passive environments such as watching sports or going to the gym. Conversation was usually superficial, containing little depth or true expression, thus, he had no real practice in telling his peers, let alone his girlfriend, how he really felt. To damage things further, his peers would tell him to 'just put up with her because she's hot'. ***These could be viewed as stereotypically male environments (m)***.

The man was a very straightforward thinker and often got into arguments with his girlfriend because she didn't see 'obvious' points of view. She failed to make sense of things and reacted emotionally. This conflicted with his rational perspective on situations. With this in mind, it didn't make sense to him to be in a relationship where there was constant conflict. He wanted to break-up even more.

During this time of confusion, and consideration of his options, he met somebody else. This woman made it clear that she was interested in him. She was open to any advance he may initiate, but was insistent that she wouldn't make the first move. He didn't either, but he liked her a lot, maybe even more than his current partner. So he innocently, (but secretly), started spending time with her. Logically, it made sense to spend time with somebody he liked, appreciated and felt would bring him some escape and enjoyment. He might have a girlfriend, but why cause problems at home by mentioning his new friend when there was really no need to? In his mind, he wasn't actually doing anything wrong as nothing physical had happened. He just knew his girlfriend would not understand. So he kept it from her to prevent any unnecessary distress. ***These are all examples of 'logical' thought processing (l)***.

It may not have been intentional, but the man had just created a situation of infidelity in his relationship. With a new secret to contend with, he was creating added guilt for himself. His 'logical' processing may have told him to break-up with his girlfriend, but it was the dominating 'empathising' brain, that worried more about how she would cope alone, that prevented it. The strength of this emotion kept him in a vicious circle. He did want to break-up with her, but experienced guilt thinking about how she would feel if she knew what he was thinking, and/or doing.

In every one of the twenty-seven different types, one of the three dimensions will ***dominate***. It is evident here that this usually plays a big part in what actually happens.

Contrary to the 'Guilty Conscience' type above, other types of men wouldn't have responded to this situation in the same way. Consider these types; what do you think would happen?

	Brain	Environment	Thought	B.E.T. code	Type
MAN 2	**BALANCED (b) (dominant)**	FEMALE (f)	INTUITIVE (i)	**B**fi	The 'Under The Thumb'
MAN 3	BALANCED (b)	**MALE (m) (dominant)**	LOGICAL (l)	b**M**l	The 'Act First, Think Later'
MAN 4	**SYSTEMISING (s) (dominant)**	FEMALE (f)	INTUITIVE (i)	**S**fi	The 'Thinker'

It is evident that each type of man has a unique B.E.T. theory combination, with one dominant dimension. Each type would react differently to the situation above. B.E.T. theory, therefore, allows an individual to assess what type of person a man really is, and maintain a romantic relationship, with a greater understanding than those without.

★★★★

After reading the chapter I was exhausted. But I understood afterwards that each influential factor had its own part to play in creating a man's type. I was beginning to see the errors made by my friends, family and myself; even my favourite characters on TV. I was ready to learn, in depth, about the different components of B.E.T. theory; and I hoped that it would also reveal a little inkling as to who Michael really was too…

++++

Chapter 16 – B.E.T. THEORY (Part 1) – Assessing a man's 'type' – The Brain

IN B.E.T. THEORY – THERE ARE THREE BRAIN TYPES		
SYSTEMISING BRAIN (male)	BALANCED BRAIN	EMPATHISING BRAIN (female)
s	**b**	**e**

The first distinction we must make is between the brain and the mind. Quite often people get them confused. Sometimes they are used synonymously, but in psychology, they are not the same thing. The brain is the physical structure inside your head. It uses electrical responses to stimulate actions in the body. Different parts of the brain process incoming sensory information and create a response to it. The brain can be touched and objectively measured. The mind, however, is different and related to thought processing. It can, for example, influence beliefs of capability on a specific task. Even though the brain may be hardwired and capable of completing the task, the mind can make it a struggle if it wants. This is more a part of self-efficacy (self-belief) than any biological drive. The distinction between the mind and the brain needs to be clear.

DIFFERENT BRAINS

Men and women have always been noted for their differences. According to recent research, one such difference is that they appear to have different brains. Also, not only do men and women differ in brain types but the twenty-seven types of men do not all share the same brain type either. This plays a huge role in the way each man behaves. After all, the organ plays a central role in all of our human actions.

It is common knowledge that men and women differ in the hormones that they produce. The way these bio-chemicals such as oestrogen, testosterone and oxytocin interact within the body and with the brain has been well documented. However, the psychologist Simon Baron-Cohen (2003), has taken this research a step further with the identification that there may be gender differences in brain ***type,*** as well as the bio-chemicals.

Baron-Cohen developed the 'Empathising-Systemising (E-S) Theory' of the brain. This concept believes that ***'on average',*** males and females tend to be born with different brain types.

The 'male' brain is predominantly hardwired to 'systemising' (s), meaning men with this type of brain are more prone to understand structures and how things work together. Based on the understanding of rules and finding the solutions to problems, this may be shown in a preference for computers, mechanics or mathematics. It also seems to be supported by the gender bias towards professions, such as engineering and science.

The 'female' brain, on the other hand, is predominantly hardwired to 'empathising' (e). This correlates well with the common perception that women are much more able to understand the emotions of others. They tend to take these emotions into account when considering their own actions. The empathising brain instinctively recognises how people are feeling. It knows how to treat people with care and sensitivity. Baron-Cohen's work has suggested that these gender differences in the workings of the human brain, can be observed in children as early as twelve months old.

In support of E-S theory, research suggests that it is evident from an early age that boys show more interest in constructional and mechanical toys. They also score better on 'systemising' tests such as following maps and building physical structures from pictures. Girls, on the other hand, by the age of six are better at considering what other people need and deciphering non-verbal communication.

Baron-Cohen goes on to argue that the difference is ***just*** a difference, however. It does not mean that one brain type is superior to the other. They are incomparable in such a way, as they both have strengths and weaknesses, with either type being more appropriate at different times. Baron-Cohen also points out that although, 'on average', males will possess a systemising brain and females an empathising one, some people have the best of both worlds. That is being equally capable in both systemising and empathising. This is known as the 'balanced' (b) brain.

However, could it be possible for a man not to fit the 'average'? Could he possess an empathising brain? This is an important factor that Baron-Cohen says does occur. And in the case of B.E.T. theory, we must consider this when understanding the varied patterns of behaviour in different types of men; for example, the common and rarer types.

★★★★

The E-S theory got me thinking about things I had taken for granted. Every girl I knew did generally lean towards things with an emotional consideration of others. And this was shown in our everyday lives. We do tend to view the characters on soap operas as real people, engrossed in their romances, fashion and relationships. We're all as bad as each other. Our status updates about reality TV give us away completely. I have always felt that women are also more sensitive to facial expressions and are much better at picking up on a 'vibe' in social situations.

My group of female friends definitely showed this empathetic interest in lots of different ways. Helen, for instance, tended to talk a lot about parenting. She would overly-concern herself with how other women raise their kids. She would get into the occasional argument when she went too far. Claire, on the other hand, was the 'horoscope queen' and the 'agony aunt' rolled into one. I could never effectively explain my compulsion to know what was going on in the

Types of men with a systemising 'male' brain

The Charmer,
The Disdainer,
The Lads' Lad,
The Manipulator,
The Opportunist,
The Rationaliser
The Stupid mistake
The Thinker,
The Visionary

lives of other people. I used to think I was just nosey, but perhaps, I just had an empathising brain. Was I hardwired to be drawn to such things? This actually made me feel a lot better.

And men; they definitely did appear systematic from my experience. From Nick, trying to explain the intricacies of the new offside rule in football, to Cameron's determination to hook his new TV to the surround sound system, without the wires being on show, of course. Even the computer games that some men seem so inescapably drawn to, have some form of systemising within them.

Perhaps I needed to consider this difference more consciously. I used to just ignore my men when they were talking about football and computer games. Most of my friends do the same. But then can we blame them for ignoring ***our*** preferences? Although very different, if neither brain type is superior, then maybe neither gender is in the wrong when some form of communication gets 'lost in translation'.

Our brains may seduce us into responding in such ways. And this may be where many disagreements and discrepancies occur between the two sexes in our relationships. However, these were only my experiences. Not all men love technology and sports. You can't tar every guy with the same 'systemising' brush. Michael also went on to describe how each type of brain comes with its own problems too.

++++

THE DRAWBACKS OF DIFFERENT BRAIN TYPES

A man's brain type can have many drawbacks in social situations, especially when it is the dominant component. Despite its obvious advantages to interpersonal relationships, having an empathising brain may make the male owner engage a little ***too*** much in the lives of other people. This can result in negative consequences such as

Types of men with a balanced 'systemising/empathising' brain

Act First, Think Later,
Back and Forth,
Easily Influenced,
The Family Man,
The Metrosexual,
The Modern Man,
Mr. Secure,
Sucker for Love,
Under The Thumb

regularly gossiping about others, knowingly excluding people from peer groups and excessively 'bitchy' remarks. Also, he may neglect his own life because of his focus on others. In the world of social networking, this is becoming increasingly more frequent and taken for granted.

On the other end of the spectrum, the man with a systemising brain may find it difficult to spot subtle changes in emotion or incorporate them into any of his subsequent responses. Some emotions are not seen as essential to his working 'system'. This can infuriate 'empathisers' who may incorrectly assume that non-empathisers should 'know how they feel', even though it may appear that they don't.

In the context of relationships, perhaps the average man is deconstructing how his ***relationship,*** (a type of system), 'should' operate and this is the consequence of having a hardwired systemising brain. Whilst the average woman is trying to understand how the ***man,*** (the individual with emotion), 'should' respond; a consequence of an empathising brain perhaps. What's more, if men, who are hardwired to understand systems, see their relationship as one, some men could try to see where cheating behaviour can fit into the system, perhaps justifying a drive towards infidelity.

★★★★

I agreed wholeheartedly with this. *With our empathising brains, women have become the masters of the verbal snipe*, I thought; *we know exactly what will hurt another person's feelings, although we all know a bitchy man too*. I felt like I was getting to grips with our brains on a superficial level, but of course, it is the interaction with the other components of B.E.T. theory which creates a man's 'type'.

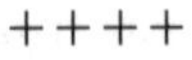

Types of men with an empathising 'female' brain

Mr. Adaptable,
The Appreciator,
The Chameleon,
The Enigma,
The Girlfriend,
The Guilty Conscience,
One Step Ahead,
The Swinger,
The Woman's Mind

STIMULATION IN THE ENVIRONMENT

Baron-Cohen suggested that stimulating environments can strengthen the biological hardwiring, making individuals more 'resistant' to change. For example, many societies encourage boys to withhold emotion whilst females are credited for expression. If boys possessed systemising brains and girls empathising ones, this social value will ***directly*** reinforce their biological drives.

However, a man who possesses an ***empathising*** brain in this situation, may be caught in a difficult position. He may have no 'acceptable' way of expelling this 'alien' emotion. Therefore, without the appropriate stimulation, he must find other methods of expression. This may mean changing his thought processes or seeking out environments which are not the stereotypical norm. In this way, the individual reaction to environmental stimulation, (or lack thereof), also influences the type of man he will become.

It appears that having a balanced brain would be the most appropriate of all. The individual would be stimulated by a range of activities. He would feel comfortable interacting with a range of different people in a plethora of situations. He should acquire skills that would allow him to solve problems efficiently, while taking the emotions of those involved into account.

QUESTIONS TO CONSIDER:

> Is he a ***people person*** or a ***planner***?
>
> What type of activities is he ***naturally*** drawn to that brings him enjoyment?
>
> At times of stress and anxiety does he want to '***do***' things or be '***near***' people?
>
> Does he '***feel***' his experiences or does he '***evaluate***' them?

★★★★

Michael's use of Baron-Cohen's research to identify differences in male brain types and possible impacts on infidelity, had laid the foundation of his B.E.T. theory. This led to the next part: the environmental influences. As I sat on my sofa and turned the page, I realised that I wasn't getting any sleep that night.

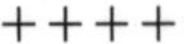

Chapter 17 – B.E.T. THEORY (Part 2) – Assessing a man's 'type' – The Environment

IN B.E.T. THEORY – THERE ARE THREE ENVIRONMENTS

MALE ENVIRONMENT	COMBINATION ENVIRONMENT	FEMALE ENVIRONMENT
m	**c**	**f**

Everybody wants to 'belong' to something or someone. Two of the most powerful human drives are survival and acceptance. That's why it's so easy for an environment to ensnare an individual. It can provide both!

The environmental influence is probably the easiest component of B.E.T. theory to understand, as we can see it happening all around us. Nevertheless, this concept requires you to look at what you may take for granted with fresh eyes. The environment acts as a ***bridge*** between the brain type and the development of thought processes. The more we allow the environment to passively influence our schemas (including the justification schema) without challenging them, the more we allow cheating behaviour to thrive.

'I AM A PRODUCT OF MY ENVIRONMENT'

For the purpose of B.E.T. theory, the 'environment' refers to the 'social environment'. This is the immediate physical and social setting where individuals live and interact daily. It includes important features such as the culture, people, institutions and knowledge that an individual interacts with. During our childhood, we don't really understand what an environment is; it's just home and school, the sights, sounds and people that characterise both. By the time we begin to question its influence, it has already taken a firm (sometimes crippling) grip on us; dictating everything from our culture to how we speak, socialise and respond emotionally.

Our environment will influence how sensitive, (or de-sensitised), we are to things that we come into contact with. Many adults misguidedly shun the impact their environment has had on them. Instead, they prefer to look for other deterministic explanations (perhaps religion, genes, in-built personality or fate), as to why things in their life occurred the way they did. In doing this, many fail to recognise the powerful environmental blueprint in their lives and continue to remain passive to its influences.

HOW POWERFUL IS THE ENVIRONMENT?

Your primary caregivers and familiar adults create your early environment. These people leave their teachings ingrained on your existence; whether you like it or not, (The Appreciator' type (**E**fi) is a good example of this). When it comes to men, no real understanding of their patterns of outward behaviour can be gained, without careful consideration of their past and present environmental surroundings. The psychologist John Watson was confident that the environment is paramount in moulding a new-born into the adult that they become in later life. He conducted a series of well-renowned experiments that supported his famous statement:

> *'Give me a dozen healthy infants, well-formed, and my own specified world to bring them up in and I'll guarantee to take any one at random and train him to become any type of specialist I might select – doctor, lawyer, artist, merchant-chief and, yes, even beggar-man and thief, regardless of his talents, penchants, tendencies, abilities, vocations, and race of his ancestors' (Watson, 1930, p.82).*

For Watson, 'nurture' (what takes place in the environment) is much more important than anything a man is born with (such as genes). Each individual is born as a 'blank slate'. Through their experiences they add behaviours to the slate via a psychological process known as 'conditioning'. Learning by association is a form of conditioning. For example, if a boy regularly observed his father and mother being physically intimate (i.e. hugging, kissing, holding hands etc.) he may associate this caring, sensitive behaviour with every romantic relationship and may be shocked if he observes anything different.

In other words, Watson would conclude that cheaters are not born, they are made; the environment is the sole determinant of this. Given the right circumstances, Watson's teachings suggest that he could create a 'Manipulator', a 'Chameleon', a 'Charmer' or anything he liked! This is a very plausible, if not simplistic explanation, as it is evident that children are very impressionable. Any such behaviours can be strengthened and become automatic through positive or negative reinforcement of the associations children make. For example, a child may receive a reward for a positive behaviour, such as getting a sticker if they do well at school. The reward acts as a reinforcement (strengthening) which will make an individual likely to behave in the same way again. Similarly, if a negative behaviour goes unpunished and the individual gains something from it, this behaviour can be reinforced in the same way too (Skinner).

It is easy to see how positive reinforcement can be beneficial in a relationship; however, it can also be used negatively. If a man is unfaithful and his partner automatically forgives him, this acts as a reward. If he can satisfy the desire for sexual variety without losing his relationship, his cheating behaviour could possibly be strengthened. So understanding the 'BET' relating to this man would require an understanding of which behaviours have been reinforced in such a way. Most conditioning occurs without an individual even realising. A clear example of how much environmental influences are taken for granted.

For a woman to understand a man's patterns, she must become ***conscious*** of the past and present environments that continue to influence his behaviour. Generally, there are three types of environment and a man will predominantly operate within one of them. Obviously, every person's social group will have unique features that do not explicitly fit these categories, but generally the majority fall into:

- **Male dominated (m):** these environments transmit patriarchal and stereotypically masculine ideals. They are competitive, with rigid patterns and group norms; physicality and sexuality are common themes.

- **Female dominated (f):** these environments are more communicative and expressive. There is an emphasis on group harmony. Intimacy is freely expressed, yet general sexuality, in comparison is slightly repressed.
- **Combination (c):** these environments are characterised by considered and thoughtful conversations. Every individual has freedom of speech. They are more flexible and dynamic; genderless perspectives are common.

THE TYPICAL ADULT MALE ENVIRONMENT

Most types of men frequent male dominated (m) environments. In Western society especially, (regardless of religion, social class or culture), there are typical characteristics of adult male environments. Most men will continue to frequent male environments for the majority of their lives. It is their realm of solace and they are socialised into it via their home parental rearing, their childhood peers, the games they play and their academic and vocational choices. Boys are nurtured into being a stereotypical 'boy', from the rejection of the colour pink, to their preference for football over dance. This clear division between genders – established ***before*** birth – creates the initial difference between male dominated and female dominated environments.

The typical male environment will vary in its form for each man depending on factors such as location, social class, ethnicity and occupation amongst others. But most of its fundamental traits will be the same and will form an integral part of every man's existence regardless of these factors. It plays a huge role in whom they become and who they remind you of. All men will share some elements that make them kindred spirits with their peers.

'JUST LIKE DADDY' (THE IMPORTANCE OF MALE ROLE MODELS)

Men have a desire to know 'who they are'. This is often depicted in 'rites of passage' movies. Children copy the behaviour of others because they need to identify with somebody else ***before*** they can form their own identity. For a child, role models act as stepping-stones towards creating an identity of their own that will conform and fit in with their social group. But this learning can have more impact depending on ***who*** presents the information. A male's role models, (whether direct or indirect), will play a huge part in the patterns of behaviour you have to deal with in a relationship.

Most young children gravitate towards people who look like them, i.e. the same gender. This makes modelling behaviour easier for them and has an extremely powerful influence. Many psychological studies have shown that throughout an individual's life, same-sex role models are instrumental in the development of aggression, addictive behaviour and views on relationships. The desire of young children to imitate same-sex role models, adds to the segregation of male and female environments in a very dynamic way.

In reference to the 'types', some men are more influenced by their role models than others. The 'Modern Man' is one type that is highly influenced by his environment as he tries to 'keep up with what's new'. Popular public figures may play a bigger part for him than they do for other men. The behaviour of the 'Family Man' also seems to be influenced heavily. If the role models for these men set a bad example, then they may automatically find more justification to embrace or reject cheating behaviour than others.

There is a potential here for a 'cycle of infidelity'.

An individual may replicate the same patterns that lead to unfaithful behaviour that he saw his role models perform. And this continues in a tautological sequence, as in time, they become the role model for others.

THE COMPETITIVE MALE ENVIRONMENT

From adolescence onwards, peers take centre stage in creating an influential environment.

Adolescence is a time ***dominated*** by stereotypes. One thing often taken for granted, is that the period of adolescence ***still*** dominates some adult males' lives. They cannot let it go. The typical male subculture is ***competitive***. It begins in pre-adolescence and extends into many adult environments; crossing all ages and cultural boundaries. Take Western society, for instance. Young and older males alike compete with each other over who is the smartest, strongest and most attractive! Sexual potency and comedic acumen are must-haves. The art of being successful without really trying is also paramount. This all explodes during adolescence.

The competition can be seen in the pursuit of females, athletic dominance and group status. Even something as simple as betting against each other is a culmination of his intellectual, common sense and financial decision-making skills; all put to the test in one swift moment. A bet is something he mustn't back down on. This is an opportunity to show his superiority!

This competition extends into his choice of sports team if he has one. Everything he supports is an extension of ***him.*** So if they lose, he loses too. He cannot be seen to make wrong decisions nor endorse 'failure', or the peer group will mock him. It could be argued, that this is a throwback to evolutionary times. Long ago, physical exertions and competition with other males were necessary for survival and reproduction. Now, psychological boasts and demonstrations, which exaggerate masculinity, are used more commonly to emerge victorious within these competitive environments.

One of the most competitive male weapons is the use of banter and ridicule. It is the 'cornerstone' of typical male groups across social settings and working environments. It has replaced physical assaults as the primary means to exhibit dominance, but leaves behind a trail of patterns. It can make men feel anxious, aggressive and insecure. But one of the most important features of this entire process is 'being able to take it like a man'. Male jokes can be vicious! But men must be able to resist the temptation to show emotion; saying a joke hurt their feelings is a no-no.

This continual repressing of emotion may explain a classic pattern in relationship behaviour. One minute, your man has disclosed a heart-warming emotional experience; you think you have 'reached' him. The next moment, he has left you feeling utterly confused by building a wall of bravado to prevent any further escape of feeling. This is because,

Types of men that frequent a 'male' environment

The Opportunist,
The Disdainer,
One Step Ahead,
The Lads' Lad,
The Swinger,
Act First, Think Later,
The Sucker for Love,
The Metrosexual,
The Guilty Conscience

regardless of how damaging the male competitive environment may be to the man, for some, it is their only place of comfort. It is all they know. For some, the expression of emotion feels like a betrayal to everything that they have been told. So they clam up, act hard and effectively go back to square one.

Sexual competition is also abundant in male subcultures. Although, in some situations this is insidious, it is mostly found in direct banter over which man is the most experienced, the most skilled, attracts the most beautiful women and whether females choose one man over another. Common male environments thus create norms and values about 'acceptable' behaviour. These involve the themes of 'honour', physical ability and sexual virility. This is a perfect opportunity to observe patterns in his behaviour, via his ***language, beliefs and attitudes***.

Many women view much male subcultural behaviour as immature, believing this 'immaturity' contributes to why some men cheat. If men behave in this way, it shows a clear refusal to grow up and relinquish the attitudes and behaviours not befitting of a responsible adult. However, it is not actually a matter of immaturity. It is more about the fact that typical male environments are governed by inherent ***insecurity***.

All adults (mature or not) ***need*** security. A common fear of most men is that appearing to not engage with the subcultural values of their male environment will result in marginalisation from their peer group; or a loss of status. They feel they will become the target of ridicule, isolation and prejudice. Therefore, conforming to the 'acceptable' behaviour of the group is more about being ***accepted*** by one's peers. This is the ***primary*** concern rather than any immature desire to engage in negative behaviours such as infidelity.

This may explain why these men appear to be, in contrast, mature and responsible in one-to-one situations with the opposite sex. He may even hold highly respectable positions of responsibility, like a doctor or a lawyer, in his professional life. But that professional status holds no weight in his male subculture. A doctor is as equal as the shop assistant.

This may make such men who have worked to obtain status in other fields, feel insecure in this one; something women need to understand. Feeling alienated from a group is something that every individual fears, (even women), and has the potential to experience.

Incorporating this knowledge into your perspective, will bring a greater understanding of masculine pressures and experiences within a male dominated environment. Empathising with it, will help you understand that these environments ***always*** create identifiable patterns.

SHOULD WE LET A MAN BE A MAN?

It is clear that most early environments for children are predominantly male or female. So why do some people assume that adult environments would not mirror this? It is almost impossible to expect a man (or woman) to change the habit of a lifetime at the drop of a hat. However, if gender roles are not challenged, and are passively built upon throughout an individual's life, automatic responses are the inevitable result. These responses become extremely difficult to adapt later on. This is especially so if the individual in question is extremely comfortable in the environments that they know. So if we encourage boys to be boys, should we let a man be a man?

For example, boys may be rewarded for building a replica toy car (stereotypically male) and girls rewarded for simulating a beautiful tea party (stereotypically female). If neither gender is encouraged to try the opposite, then a norm will be created. This norm may hinder the ability to deal with ***unfamiliar*** situations in the future. A woman may not be able to change a car wheel, and a man may struggle to arrange a dinner party, even though neither task in itself is difficult. But we may chastise an adult for this inability.

Society has tried to encourage more equality for girls, pushing them towards sports such as football, for example. This allows them to experience a different type of environment. However, this is not encouraged in boys and thus, places them at a social and emotional disadvantage. They aren't encouraged to try cheerleading and netball. The same could be said about dress sense. Females can easily wear stereotypical male attire, but the reverse would be questioned. Although this is taken for granted, these norms and values in society reaffirm a masculine environment onto men with its typical traits of insecurity and competitiveness.

For some men in romantic relationships, it may be too late. The inevitable challenge to his automatic responses from a female partner comes at an advanced stage in his life. He feels he can't help but rigidly stick to what he knows. He is not willing to adapt. In this way, it's evident why some men only feel comfortable in male environments. The challenges to his comfort zone – i.e. his partner questioning why he prefers to watch football regularly rather than spend time with her – are viewed as his partner moaning at him. She does not give him the space to do what he wants to do. She is trying to control him; so he seeks his male environments, where he knows what to expect. Ironically, why does the same wife, who chastises a husband about watching football, then encourage her son to take a full part in the school team? The cycle continues.

Many men resist opportunities to change. This is because for some, they fear it or see the chances to do so as being few and far between. These men have learned to be helpless, choosing to remain in their comfort zone. Some women may see this as weak; others habitual. After years of influence from same-sex role models and competitive peer groups, being in a committed and emotionally open relationship, can be an alien situation which shakes a man's equilibrium.

It is important to realise that the sometimes hostile and competitive male environment, where men have been nurtured, may be the only place that provides any form of security. Being constantly told to 'grow out of it' may not be an appropriate response as he searches for his own personal identity – which in reality may be many years away – even if you demand it now. We all know certain responsibilities (i.e. children) cannot wait for him to do so.

The result of this emotional turmoil can be poor decision-making on his part in relation to things such as infidelity. This again depicts how powerful the environment can be on adult male behaviour. For example, 'Easily Influenced' types sometimes actually try ***harder*** to reinforce stereotypical behaviours and norms, even when it is not appropriate. This may be an attempt to fit in or to receive some form of recognition from his peers – even if it may be at the expense of his romantic relationship.

The suggestion of B.E.T. theory is that this male environmental influence (m) reinforces the drives of the hardwired 'male' systemising (s) brain; which may create men who are more susceptible to engaging in stereotyped behaviours. However, this does create familiar patterns which overall, are much easier for you to spot.

However, when dealing with a man with a systemising brain combined with a ***contradictory*** female environment (f), patterns are created within a man that may be harder to identify. This could be because he hides them or they are just not as frequent. The task of identifying patterns is also more difficult in men possessing an empathising brain (e). These types of men may feel excluded by a dominant character in their male environments and thus seek out completely new, potentially female milieus. In these situations, men gain a greater understanding of the female sex, but at the same time, gain an alternative perspective of their male peers. This forces you to take a new direction on the path of identifying his patterns.

FEMALE AND COMBINATION ENVIRONMENTS

Although they are in the minority, some men are raised and constantly find themselves in female dominated environments. But the factors of role models and socialisation still apply. However, this increased female interaction may create a psychological conflict within a man. He may feel confusion and emotional turmoil. Especially, when he realises that he doesn't fit in with the norms and expectations of the male subcultures he will inevitably be pushed towards. Society in general may impose certain gender roles onto his identity. He may feel completely out of sync with this and some men are unable to effectively cope with the dilemma. This will undoubtedly influence his journey towards personal identity.

Types of men that frequent a 'female' environment

Under the Thumb,
The Charmer,
The Thinker,
The Manipulator,
The Appreciator,
Back and Forth,
The Woman's Mind,
Easily Influenced,
The Enigma

In order to remove those feelings of uncertainty, a man raised in a female (f) dominated environment, (for example, growing up with a single mother and all siblings being older and female), will also search for a comfort zone. It may encourage him to seek out similar female environments in his adult life, which remind him of the comfort of his childhood ones; such as beauty salons and female-orientated workplaces. In this example, we can see that socialisation doesn't always occur in the stereotypical manner, for males, that Western civilisation suggests. The environmental impact, however, retains its power over these individuals; preventing some men from adapting well to stereotypical male peer groups in their adult lives.

As well as male and female dominated environments, there are also combination environments (c). These are equally balanced in gender-role socialisation. Parents in these situations encourage their children to engage in a range of activities and develop skills which break down traditional gender barriers. For example, many young boys in a combination environment will learn to cook and clean alongside their female siblings. They may engage in sports and activities which are now considered unisex, such as gymnastics. They are encouraged to express their feelings and uncover solutions to address any problems. This type of environment allows an individual to thrive in both familiar and unfamiliar situations. They gain a greater knowledge of their identity much earlier in life. They continue this by participating and facilitating the development of combination environments in their adult lives. However, despite their obvious benefits to a gender equal society, totally combined environments are unfortunately not as common as the others.

UNIQUE PATTERNS OF BEHAVIOUR

There are, of course, men who do not seem to fit into any of these categories; or those appearing to fit into them all. Nevertheless, B.E.T. theory relies on the identification of patterns and every type of man ***will*** show recurring behaviours. The cheaters are no exception. Most environments create predictable patterns approximately 95% of the time.

Types of men that frequent a 'combination' environment

The Family Man,
The Girlfriend,
The Rationaliser,
Mr Secure,
Mr Adaptable,
The Stupid Mistake,
The Visionary,
The Chameleon,
The Modern Man

It is this that we are trying to understand, not the 5% of the time when something unexplainable occurs.

The predictable behaviour creates a blueprint.

When faced with a new situation, an individual will try to respond or adapt to the circumstances. Adaptation usually involves utilising what the individual believes to be a recently acquired ***new insight;*** a philosophy or behaviour that defies what they have known previously. But in order to adapt and use any new information, they will ***still*** rely on and modify their ***existing*** behaviours. The environment still retains its grip.

This is why some men believe they have changed, when actually, they haven't. They may even make proclamations of changes to their behaviour and attitudes. But in reality, everything remains the same, especially if their environmental influences have not changed in the slightest. A dominant environment type may be the most difficult aspect of all 'BETs' to break.

QUESTIONS TO CONSIDER:

Who are his ***past and/or present*** role models?

What were the ***real*** significant features of his socialisation?

What are the ***passive*** (taken for granted) influences on him?

What are the norms and values of the subcultures ***he*** deems important?

****

Environmental influences really do impact everyone more than we know, that's clear, I thought to myself. Everybody has a story of this. Take Sasha, for instance. She hardly ever listened to her mum's pleas for her to be more feminine; Sasha wanted to be like her dad. It helped that he used to slip her cash and chocolate whenever she watched the football with him or helped fix the car. Spending time with him, she had become accustomed to many stereotypical male behaviours too; whilst the rest of us found these offensive, (like men who sat with their hands down their pants), she was desensitised to it all.

Guys seemed to like her for her 'liberal' attitudes.

This is definitely interesting, I thought, *but it's too simplistic to explain everybody's behaviour*. Not everyone can be ***that*** passive to their environment. If this was the case, then nobody from an environment littered with poverty and a lack of educational opportunities would be able to escape. I supposed that's why there were twenty-seven different types of men. Each use their brain and environmental stimuli slightly differently, which in turn, influences the path that they walked. Michael went on to state how our individual differences in thought processing provided the final piece of the puzzle.

++++

B.E.T. theory emphasises the suggestion that it is ***how*** men think, and interpret, their environments that is the key to understanding the twenty-seven different types. Although the environment can be dynamic, it is more influential on a passive level. It is also hugely affected by how men ***perceive*** incoming information. His preferred thought processing strategy (T) completes the triad of your 'BET'.

Chapter 18 – B.E.T. THEORY (Part 3) – Assessing a man's 'type' – Thought Processing

IN B.E.T. THEORY – THERE ARE THREE THOUGHT PROCESSING TYPES		
LOGICAL THOUGHT	AMALGAMATED THOUGHT	INTUITIVE THOUGHT
l	**x**	**i**

****

I was lounging on my sofa with the book on my lap, when the phone vibrated next to me. It was Claire again.

"Why haven't you called me back yet?"

"I'm sorry, I was reading. What are you doing up this late?"

"Well I know that. If you hadn't called me back, you could only be in ***that*** book," she sighed. "Anyway, you know I don't have work tomorrow, remember? I booked the weekend off, thinking Derek might whisk me away. He didn't. Does the book tell you what kind of idiot guy would act like that?"

"I'm not sure yet, I've not finished it..."

I was dying to get off the phone. I loved Claire to bits, but I wasn't in the mood for her that night. She was interrupting my flow and if we didn't talk about the book, then she was going to complain about Mr. Lawyer. I definitely didn't want to hear that either. So after a little white lie about not being able to keep my eyes open, Michael and I were engaged again.

++++

INTRODUCTION – THE KEY TO THE VAULT

If the brain type (B) is the foundation, and the environmental influences (E) are the walls protecting the secret of a man's 'type'; then the thought processing strategy (T) is the key that opens the door. Individual thoughts are impossible to measure; however, patterns in language and behaviour, (which are the consequences of thoughts), are not.

Cognitive Psychology recognises that environmental and biological explanations alone, are too simplistic to explain all human behaviour. Although habitual, humans aren't passive creatures; we ***always*** interact. The development of cognitions and schemas are a big part of this interactive process. For some, the development of cognitive thought is the latest facet in human evolution, which aids our survival.

Cognitions can be explained as any incoming information gathered from our sense organs that can be: transformed, reduced, elaborated, stored, recovered and/or used. This means everything we see, smell, taste, touch or hear is changed into a format, such as an image, sound or emotion. They are linked very closely to memory, attention and problem solving.

The interpretation of these cognitions, (and the impression they leave an individual with), depends on that person's unique personality traits and experiences. This is then retained in the memory for them to use later on, if they choose to. All behaviour is directed by some form of cognitive thought process.

The essential feature to be understood here is how the individual uniquely ***interprets*** their environment. For example, Emery (1988) argues that divorce has a bigger impact on children than if they experience mourning; and suggests that children from divorced homes will have more psychological problems in later life. However, many people, based on their own experiences, would argue that the opposite is true, that death has a more profound impact on a child than divorce. The outcome all depends on how the events are processed by the individual.

THOUGHTS AND ENVIRONMENT INTERTWINED

It is clear that any man's thought processes, and his environment, are extremely difficult to disentangle. They interact so dynamically that only through considered examination of both, can a man's patterns be truly understood.

His schemas allow him to organise numerous pieces of information, (for example, his views concerning men, women, infidelity and relationships), and then make 'sense' of it all. He will then interpret how he ***thinks*** he should behave, in any given situation, based on his schemas, (which may only make sense to him). The result is him forming a set of personal cognitive assumptions. These are based on his prior experiences and make his decision-making process as smooth, and as comfortable, as possible for him.

The psychologist Bartlett found that pre-existing schemas are always used to process ***any*** new incoming information from the environment. The pre-existing schemas also have the ability to ***adapt*** the information, allowing an individual to handle unfamiliar situations/circumstances in a way that is more familiar to them; ***even if this is not an accurate representation of the real situation or circumstances.*** In other words, the mind made something up that wasn't real or correct.

Take this scenario to illustrate the way schemas can adapt new situations:

One of the men interviewed for this book, was a young, recently married professional man. He was away on business for the weekend. In his hotel, he was propositioned by an average-looking woman who was aware that he was married, but was only interested in a one-off 'no strings attached' sexual encounter. He had never been in a situation like this before; his only pre-existing environmental schemas for such circumstances were based on a few stories from work colleagues and examples from film and TV characters.

Up until this point he had never thought about any of these influences; nor seriously considered cheating on his wife beyond a few fantasy conversations with friends. But in this moment, they guided his decision-making. He thought that none of the men he knew, or had seen on TV, had ever been caught and he assumed the same would be true for him on this occasion. The woman didn't want to see him again, so he believed there was nothing wrong with it. He accepted the woman's proposition.

THE DEVELOPMENT OF A NEW SCHEMA

Based on this experience, it is likely the man created either, a wholly new schema or made an adaption to his pre-existing one. This will dictate how he behaves in similar cheating situations in the future; as he uses his new or adapted schema over and over again, until his experiences motivate him to replace or alter it once more.

Although his behaviour may seem similar to that of any other cheat, his new schema is unique to this man.

His personal environmental experiences ***combined*** with the processing strategy he used to interpret the event, (i.e. logical, intuitive or amalgamated). This created something completely exclusive in his mind.

But because his behaviour will definitely appear to be that of 'just another cheat'; and his views very similar to those held by other men, this explains why understanding B.E.T. theory is important. Recognising this ***individual*** man's thought processing strategy, can possibly highlight the patterns he displays and the possible schema he developed. For example:

If the man in this scenario used a 'rational' processing style, there may be many interpretations which could have influenced his schema development. He may now think:

- No strings attached situations with strangers are unlikely to cause any problems in his relationship, as long as he is careful. He can continue to partake.
- That it was easier than he thought to not get caught. He may then actively search for similar opportunities quite freely.
- He may become apprehensive and cagey, believing that by the law of averages, the more he engages in this type of behaviour, the more he increases the chances of getting caught.
- He may decide he was lucky on this one occasion and decide not

to take such risks in future; putting it completely behind him.

If the man used 'a gut reaction' thought processing strategy in the situation with the woman he may now:

- Crave excitement and other dangerous liaisons to satiate the feelings he gets. The situations may also give a desirable ego boost. He may engage again if it feels right.
- In an attempt to mentally protect himself from the guilt, he justifies it in his mind. He views it as a meaningless indiscretion that many people do. He denies the guilt by engaging in the cheating behaviour further, or less, to prove it means nothing.
- He does not actively seek out these opportunities, but if presented with the same situation, will respond depending on how he feels at the time.

Patterns in his behaviour will subsequently be revealed if the man developed any of these schemas. However, the new schema may also have a foundation in ***all*** of the man's previous environmental experiences.

WAS IT HIM OR WAS IT HER THAT CHANGED HIS THOUGHTS?

Although we tend to focus on the act of infidelity because of its emotional significance, the new schema may actually have ***nothing*** to do with the event itself (being propositioned by the woman or cheating on his wife). Remember, infidelity (when considered objectively) is just another behaviour; although we as humans do attach huge emotional significance to it.

The new schema, created to interpret situations related to infidelity, may actually be a new manifestation of some ***other*** aspect of his past, personality or experiences of the world.

For example, the development of the new schema may actually be a response to any of the following environmental factors and the cheating behaviour was just a circumstantial incident within it:

- What his previous experiences of guilt and remorse are
- The level of excitement and fun he perceives in his life

- His perspective on keeping secrets
- The value he places on relationships
- Whether he is experienced in thinking on his feet
- How well he has handled stressful situations in the past.

This once again demonstrates how difficult the environment and thoughts are to disentangle. ***And just like the environmental influences, if a schema is not challenged, it is likely to become automatic.***

Beginning as a conscious choice, the often used schema quickly leaves the man having little or no awareness of its effect. Its mental trace on his brain becomes absorbed with his millions of other memories, to be used at a later date. They influence his decisions as and when necessary. For example, it may appear that cheating men consciously expect a desirable outcome from their infidelity. Why else would they do it? However, his decision-making responses may be ***so*** automatic, that they have been activated before he can even ***think*** about whether he is actually going to 'enjoy' the experience or not. As we know, some men are more prone to this than others.

NEITHER STYLE IS BETTER

In B.E.T. theory, all schemas are influenced by one of the main decision-making strategies. These are either logic, (the use of reasoned thought) or intuition, (thought without reason). What's more, a number of men have the propensity to combine logic and intuition effectively in the right situations. This is the 'amalgamated' (x) thought processing strategy.

In modern society, we hear more about logic than intuition. Children are taught to think logically from an early age. This can be observed in their schoolwork for instance, when they complete mental maths and scientific experiments. Intuition, on the other hand is almost viewed as some 'mystical' property, which is not as widely recommended. With this in mind, many may think that using logic is the better method of processing information. However, this is incorrect. In fact, most automatic daily activities rely more on intuition; such as when life requires you to improvise unexpectedly. For example, if you trip suddenly, breaking the fall may rely more heavily on intuition than logic.

It is clear that many men hold rational and irrational views about infidelity. Sometimes, his argument makes little sense, implying that his processing strategy has been used ineffectively. Nevertheless, no matter how he has interpreted the information around him, that does ***not*** mean you can just ignore the fact that there was ***still*** a strategy behind his thinking. This strategy is important to discovering his patterns.

Clearly, these methods of processing incoming information illustrate that there are many different ways of perceiving infidelity by an individual whether you agree with them or not.

2 + 2 = 4: THE 'LOGICAL' THINKING MAN

A lot of men are 'logical' thinkers (l). It could be argued that this is the predominant male method, aligning well with the stereotypical male systemising brain. Logic is closely linked to the rules of science and mathematics. A man may see a relationship problem as being similar to an equation that must be solved. They want to deal with the issue at hand, not go around in circles with unnecessary dialogue. They appreciate rules and use them to support their actions. Solving problems makes sense.

The use of logic is productive and, by consequence, valued and encouraged as the user sees a clear route of progression. Therefore, if it works, he would never need to adapt this strategy or the schemas related to it. For example, if a cheating man, that uses 'logical' thought processing (l), has discovered that possessing two mobile phones will solve the problem of his partner reading his private messages, then he is likely to consider this as a viable option.

Logical thinkers will tend to avoid people who aren't. They see these people as annoying and frustrating. This is a difference that could easily create a potential rift between couples. Defenders

Types of men that tend to use a 'logical' thought process strategy

Act First, Think Later,
The Rationaliser,
Mr Adaptable,
The Family Man,
The Lad's Lad,
The Manipulator,
Back and Forth,
The Enigma,
The Guilty Conscience

of logic often argue that other thinking strategies – that do not use a solid base of reasoned thought – are inferior. They view people who rush into making decisions; act impulsively; or depend on 'blind' hope, as irrational and perhaps even dangerous. They find logic can be extremely difficult to use with people who display this kind of unpredictability. This conflict is the source of many daily arguments.

At times like these, logical thinkers are clearly exposed. This is when many of their behavioural patterns will be revealed. They will be clearly flustered by non-logical thinkers, especially those men whose B.E.T. theory combination is ***dominated*** by logic.

However, although logical thinking can be fruitful, it can also undo cheating men who routinely rely on it. Personal situations are not mathematical equations. When there are people involved there is ***never*** just one possible outcome to take into consideration. Numerous unknown variables can change the direction of the best laid logical plan, at any given time. For example, no matter how much logic has been used to bed the new office secretary without being caught, it is unlikely that the man can always know who is acquainted with whom; who was watching and who was listening. This is the exact nature of all human interactions, it is impossible to factor in every eventuality. ***This is a good way to spot patterns, by understanding those men who think they can.***

Nevertheless, the use of logic is just a strategy based on schemas and the input of environmental experience. Indeed, a person may have interpreted some circumstance by using a 'logical' strategy, but that doesn't mean the output will make justifiable sense to anyone else. This may be why some people reject the use of logic preferring something a touch more personal. Many feel there is no depth or emotional commitment implied from using logic as a strategy, especially in relationship situations. Logic can make a man seem calculated and robotically inhuman. Some people prefer to make decisions relying on a more 'unexplainable feeling' which doesn't fit with the rules of logic, but has more of a ***connection*** associated with it; something which comes from intuition.

IF IT FEELS RIGHT: THE 'INTUITIIVE' THINKING MAN

Surprisingly to many, some men are purely 'intuitive' thinkers (i);

even though this method is widely associated with women. Intuition usually involves emotional responses driven by a gut feeling that cannot fully be explained. In the absence of reason and rationality, it is implied that this thought processing strategy works at a level running 'just beneath logic'.

Alongside the empathising brain type (e), the common phrase 'women's intuition' indicates the involvement of emotional expression within this thought processing technique. However, neither the empathising brain, nor intuitive thought processing are exclusive to the female sex.

It may be surprising. A man who disregards practical evidence to rely on what 'feels' more appropriate does not conform with the common stereotype. But even so, some men interpret events in such a way that they get a 'feel' for how a situation will be resolved. They understand that there is a correlation between familiar events, and this allows them to sense how they should behave next time round.

In regards to relationships and infidelity for example, some people can intuitively sense when there is an attraction between two people. Nothing overt has been said or done, but there are signs that are detected; a prolonged hug for instance. Intuitive people, in their own relationships, believe they can sense when something is wrong. They don't need anybody to tell them or to think about it logically.

Using intuitive processes in this manner can be valuable for the male user. He can make short-term predictions that are 'correct enough' to improve his understanding of his surroundings. When others are 'wasting time' calculating the correct answers, and whether the circumstances make sense, intuitive thinkers have already made their decision. Using intuition may not be able to give a factual explanation as to 'why' he feels something. However, if his intuition is correct, the

Types of men that tend to use an 'intuitive' thought process strategy

The Thinker,
The Stupid Mistake,
The Swinger,
The Appreciator,
The Girlfriend,
The Modern Man,
The Sucker for Love,
The Opportunist,
Under The Thumb

resulting schemas can be used to either initiate or avoid cheating behaviour. Using intuition also acts a valuable mechanism to express emotion, especially for those men where it dominates.

AMALGAMATED STRATEGY

An 'amalgamated' strategy (x) is the ideal. It combines the best elements of both logic and intuition at appropriate times. The men that use this type of processing possess more choice in their cognitive strategies. They are not bound by the limitations of logic or intuition, as they can adapt between them both. Thus, their schemas also have more room to adapt effectively and they are less likely to look for excuses. The men who use this have the potential to become masters of human relationships and interpreters of situations. Nevertheless, they can still use this knowledge for both positive and negative effect.

FEAR AND INFIDELITY

One final thing to consider is that in ***all*** people, ***fear*** is an essential factor in the decision-making process. This is regardless of their thought processing strategy. With the acquisition of cognitive thought in humans, it could be argued that psychological fear has more impact on individual schemas and relationship decision-making, (including the choice to cheat or not), than anything else. Some men are driven by fear; responding to social situations with a ***defensive*** fear response, whereas other men ***attack*** because of fear. The 'five factors of psychological fear' play havoc with the decision-making of many men.

The five factors include: the fear of change; the unknown; the obvious; of loss; and the fear of knowledge (Stewart 2001).

Types of men that tend to use an 'amalgamated' thought processing strategy

The Charmer,
The Visionary,
One Step Ahead,
The Chameleon,
Mr Secure,
The Disdainer,
The Woman's Mind,
The Metrosexual,
Easily Influenced

An irrational fear of any these factors tends to abound from an overreliance on an automatic schema; this creates anxiety, impairing the decision-making process. For instance, a 'Manipulator' who cunningly creates social situations to his own design may be driven by an intense fear of ***losing*** this control, whereas a 'Charmer' who automatically uses charisma and seduction on women, may become anxious at a fear of ***changing*** circumstances; when he has to give that lifestyle up for a committed, monogamous relationship. Being privy to information about any psychological fear in a man, will give you a huge insight into his behaviour patterns, including those related to infidelity.

QUESTIONS TO CONSIDER:

Is he a ***rigid, fixed*** thinker or is he ***flexible and open to change***?

Is he more of a believer in things *like* ***fate, luck and destiny*** or does he believe in **personal** ***choice, control and responsibility*** for his decisions?

Do things have to make ***sense*** for him to understand or can he let them 'play out' their ***natural*** course and see where it goes?

Do his thoughts tend to use a strategic form of ***plan*** or is he more of a 'think in the ***moment***' type of character?

★★★★

I used to think that B.E.T. theory was complex, but after reading the chapters, it completely made sense. I'll definitely be reading them again just to consolidate everything. The most surprising revelation for me was the idea that some men regularly use ***intuition***. I had liked that intuition was seen as a female advantage. It angered me that the male species could use it to cheat on us if they wanted. Could intuitive men be more prone to infidelity than logical men? At least logical thought processes may be restricted by the 'rules' of commitment.

I knew that a lot of women wouldn't like the ***realism*** of this theory.

We all like the idea that men are just stupid idiots whose brains are below the belt. What other topic would get us all so passionate on a Wednesday night?

However, I had to be honest, especially in regards to my own relationships. I could now see areas where I had gone wrong. If I had taken a little more time in the courting period with Ramone and Nick, I don't think I would have been so easily seduced by their charm and manipulative ways. Granted, using this new concept would take a lot of willpower. Many women wouldn't take it any further than superficial escapism. *But we cannot stay blinded by good looking men anymore!* I thought. I made a deal with myself to keep aware of my 'BETs' in future relationships. However, even if I bent a few of my own 'rules' and altered my standards… men will still cheat!

Well, some will. B.E.T. theory demonstrated that not all men fitted into this cheating category. Women have typically been looking out for ***one*** stereotypical loser to avoid. They have mixed all of the traits associated with infidelity into one 'type': opportunism, manipulation, deceit, lack of empathy, immaturity, disdain for women, etc. However, it is unlikely that any man would possess ***all*** of these traits. So whilst women have been attempting to avoid a ***myth*** and still coming up short; B.E.T. theory paints a ***realistic*** target, outlining traits that indeed appear to separate men into twenty-seven types. And perhaps only a small number of the twenty-seven should be highlighted – not all.

Uncovering the interaction within an individual man, that results in his patterns of behaviour, is what is meant by understanding my 'BET'. I had got it now! The dynamic combination of the brain, environment and thought processes all contribute to his habitual patterns, and what type of man he really is. It also explains why some women get different types of men mixed up, as some are so similar to each other.

As Michael said in the bar, a *'Manipulator' may be charming and a 'Charmer' may manipulate; but that doesn't mean that they are the same type of man.* Many of us didn't understand this. *But we do now*, I thought. So all I needed to know was which types were more likely to cheat; an 'eci' or a 'scl'? An 'efi' or a 'bml'?

++++

Figure 5 – Diagram to show the twenty-seven different type combinations (capital and bold letter denotes the dominant component)

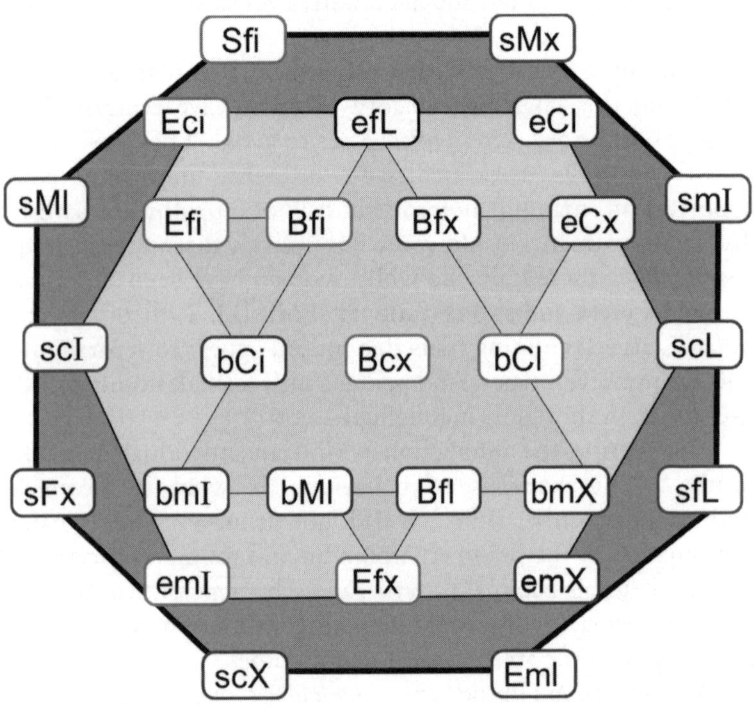

Table to show each of the twenty-seven different types with their dominant component shown in bold and capital letters.

TYPE	CODE	TYPE	CODE
Mr Adaptable	e**C**l	Guilty Conscience	**E**ml
The Stupid Mistake	sc**I**	The Manipulator	sf**L**
Under the Thumb	**B**fi	One Step Ahead	em**X**
The Charmer	s**F**x	The Swinger	em**I**
The Family Man	b**C**l	The Chameleon	e**C**x
The Visionary	sc**X**	The Appreciator	**E**fi
The Lads' Lad	s**M**l	Back and Forth	**B**fl
The Rationaliser	sc**L**	The Girlfriend	**E**ci
The Thinker	**S**fi	The Modern Man	b**C**i
Act First, Think Later	b**M**l	The Disdainer	s**M**x
Sucker for Love	bm**I**	The Woman's Mind	**E**fx
The Metrosexual	bm**X**	The Enigma	ef**L**
Easily Influenced	**B**fx	The Opportunist	sm**I**
Mr Secure	**B**cx		

Chapter 19 – What Men REALLY said about cheating – The Results in short!

THE STATISTICS

The men who formed the basis of this book were selected using an opportunity sample. This aimed to give a wide general consensus about cheating behaviour and to gain differing perspectives, attitudes and experiences of infidelity. Men from all ethnic groups, cultures, religions, ages and social classes were invited to contribute from several UK cities. Below are some very brief statistical results from the 547 men. Some gave very short questionnaire answers while others agreed to provide detailed insight from interviews and psychological testing via analysis of personality and cognitive functioning.

STATISTICS CODE:

1) **The bad news – the 'more prone' types**
2) **The good news – the 'less prone' types**
3) **More good news – the normal distribution – the 'average' types**
4) **How many men think about or actually have cheated?**
5) **What men really think about cheating**
6) **Do men believe they are born to cheat?**
7) **Do men think women will date a man, (or take a man back), who has cheated?**
8) **How often do men think about sex with other women?**
9) **The reasons (excuses) men give for their cheating**
10) **How and where do men do their cheating?**
11) **How do men feel after cheating?**
12) **General male views on cheating**
13) **Summary of the types**

1) THE BAD NEWS – The 'more prone' types

- Of the 547 men interviewed or questioned, 251 stated that they had cheated on their wife or girlfriend at some point in their lives. This equates to 46%.
- 27% of men also admitted to cheating on their ***current*** partner.
- Based on the in-depth interviews and questionnaires, of the twenty-seven different types of men identified, five types are ***more*** prone to cheating behaviour (This equates to 18% of the men sampled).

These types are:

'The Opportunist'; 'The Lads' Lad'; 'The Manipulator'; 'The Stupid Mistake'; 'The Disdainer' (five out of twenty-seven).

It appears that these men make inappropriate decisions and more likely than not will openly court the opportunity to cheat. They either frequently search for opportunities to do so or they do not hesitate to take the chance when it presents itself.

THE GOOD NEWS – The 'less prone' types

- 73% of men stated that they have been faithful to their ***current*** partners.
- Based on the in-depth interviews and questionnaires, of the twenty-seven different types of men identified, eight types are ***less*** prone to cheating behaviour (This equates to 30% of the men sampled).

These types are:

'The Family Man'; 'Mr Secure'; 'The Thinker'; 'Under the Thumb'; 'The Appreciator'; 'The Girlfriend'; 'The Swinger'; 'The Woman's Mind' (eight out of twenty-seven).

This suggests that there is ***not*** one type of man that you can be with who will remain faithful. There is not just one type of 'knight in shining armour' waiting.

3) MORE GOOD NEWS – THE NORMAL DISTRIBUTION – The 'average' types

- Of the 547 men interviewed or questioned, 296 stated that they had ***never*** cheated on any partner at any point in their lives. This equates to 54%, a slight majority.
- Based on the in-depth interviews and questionnaires, of the twenty-seven different types of men identified, thirteen are ***average types*** (49%). These men are your normal everyday men who may or may not cheat, depending on the relationship ***situation and circumstances***. They are not special nor are they 'weird'. You are more likely to find happiness with one of these types of men, by continually working at your relationship to maintain its success.

These types are:

'The Rationaliser'; 'Easily Influenced'; 'The Charmer'; 'The Modern Man'; 'The Sucker for Love'; 'Mr Adaptable'; 'Back and Forth'; 'The Chameleon'; 'Guilty Conscience'; 'Act First, Think Later'; 'The Metrosexual'; 'The Visionary'; 'One Step Ahead' (thirteen out of twenty-seven).

These men are not immune to cheating. They may commit infidelity or they may remain faithful. The key to which decision they make, (whether rightly or wrongly), depends on the dynamics and strength of the relationship situation.

****NOTE** – 'The Enigma' could not be placed as either less prone, an average type or more prone to cheat. His behaviour patterns were erratic.

4) HOW MANY MEN THINK ABOUT OR ACTUALLY HAVE CHEATED?

- 251 out of 547 men admitted to cheating at some point in their life.
- 72% of men said that they 'have thought about cheating'.
- 28% said that they have 'not thought about cheating'.

- 46% of men stated that they 'have cheated in their adult life'.
- On average, most cheating occurs between the ages of twenty-four – twenty-nine (24%).
- On average, there is then a drop in the numbers of men that cheat, (between the ages of thirty – thirty-five), and it increases again between ages forty-one – forty-five (21%).

Table to show the percentages and ages of men who admitted cheating

Age	18 – 23	24 – 29	30 – 35	36 – 40	41 – 45	46 – 50	50+
% of men who admitted cheating	14%	24%	11%	14%	21%	7%	9%

These figures suggest that the desire to have sex with other women remains, despite men being in a committed relationship. This would be a strong argument made by evolutionary psychologists.

5) WHAT DO MEN REALLY THINK ABOUT CHEATING?

- Nearly two thirds of men (59%) said that when they hear about cheating on TV, newspapers or in the media, it 'hardly registers with them'.
- Only 11% of men think that it is 'really bad' when they hear about cheating behaviour in the media.

On the debate whether 'cheating is acceptable or not in society', men are almost evenly split in their opinions.

- 33% of men believe that 'most people' view cheating as ***unacceptable***.
- 37% of men believe that 'most people' view cheating as ***acceptable***.
- The other 30% said most people '***tolerate***' cheating as long as it does not affect them personally.

This suggests that most men have become desensitised to the notion that cheating is wrong. Environmental influences such as the family, media and general society – which may ***not*** condone cheating – do not appear to have a strong impact on their perspectives. This then may influence the use of the justification schema to act on their desire for sexual variety.

6) DO MEN BELIEVE THEY ARE BORN TO CHEAT?

When asked if cheating is a biological drive or not:

- 78% believe that cheating ***is not*** biological
- 22% believe it ***is*** biological to cheat

This implies that the majority of men ***believe*** that cheating behaviour is something that can be controlled and is not an instinctual response.

7) DO MEN THINK WOMEN WILL DATE A MAN (OR TAKE A MAN BACK) WHO HAS CHEATED?

A large majority of men believe that ***most*** women would start a relationship with a man that they know has cheated in the past.

- 25% of men said, 'Yes, definitely, all women would'.
- 51% of men said, 'Probably, most of them would'.

They also feel that the majority of women (67%) would 'probably' or 'definitely' take a man back that had cheated on them. Only 6% said, 'No, not a chance a woman would take a man back if he cheated'.

This suggests that most men believe that cheating will be forgiven, or forgotten by women, again perhaps justifying the schema to act on their desire for sexual variety.

8) HOW OFTEN DO MEN THINK ABOUT SEX WITH OTHER WOMEN

- 15% of men stated that they think about having sex with

different women 'all of the time' even if they are (have been) in a relationship.
- 60% of men stated that they think about having sex with different women 'regularly' even when if they are (have been) in a relationship.

This suggests that despite being in a relationship, the **desire** for sexual variety continues to exist.

9) THE REASONS (EXCUSES) MEN GIVE FOR THEIR CHEATING

Of the men that cheated, when asked to provide a 'reason' why they had done so, there were many different excuses. Below are the most popular:

- It doesn't mean anything it is just sex. I still love my girlfriend (21%)
- I can't help it. I just love women (14%)
- She won't find out (9%)
- It's too easy. They put it on a plate (19%)
- I was bored (13%)
- I need more sex. She has let herself go / She doesn't give me enough (10%)
- Cos I'm a man, we all do it (7%)
- Because I can get away with it (7%)

This suggests that a lot of men are unaware of the real reason why some of them cheat, or are not prepared to acknowledge it. They will make excuses to protect the automatic justification schema.

10) HOW AND WHERE DO MEN DO THEIR CHEATING?

Men also stated where, and when, most cheating occurs:

- It is planned / a regular meet (38%)
- At work (28%)
- Nights out (21%)

- On holidays (13%)

11) HOW DO MEN FEEL AFTER CHEATING?

When those men who admitted cheating were asked how do/did you feel after you had cheated on your partner

- 52% said 'a little guilty'
- 32% said 'nothing'
- 16% said 'very guilty'

Again, this is evidence that a lot of men have become desensitised to the effects of their cheating behaviour, if they have committed infidelity. Some, (almost one-third), have reached the point where their act(s) of infidelity doesn't bother them at all.

12) GENERAL MALE VIEWS ON CHEATING

- 14% of men said that they have been caught cheating but would still do it again anyway.
- The results found that 89% of men do not think badly of other men that cheat.
- However, 79% of men also believe that 'men should ***not*** cheat'.
- When asked what would stop them from cheating again, 88% of men said that they would not even consider cheating, if they knew that their partner ***really*** would not stand for it.
- 98% of men said that cheating is under each man's conscious control and they choose to cheat.
- 75% of men stated that they have male family members who cheat.
- 84% of men said that they believe 'quite a lot of other men' cheat.
- 90% of men said that they have close friends that cheat.
- However, 88% of men said they do not challenge their friends and/or family on their cheating.
- Of the men that said they do not challenge their friends and family on cheating, the reasons given were:
    - 54% of men believe it is 'none of their business'.

- 21% said they would 'feel hypocritical because they cheat themselves'.
- 14% believe 'their family and friends wouldn't listen'.
- 11% believe 'there is nothing wrong with cheating'.

13) SUMMARY OF THE TYPES

Figure 6 – Pie chart to show the percentage of different group types of men

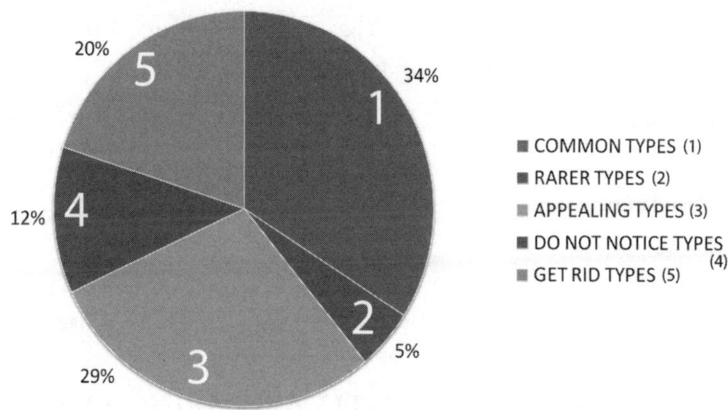

The Common Types	The Rarer Types	The Appealing Types	The Do Not Notice Types	The Get Rid Types
The Opportunist	One Step Ahead	The Secure Man	The Guilty Conscience	The Lads' Lad
The Rationaliser	The Swinger	The Modern Man	Mr Adaptable	The Manipulator
Easily Influenced	The Enigma	The Family Man	Under The Thumb	The Metrosexual
The Charmer	The Woman's Mind	The Appreciator	The Girlfriend	The Disdainer
The Sucker For Love		The Thinker		The Stupid Mistake
Back and Forth			The Visionary	Act first; think later
				The Chameleon

The FIVE MOST FREQUENTLY APPEARING TYPES OF MEN ARE:

(In no particular order) 'The Rationaliser'; 'The Family Man'; 'The Modern Man'; 'Easily Influenced'; 'The Opportunist'.

The FIVE LEAST FREQUENTLY APPEARING TYPES OF MEN ARE:

(In no particular order) 'The Swinger'; 'The Woman's Mind'; 'The Enigma'; 'One Step Ahead'; 'The Disdainer'.

***Note – All individual names and personal details in this book have been changed to ensure confidentiality and anonymity.**

Chapter 20 – Case Study: Explaining how B.E.T. theory can work

PROFILE

Name – Brian
Age – Thirty-three
Born – Leeds, England
Resides – Birmingham, England
Occupation – Recruitment Consultant
Ethnicity – White British
Partner – Joanne, aged twenty-nine
Children – Two girls – Rebecca, aged four and Chelsea, aged two

GENERAL ASSESSMENT

As a successful Recruitment Consultant, Brian knew that he could provide for his family. The extra cash he had for his own lifestyle was a great perk too. Even though he had to work and live 100 miles away in London during the week he wasn't complaining. Brian didn't particularly enjoy being away from his family and made the long journey home each weekend; but when asked if he would give up his current job, his answer was emphatic:

"Not a chance! Not yet anyway. I'm having too much fun with the life and money. The travelling is a pain, but the sacrifice is worth it in the end."

Joanne was on a night out with work when Brian charmed her with a few neat one-liners. He ended up proposing on their eldest daughter's first birthday. Some might consider this romantic. It was soon followed by the purchase of their own semi-detached home in a nice suburb. A little sister for Rebecca followed two years later. After five years together, the relationship was still going strong. Joanne had given up work to look after the children, meaning the financial burden was completely on Brian's shoulders. But with his substantial wage, there was always enough for Joanne to be treated when they spent quality time together. The rewards for hitting quarterly targets at Brian's firm included free trips abroad to Dubai and New York, champagne baskets and vouchers to designer stores.

"To be honest, working in recruitment consultancy is a job full of confident, young people who make a lot of money. There's lots of partying, alcohol, casual sex and other things going on. Whether you're into it all or not, it's in your face."

Joanne rarely got the chance to visit him during the week because of her childcare responsibilities. Lacking these daily parental duties however, Brian took full advantage of the extensive social life on offer in the capital. After honing his communication skills in meetings, business lunches and sales pitches, women in a bar were no comparison. Brian loved using his persuasive utilisation of language.

"We're out socialising in bars several days of the week! I have to go home at the weekend, so I make the most of the weekdays. There are always girls who are 'up for it', because there's loads of cash being splashed."

Brian had always been a good listener, understanding what other people are experiencing. Maybe this is why he was such an effective communicator. He would pre-empt the thoughts of people before they even uttered a word. He was truly engaging in conversation; this was his skill and he was ambitious in making the most of it. He was an adept storyteller, capable of painting a realistic picture in the mind of most.

He knew that his working life was the one he really wanted instead of the one at home, nevertheless, he still understood that his wife felt isolated alone. Whilst he was partying she was practically living as a single parent. Ironically, he felt guilty and lonely whilst he was away, but found ways to force the emotions to the back of his mind. These 'ways' usually involved the company of an attractive female. He was aware that his liaisons in the capital may be superficial, but they fulfilled his selfish need.

"I love meeting new people on the job. The socialising is a big part of it. There are too many opportunities; I'm living a different life to my one at home."

His work colleagues were unashamedly promiscuous, both the

men and the women. A night out was considered wasted if someone from the office didn't sneak off with a complete stranger. And if it wasn't a stranger, then it was each other. There was always some form of scandal in the office; Brian tended to swerve the one-night stand route, although he had participated at least once or twice:

"With friends like these, something is bound to rub off. I'm not as bad as them though."

Brian preferred short-term 'relationships or flings'. He used these in an attempt to nullify his loneliness. He engaged with the women only slightly more than just physically. He liked to play a dangerous game, well aware of how much he had to lose. He justified it with a concoction of rational thought and over-confidence. He took risks, but not stupid ones.

"As if she's going to find out; Jo's the unassuming type. As long as I'm home every weekend, she isn't going to go looking for anything. Besides, I'm careful. I never use my real name and I don't do the social networking thing, so that won't cause any problems. What she doesn't know can't hurt her."

Dana, the confident brunette from the nearby solicitor's office, knew nothing about Joanne, the children, or his life back home. They had been sleeping together for eight weeks, and Brian was constantly reserved about his previous life or relationships. He told Dana that he 'doesn't like to dwell in the past'. Brian regularly wormed his way out of awkward questioning, providing slick responses about his weekend whereabouts. Dana believed that he lived in London and worked away in the north, not the other way round.

When asked why he continued to cheat with Dana, Brian stated:

"It's just new and exciting. I love Jo and I'd never leave her. And I'm going to stop one day, probably when I move back to Birmingham. I know I'm the one in the wrong, but I kind of miss having somebody around all the time. But at the same time, if I'm honest, I'm not ready to completely give up what I have here. I want both. It's confusing. I only cheat when I am in London; it's hard, because it would probably make more sense to have 'no strings attached' sex

with girls. But I just love how the girls want me. Besides, if I was just sleeping with loads of random girls, I know I'd feel dirty. I get a buzz off the connection I get, like I have with Dana. But, I have to cut if off before she gets too attached and finds out too much about me. I know if I'm careful though, Jo will never find out, so there's no reason to stop. I don't mess around when she's visiting or when I'm back home; I treat her well."

BRAIN TYPE

When taking part in the study, Brian agreed to be assessed in a range of tests that would cover social skills, personality and intelligence amongst others. These aimed to uncover whether he had an empathising or systemising brain. His results were surprising, considering the high powered and organised nature of his job. Brian scored average on systemising tasks, but well above average on empathising ones.

Brian's brain made him think about the feelings of others. Even though some of his behaviour was questionable, when interviewed, it was clear that this was the case. It doesn't explain why he cheated on Joanne, or why he strung Dana along either, but perhaps it illustrates why he 'knew' his wife needed him home on weekends. A cynic would claim that this was solely to keep his cheating lifestyle going. However, maybe he felt like he could have both the commitment and the fun, without really upsetting anyone. Regardless, he appeared to understand how people feel. His strength on empathising tasks may also explain why he also understands the needs of his clients, making him so successful at his job.

Test	Score
Empathising	Well Above Average
Systemising	Below Average
Non-verbal reasoning (systemising)	Average
Language (verbal reasoning) (empathising)	High

Why did he think he felt the need to cheat on Joanne?

"I wouldn't if she was here. It's probably because she isn't, like I said Jo's not the type to suspect anything. She trusts me completely. I feel bad for her; she's a lovely girl, but is slightly naïve at times. We've spoken about that in relation to other things. I'm pretty sure she'll never catch me out."

What would he do if she found out?

"I know she'd be devastated if she did find out. I don't want to put her through that. But I'd convince her to give me another chance. Maybe I'm just not mature enough for the things she wants from me right now. I try to think about it, but I just can't explain why I still get a buzz from introducing myself to new women. I don't love them like Jo, but I get a great feeling when I get them, especially when they've said no the first time… It's a mission for me. I love it. I just tell them whatever they want to hear. When I do that, they open up to me and then I know I've got them. I suppose it's like an ego boost. I don't want to do this forever though; it's just while I am working away. Once the kids are older and Jo goes back to work, I'll move back home and I'll stop. I know they need me but I suppose, if I'm being honest, I just like the attention."

It is evident through his answers that Brian had considered the feelings of his wife, but he had also thought about his own feelings, and those of the women around him. He didn't seem overly planned or rigid in this thinking but his selfish drive for the 'buzz' simply overpowered his want of commitment.

Nevertheless, overall, Brian's brain was hardwired for empathising (e).

ENVIRONMENT TYPE

Growing up as the middle of three children, you can sometimes be missed. Brian felt he had to make an extra effort to gain attention away from his older brother, (aged thirty-six) and younger sister (aged twenty-seven). His parents were both teachers and he was raised in an affluent middle-class area of Leeds. His family provided a supportive and loving environment, until the day his mother left his father for another man. This man wasn't a stranger; he was a close family friend. In Brian's own words:

"It smashed everyone's happy existence. Nobody saw it coming, it came out of nowhere."

His parents were married for the majority of his childhood. What hurt Brian the most about the break-up was how badly it had hurt his father and siblings. Years later, Brian could understand how his mother had felt when she'd explained how she had been trapped in an unloving, hollow relationship. His brother, on the other hand, couldn't. The hammer blow to his dad's manhood and confidence had been difficult to watch. Knowing a 'friend' had let his father down so badly had a profound impact on Brian. He had to become a rock for his younger sister, as her tender years had made it difficult for her to comprehend the turmoil. Brian recalled the biggest change, being the financial strain, that suddenly enveloped the family. This was the catalyst that fuelled his ambition to pursue a highly paid job.

It may come as a surprise, but Brian was never one to crave popularity during his teens. Although he was very confident with people, this may have had something to do with moving schools twice and being forced to make new friends because of the divorce. When asked about his peers, Brian claimed:

"I wasn't popular, but I wasn't unpopular. I was a guy in the middle who learned to adapt to others. I had to make new friends because I moved to different areas; having to 'start again' more than once meant that paying attention to others became an extremely important tool."

His communication skills definitely improved through his performance in sports, drama and musical productions. His part-time job in the local corner shop also helped him take responsibility for his own money early on; as well as providing interaction with the general public. His time at university was commandeered by organising student parties and club nights. Getting on with everybody, he formed a strong network of both male and female friends, but with a core group of male mates. He was never the dominant personality however, usually acting as the voice of reason.

After university, he tried job after job, before landing his current role in recruitment. Brian's working environment is quite volatile due to the competition to make money, but he is well liked.

Although there are a few women in the firm, Brian's company is a very male dominated environment. This is Brian's explanation why, in his own words:

"Recruitment consultancy is an ego-driven environment with a lot of competition, envy and backstabbing. You have to be confident. Everybody is out to impress; even the women act like men. They are bossy, cocky and assertive. They want to be just as, if not more successful, than the guys. You have to be thick-skinned."

Besides working, Brian's passion was football. An avid supporter of his hometown team, he would watch them whenever he could. He also enjoyed a touch of class when he went out on the town, impressing friends and colleagues in expensive restaurants and bars. He liked to get to know the staff well too. Nevertheless, he wasn't averse to the simple things either, like listening to music, reading and going to the cinema. All in all, Brian was a well-rounded guy; one of the lads, but also knowing how to treat a lady. Both Joanne and Dana seemed to be swept off their feet with his charm and individuality.

Did Brian believe that there were any influences from his environment that impacted on his cheating behaviour?

"I've always been told I have the 'gift of the gab'. I find that women love men who are confident but not cocky; I've always been like this. I'm not a typical lad though; I have lots of interests, I like learning about new things. I've always been good at understanding people's feelings, and I suppose that is one of the ways that I meet women. I listen to what they say and then try to give them what they want. Having a job that requires me to talk a lot tends to help lead a lot of conversations. I suppose that is probably the biggest influence from my environment that I use on women: being able to hold a good conversation! I suppose one of the main things as well is that Jo is so laid back. If she was on my case all the time, I probably wouldn't even dare."

From Brian's answers, it is evident that his work environment has enhanced his talking skills. His empathising brain encouraged him to seek socialising experiences that not only included the regular views and company of females; but also demonstrated understanding and respect of their viewpoints, without compromising his integrity amongst male peers. This is shown by him often being the mediator. Both influences are strong on his decision-making.

In conclusion, Brian frequents 'combination' (c) environments.

THOUGHT PROCESSING TYPE

School was a no-brainer for Brian. He was a talented student, collecting a successful string of A's and B's. He actually enjoyed school, possessing a natural flair for all his subjects from Maths to History, Economics to Art. You could say he was a jack of all trades. This was more than enough to make him a success at a top university, where he came out with a 2.1 in Business Studies. This academic history demonstrates Brian's ability to think in a logical manner, but also to demonstrate creativity and flair when it was necessary. His choice of Business Studies, as an area of academic focus, suggested this intuitive and creative spirit perfectly. Entrepreneurial decisions rely on more than just reason. It is evident that he could see opportunities before they were presented, and he was well equipped to take advantage of them.

"There are plenty of women out there and they're all looking for something. You just need to find out what that is..."

Brian loved socialising, both on nights out and in a more general manner. Sometimes he was the watcher, scoping his next target, learning about them without them realising. Sometimes he outsmarted other men who were competing with him, mixing a potent combination of wit and charm to make the girls flock to him. He would remember a girl's favourite drink and didn't need social networking prompts to recall her birthday. Always the listener, paying attention and aware of the next person's needs; his subtle approach is seductive, lowering defences in social circles. He often has the upper hand, sensing when a woman is wary of guys in general. Some would say he possesses a silver tongue, but mostly his persona displays that of a genuine and believable guy with an uncanny feel for situations.

Brian's personality assessment showed a range of strengths,

demonstrating that his thinking patterns are not limited to one strategy to direct his behaviour. He scored highly on conscientiousness and believed he had control over his choices; both of which are linked to logical thought processing. Nevertheless, his understanding and relaxed approach, guided by a glut of 'Type B' characteristics, such as being laid back and easy going, suggest that he is not overly reliant on a plan. The only characteristic he scored below average on was 'openness'; a personality trait linked to the willingness to try new things. He had no overbearing desire for this. He may be a creature of comfort and, maybe, had an irrational fear of changing circumstances. Although he can think intuitively, it is evident that his use of logic tells him not to err too much from what he knows.

What did Brian think about when he was with the other women and away from Joanne?

"To be honest, I don't really think about Jo until afterwards. It doesn't make sense to be worrying about what I'm doing and who I'm doing it with, because then I'm not going to behave naturally. Besides, I actually enjoy Dana's company. It's not going to go anywhere. She doesn't know that – so we still have fun. I don't want to upset her on purpose and I'll end things before they get too serious, so she doesn't get attached and things don't get messy. Sometimes, I feel myself getting slightly attached too. But then I end it straight away. If I start thinking like that I am just asking for a world of trouble. It's better to just find someone else."

The way in which Brian seemed to 'go with the flow' when he was with Dana, shows that intuitive thought processes were present. However, the way in which he plans to call it off before any problems occur also shows logic behind his thinking.

Considering all factors, Brian shows he has 'amalgamated' thought processes (x).

IN CONCLUSION:

Brian's empathising brain (e), his combination environment (C), and his amalgamated thought processes (x) give him a B.E.T. theory code of: eCx – Brian is 'The Chameleon'.

THE CHAMELEON

A 'GET RID' TYPE

WHITE FLAGS

He is a charismatic, charming and effective communicator. A very good listener with a believable persona!

Initially, it may appear that he does not have any 'long-term history' i.e. he may move house a lot or no long-term exes. children, mortgages

YELLOW FLAGS

You discover he is talented at telling stories or pulling the wool over other people's eyes.

He is intelligent, with a high level of social aptitude, (also he has the gift of the gab).

RED FLAGS

He appears and disappears frequently, maybe due to 'working commitments'. He may have a secret.

Too many lies have caught up with him. You find too many holes in his stories, – and perhaps a history of disillusioned exes

When in Rome, do as the Romans do. Loosely translated - this type of man will be whatever the girl wants him to be; whatever she wants to see, hear or experience at that time. His dominating **COMBINATION** environments allow him to adapt efficiently, understanding the behaviour of both men and women well. He can relate to the person's needs and fit seamlessly with them. This is until it becomes time to move to the next girl, and be who she wants him to be. His hardwired **EMPATHISING** brain enables him to spot cracks in women's emotional armour; because of this he doesn't tend to cheat in a one-night stand manner, preferring rather to cater towards their weakness. His thought processes are such a fluid concoction of **LOGIC** and **INTUITION.** His stories are always believable and you never really know who he is. You may find he is living a lie i.e. a dual life with a relationship/family elsewhere.

B.E.T. THEORY TYPE – eCx

THE CHAMELEON - eCx

How this type looks / or comes across to women

This type of man seems to be 'normal' and safe. They fit in well to the environment where you first meet them, i.e. work or a social gathering. They are not over the top with their behaviour, but they are not understated. They appear to have a typical, engaging, everyday existence. They try to get a good balance between their responsibilities, whether this includes education, work, family, hobbies, whatever. Nothing seems to be amiss… at first. **His insecurity relates to 'not being ready' to settle down, have a family, to compromise, get married, be completely responsible, etc. He may have a life that includes all of these things currently, but he may do this just to keep up appearances. In reality, 'he just wants to do him'. He may feel slightly trapped, want to sample the spice of life or just want to be free with no constraints. So he adapts to every situation that allows him to do that; 'playing the game' expertly and being whatever he wants to be whenever he wants.**

Chapter 21 – The 'Sure Fire' signs – a quick guide to identify a man's type

The intention of this book is not to turn the female readers into 'bunny boilers' like the infamous scene from the film *Fatal Attraction*. Nor is it designed to send male readers crazy with paranoia. The aim is to try and encourage self-awareness and self-development – even though the information provided here is simultaneously designed to take you out of your comfort zone, and keep you on your toes!

Relationship problems tend to occur because both parties do not take equal responsibility at maintaining the union. This may or may not lead to infidelity. But the majority of the twenty-seven types of men are 'average' types and their decisions are heavily influenced by the state of their relationships. Therefore, making a better choice at the beginning may minimise the chance of problems later. ***However, be sure not to use these 'sure fire' signs just for the negative purpose to stigmatise or pigeonhole the males that you know.*** That is ***not*** the intention here.

This book is not a witch-hunt to catch men out. It should not be used to sabotage or entrap. It is an intellectual guide, to provide the reader with more knowledge, to make informed future decisions. So, if a man is ***not*** giving you any cause for alarm—***do not go looking for the bell!*** Don't ***search*** for 'evidence' based on an assumption or suspicion without any factual information. You may interpret information the wrong way by using negative schemas to back up your views. ***Don't go looking for trouble when none exists – or your mind just might create it***.

Nevertheless, there is nothing wrong with being wary; and that being said, you are bound to see some identifying signs. White flags are nothing to worry about. However, a relationship trail with a series of warning signs, i.e. white, then yellow leading to red flags, does mean some action will have to be taken. You definitely have a decision waiting to be made. This decision may be positive or negative... depending on the type of man of course! If you have stumbled across 'Mr Right' the decision is ***how*** you are going to keep him!

The research on B.E.T. theory and the identification of the behaviour patterns of the twenty-seven different types of men found that 18% of men are ***more*** prone to cheating, (regardless of whether the relationship situation they are in is good or bad – **THESE TYPES ARE IDENTIFIED WITH A ●**

49% of men are average types who may or may not cheat. (Their choices are ***dependent*** on whether the relationship situation is good or bad) – **THESE TYPES ARE IDENTIFIED WITH A ◆**

30% of men are ***less*** prone to cheating, (regardless of whether the relationship situation they are in is good or bad) – **THESE TYPES ARE IDENTIFIED WITH A ■**

3% of men are identified as 'The Enigma' and their behaviour patterns were wholly unpredictable and they were not able to be classified– **THIS TYPE IS IDENTIFIED WITH A →**

SUREFIRE 1 (white flag) W	**SUREFIRE 2 (yellow flag) Y**	**ALMOST A CERTAINTY (Red Flag) R**
Not a cause for alarm but start paying attention	There will probably be consistent patterns in behaviour that need to be addressed	You are quite sure of the type. So you have a decision to make. Whether positive or negative

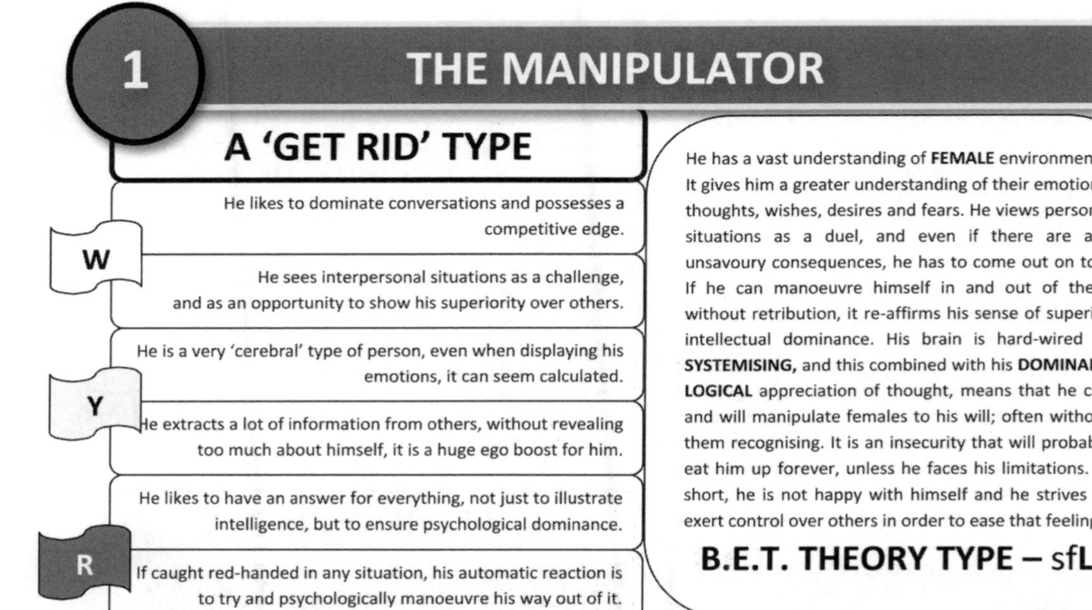
1
THE MANIPULATOR
A 'GET RID' TYPE
W
Y
R
He likes to dominate conversations and possesses a competitive edge.
He sees interpersonal situations as a challenge, and as an opportunity to show his superiority over others.
He is a very 'cerebral' type of person, even when displaying his emotions, it can seem calculated.
He extracts a lot of information from others, without revealing too much about himself, it is a huge ego boost for him.
He likes to have an answer for everything, not just to illustrate intelligence, but to ensure psychological dominance.
If caught red-handed in any situation, his automatic reaction is to try and psychologically manoeuvre his way out of it.
He has a vast understanding of FEMALE environments. It gives him a greater understanding of their emotions, thoughts, wishes, desires and fears. He views personal situations as a duel, and even if there are any unsavoury consequences, he has to come out on top. If he can manoeuvre himself in and out of these without retribution, it re-affirms his sense of superior intellectual dominance. His brain is hard-wired to SYSTEMISING, and this combined with his DOMINANT LOGICAL appreciation of thought, means that he can and will manipulate females to his will; often without them recognising. It is an insecurity that will probably eat him up forever, unless he faces his limitations. In short, he is not happy with himself and he strives to exert control over others in order to ease that feeling.
B.E.T. THEORY TYPE – sfL

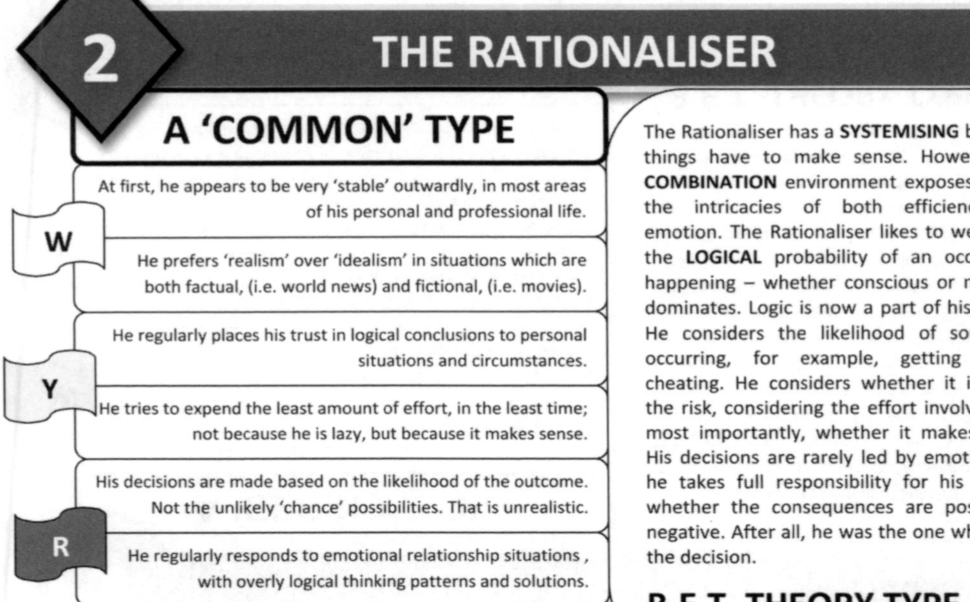
2
THE RATIONALISER
A 'COMMON' TYPE
W
Y
R
At first, he appears to be very 'stable' outwardly, in most areas of his personal and professional life.
He prefers 'realism' over 'idealism' in situations which are both factual, (i.e. world news) and fictional, (i.e. movies).
He regularly places his trust in logical conclusions to personal situations and circumstances.
He tries to expend the least amount of effort, in the least time; not because he is lazy, but because it makes sense.
His decisions are made based on the likelihood of the outcome. Not the unlikely 'chance' possibilities. That is unrealistic.
He regularly responds to emotional relationship situations , with overly logical thinking patterns and solutions.
The Rationaliser has a SYSTEMISING brain, so things have to make sense. However, his COMBINATION environment exposes him to the intricacies of both efficiency and emotion. The Rationaliser likes to weighs up the LOGICAL probability of an occurrence happening – whether conscious or not. This dominates. Logic is now a part of his nature. He considers the likelihood of something occurring, for example, getting caught cheating. He considers whether it is worth the risk, considering the effort involved, and most importantly, whether it makes sense! His decisions are rarely led by emotion, and he takes full responsibility for his actions, whether the consequences are positive or negative. After all, he was the one who made the decision.
B.E.T. THEORY TYPE – scL

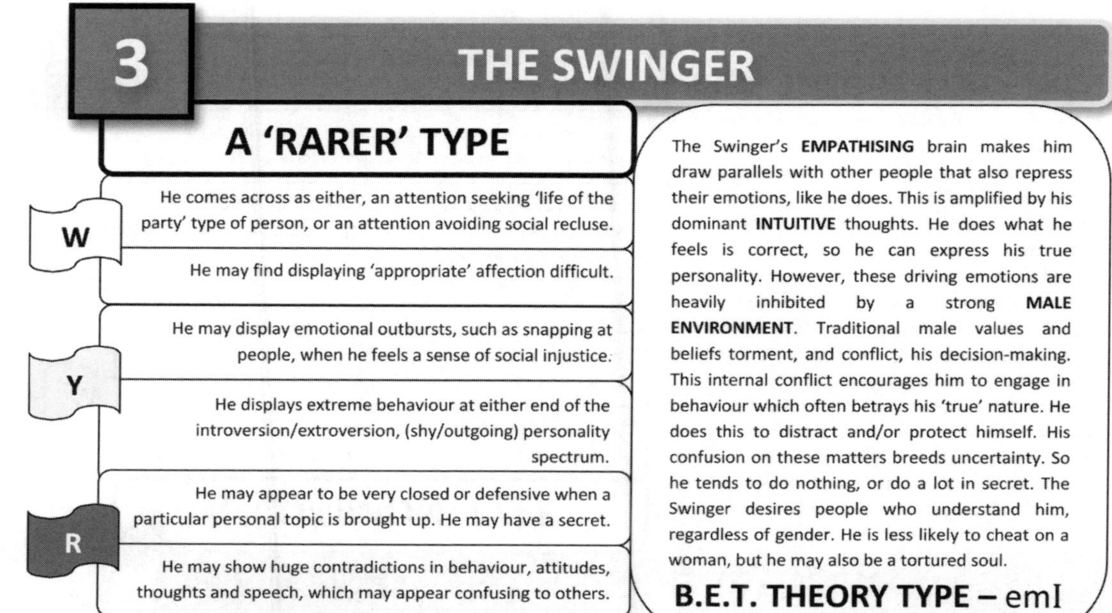
3
THE SWINGER
A 'RARER' TYPE
W
He comes across as either, an attention seeking 'life of the party' type of person, or an attention avoiding social recluse.
He may find displaying 'appropriate' affection difficult.
Y
He may display emotional outbursts, such as snapping at people, when he feels a sense of social injustice.
He displays extreme behaviour at either end of the introversion/extroversion, (shy/outgoing) personality spectrum.
R
He may appear to be very closed or defensive when a particular personal topic is brought up. He may have a secret.
He may show huge contradictions in behaviour, attitudes, thoughts and speech, which may appear confusing to others.
The Swinger's EMPATHISING brain makes him draw parallels with other people that also repress their emotions, like he does. This is amplified by his dominant INTUITIVE thoughts. He does what he feels is correct, so he can express his true personality. However, these driving emotions are heavily inhibited by a strong MALE ENVIRONMENT. Traditional male values and beliefs torment, and conflict, his decision-making. This internal conflict encourages him to engage in behaviour which often betrays his 'true' nature. He does this to distract and/or protect himself. His confusion on these matters breeds uncertainty. So he tends to do nothing, or do a lot in secret. The Swinger desires people who understand him, regardless of gender. He is less likely to cheat on a woman, but he may also be a tortured soul.
B.E.T. THEORY TYPE – emI

4 THE SUCKER FOR LOVE

A 'COMMON' TYPE

W

He is usually perceived as physically attractive by the opposite sex, this provides many opportunities for 'love'.

He shows many excessively 'romantic' gestures, in the early stages of dating and/or relationship.

Y

He conveys the impression to you, and others, that he is an exceptionally good listener.

He seems considerate of other people's feelings and emotions; but can come across as a bit of a 'dreamer' with his ideas.

He has intense expressions of thoughts/emotions towards you in the early stages of a relationship. Sometimes too early!

R

After a relatively short period of time, he doesn't do any of the above behaviours anymore, likely to disappear off the radar.

Driven by his dominant **INTUITIVE** thought, this man takes chances on his gut feelings. In any specific moment, if it feels right; it's right. His **BALANCED** brain means he can feel, and sense, what another person enjoys; but can also systematically work out what is the best outcome for him, whether this outcome is selfish or not. The **MALE ENVIRONMENT** makes him fully aware of his peers' thoughts on his behaviour, so he may keep his intense addictive personality to himself. This man falls emotionally for people during intense moments of connection, usually relating to proximity, similarity or physical appearance. He falls for you very quickly! He forgets everything, and everyone, before that important moment occurred. It is like he is living in a continual holiday romance... until he gets bored.

B.E.T. THEORY TYPE – bmI

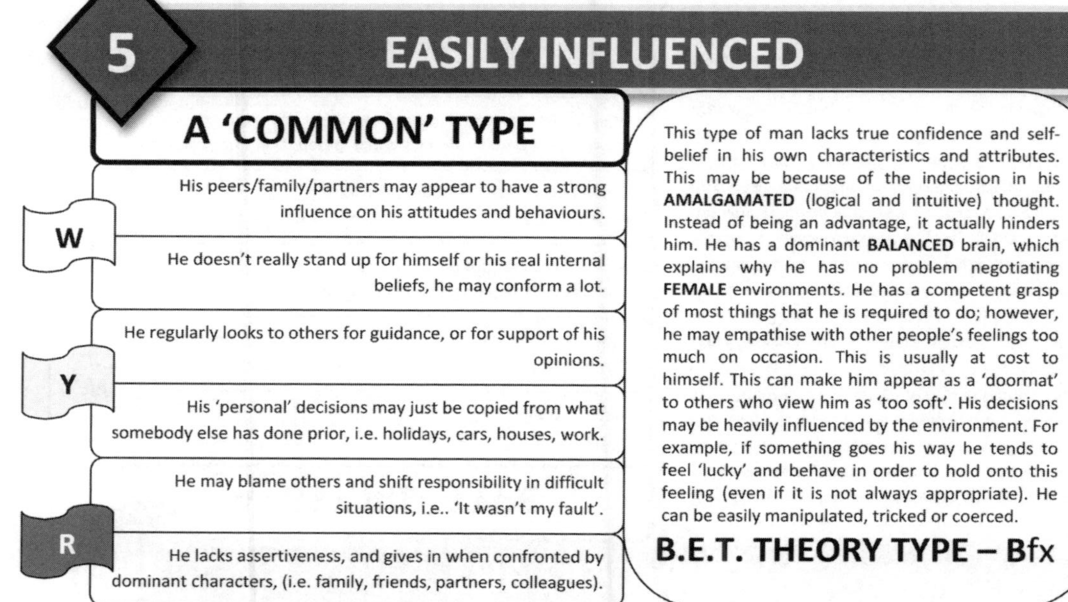
5
EASILY INFLUENCED
A 'COMMON' TYPE
W
His peers/family/partners may appear to have a strong influence on his attitudes and behaviours.
He doesn't really stand up for himself or his real internal beliefs, he may conform a lot.
Y
He regularly looks to others for guidance, or for support of his opinions.
His 'personal' decisions may just be copied from what somebody else has done prior, i.e. holidays, cars, houses, work.
R
He may blame others and shift responsibility in difficult situations, i.e.. 'It wasn't my fault'.
He lacks assertiveness, and gives in when confronted by dominant characters, (i.e. family, friends, partners, colleagues).
This type of man lacks true confidence and self-belief in his own characteristics and attributes. This may be because of the indecision in his AMALGAMATED (logical and intuitive) thought. Instead of being an advantage, it actually hinders him. He has a dominant BALANCED brain, which explains why he has no problem negotiating FEMALE environments. He has a competent grasp of most things that he is required to do; however, he may empathise with other people's feelings too much on occasion. This is usually at cost to himself. This can make him appear as a 'doormat' to others who view him as 'too soft'. His decisions may be heavily influenced by the environment. For example, if something goes his way he tends to feel 'lucky' and behave in order to hold onto this feeling (even if it is not always appropriate). He can be easily manipulated, tricked or coerced.
B.E.T. THEORY TYPE – Bfx

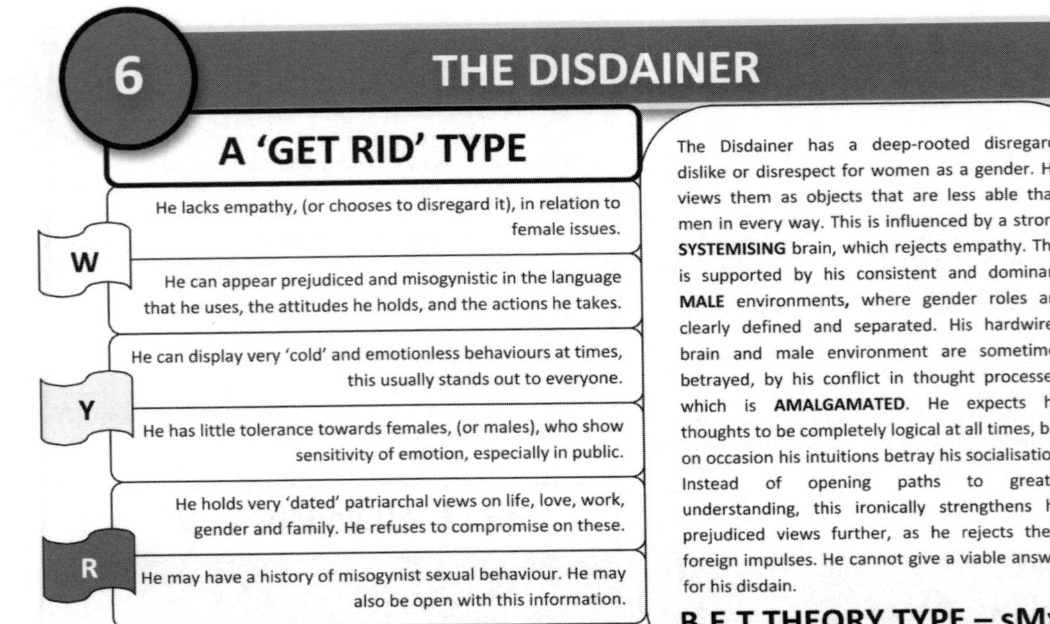
6
THE DISDAINER
A 'GET RID' TYPE
W
Y
R
He lacks empathy, (or chooses to disregard it), in relation to female issues.
He can appear prejudiced and misogynistic in the language that he uses, the attitudes he holds, and the actions he takes.
He can display very 'cold' and emotionless behaviours at times, this usually stands out to everyone.
He has little tolerance towards females, (or males), who show sensitivity of emotion, especially in public.
He holds very 'dated' patriarchal views on life, love, work, gender and family. He refuses to compromise on these.
He may have a history of misogynist sexual behaviour. He may also be open with this information.
The Disdainer has a deep-rooted disregard, dislike or disrespect for women as a gender. He views them as objects that are less able than men in every way. This is influenced by a strong SYSTEMISING brain, which rejects empathy. This is supported by his consistent and dominant MALE environments, where gender roles are clearly defined and separated. His hardwired brain and male environment are sometimes betrayed, by his conflict in thought processes, which is AMALGAMATED. He expects his thoughts to be completely logical at all times, but on occasion his intuitions betray his socialisation. Instead of opening paths to greater understanding, this ironically strengthens his prejudiced views further, as he rejects these foreign impulses. He cannot give a viable answer for his disdain.
B.E.T THEORY TYPE – sMx

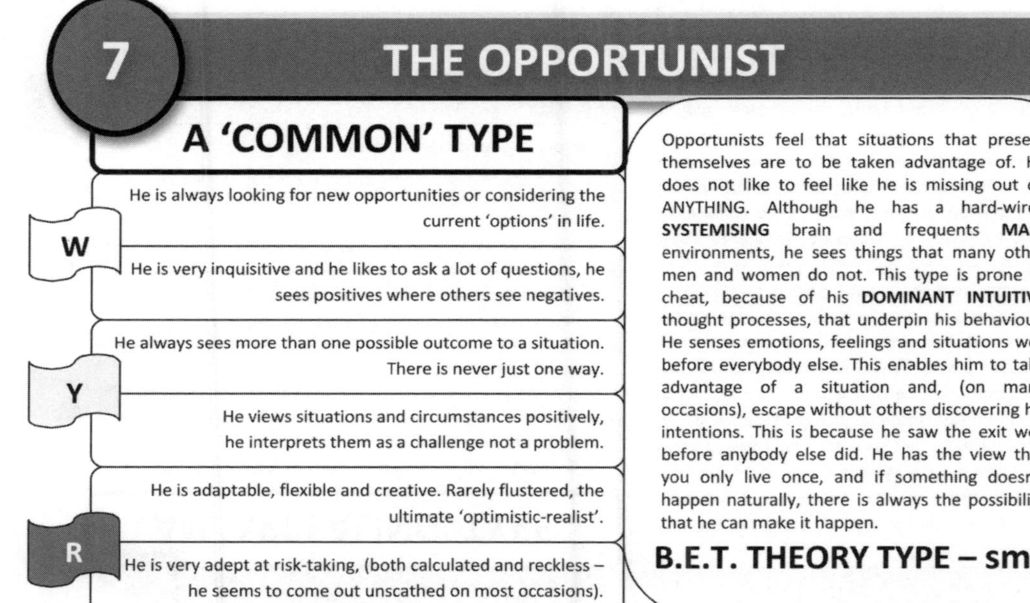

7 THE OPPORTUNIST

A 'COMMON' TYPE

W

He is always looking for new opportunities or considering the current 'options' in life.

He is very inquisitive and he likes to ask a lot of questions, he sees positives where others see negatives.

Y

He always sees more than one possible outcome to a situation. There is never just one way.

He views situations and circumstances positively, he interprets them as a challenge not a problem.

R

He is adaptable, flexible and creative. Rarely flustered, the ultimate 'optimistic-realist'.

He is very adept at risk-taking, (both calculated and reckless – he seems to come out unscathed on most occasions).

Opportunists feel that situations that present themselves are to be taken advantage of. He does not like to feel like he is missing out on ANYTHING. Although he has a hard-wired **SYSTEMISING** brain and frequents **MALE** environments, he sees things that many other men and women do not. This type is prone to cheat, because of his **DOMINANT INTUITIVE** thought processes, that underpin his behaviour. He senses emotions, feelings and situations well before everybody else. This enables him to take advantage of a situation and, (on many occasions), escape without others discovering his intentions. This is because he saw the exit well before anybody else did. He has the view that you only live once, and if something doesn't happen naturally, there is always the possibility that he can make it happen.

B.E.T. THEORY TYPE – smI

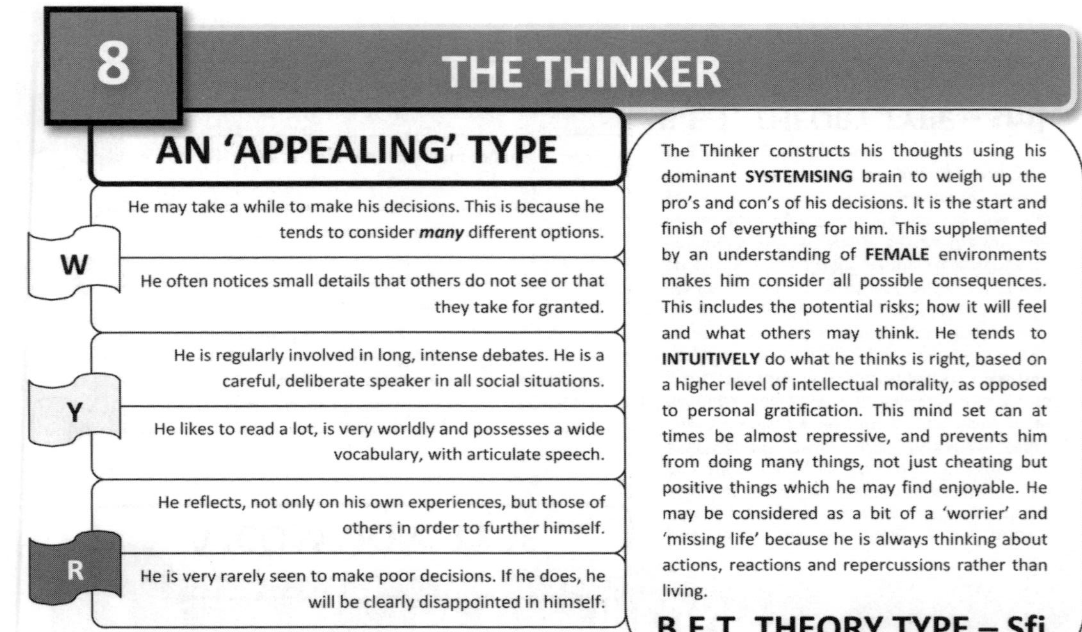
8
THE THINKER
AN 'APPEALING' TYPE
W
He may take a while to make his decisions. This is because he tends to consider ***many*** different options.
He often notices small details that others do not see or that they take for granted.
Y
He is regularly involved in long, intense debates. He is a careful, deliberate speaker in all social situations.
He likes to read a lot, is very worldly and possesses a wide vocabulary, with articulate speech.
R
He reflects, not only on his own experiences, but those of others in order to further himself.
He is very rarely seen to make poor decisions. If he does, he will be clearly disappointed in himself.
The Thinker constructs his thoughts using his dominant **SYSTEMISING** brain to weigh up the pro's and con's of his decisions. It is the start and finish of everything for him. This supplemented by an understanding of **FEMALE** environments makes him consider all possible consequences. This includes the potential risks; how it will feel and what others may think. He tends to **INTUITIVELY** do what he thinks is right, based on a higher level of intellectual morality, as opposed to personal gratification. This mind set can at times be almost repressive, and prevents him from doing many things, not just cheating but positive things which he may find enjoyable. He may be considered as a bit of a 'worrier' and 'missing life' because he is always thinking about actions, reactions and repercussions rather than living.
B.E.T. THEORY TYPE – Sfi

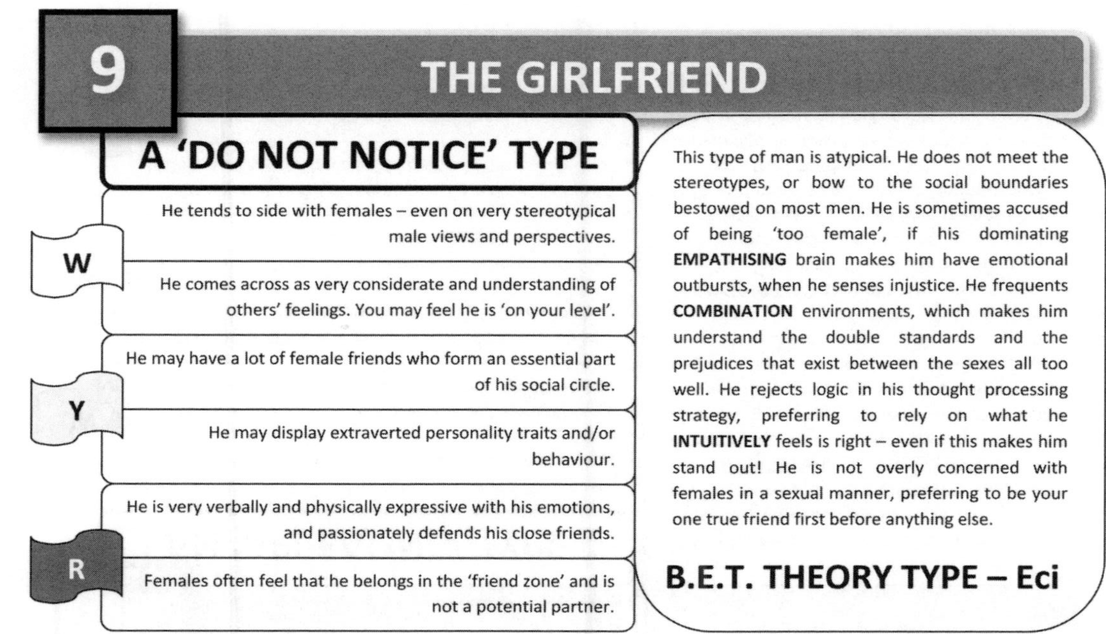

9 THE GIRLFRIEND

A 'DO NOT NOTICE' TYPE

W

He tends to side with females – even on very stereotypical male views and perspectives.

He comes across as very considerate and understanding of others' feelings. You may feel he is 'on your level'.

Y

He may have a lot of female friends who form an essential part of his social circle.

He may display extraverted personality traits and/or behaviour.

R

He is very verbally and physically expressive with his emotions, and passionately defends his close friends.

Females often feel that he belongs in the 'friend zone' and is not a potential partner.

This type of man is atypical. He does not meet the stereotypes, or bow to the social boundaries bestowed on most men. He is sometimes accused of being 'too female', if his dominating **EMPATHISING** brain makes him have emotional outbursts, when he senses injustice. He frequents **COMBINATION** environments, which makes him understand the double standards and the prejudices that exist between the sexes all too well. He rejects logic in his thought processing strategy, preferring to rely on what he **INTUITIVELY** feels is right – even if this makes him stand out! He is not overly concerned with females in a sexual manner, preferring to be your one true friend first before anything else.

B.E.T. THEORY TYPE – Eci

10 THE VISIONARY

AN 'APPEALING' TYPE

He sees a bigger 'widescreen' picture of the world, that others may fail to acknowledge, or are incapable of comprehending.

W

He has big plans for the future, is worldly and likes gathering information and knowledge, (maybe on a specific topic).

He thinks outside of the box, in terms of solutions to problems and suggestions of ideas. He is unorthodox.

Y

He is 'spiritual', if not overly religious. He believes in hidden human potential and ***regularly*** achieves his.

He is calm under stressful circumstances. He is not constrained by the usual societal boundaries, that can limit experiences.

R

Discussions with him leave you 'enlightened', considering alternative perspectives and options to your own norms.

The Visionary has a **SYSTEMISING** brain which encourages him to have structure to his life. However, the experiences shaped by his **COMBINATION** environments and thought processes have been diverse and nourishing. He makes the most out of every life situation. He can see opportunity and negative consequence long before they have presented themselves. And even when negativity is upon him, his dominant **AMALGAMATED** thought processing, knows how to deal with the situation. He makes appropriate decisions relating to all people involved. His goal is to achieve maximum joy, with minimum pain; gaining optimal output out of the minimal input. He believes knowledge is power. His vision is immense, unrestricted and unlimited.

B.E.T. THEORY TYPE – scX

11 THE CHARMER

A 'COMMON' TYPE

W

He always seems very sweet and appreciative...especially when females are around.

He puts himself out for you and the people close to you, i.e. family and friends. At times it may seem too nice/too much.

Y

He attracts attention and may have a lot of female 'friends', who indirectly, (or directly), vie for his time.

He talks a good game and listens attentively. He says all the right things. He clearly gains self-reward from this.

R

He may be irresponsible and reckless at times, especially with the promises that he makes.

He uses flattery, (verbal and materialistically), as an essential part of his social armoury. It is usually an automatic response.

His thought processes are in tune with most people around him; a perfect **AMALGAMATED** concoction of logic and intuition. But, females are attracted even more, as he has a strong understanding of **FEMALE** environments. This dominates his actions. His game puts women first, lowering their defences with his wit and willingness to go that step further for them. He loves doing it, so it is easy. But his problem is that he can't help but do it to everybody! The Charmer's ego is heavily stroked by being able to please women. It is like a drug to him. By giving them what they want and what they desire, – in the short term – his goals are achieved. It provides him with a sense of self-worth and it is a **SYSTEM** that he knows will work more often than not, so he keeps doing it.

B.E.T. THEORY TYPE – sFx

12 THE GUILTY CONSCIENCE

A 'DO NOT NOTICE TYPE'

W

He will make 'serious' efforts to make up 'minor' indiscretions to you.

He may be a little bit of a worrier, (even anxious or neurotic at times).

Y

He may be quite organised in most areas of his life. He rarely makes or commits to reckless decision-making.

The mistakes he does make tend to be 'silly', (rarely malicious), probably because he can overthink at times.

R

He generally has a good heart, but can sometimes have a hard time letting go of any errors he has made.

He will regularly feel that he has contributed more to any problems with people than he actually has.

The reason why this man cheats is usually situational. He possesses a reflective personality, and with his dominating **EMPATHISING** brain he understands all too well how other people feel. He does not like to treat others how he wouldn't like to be treated himself. However, his **MALE DOMINATED** environments and peers regularly contradict his brain type. This means that he may on occasion be susceptible to misbehaviour. **LOGICALLY,** he is able to dismiss any indiscretions he participates in from his mind, but this is only for a short period of time. It will not be long before he starts to feel extremely guilty about his decision-making, and keeping the secret makes the stress build up. He does not handle relationship anxiety well. He may confess to make himself, (not you), feel better...then try immensely hard to make it up to you. He may even give certain things up for you, (because of the guilt).

B.E.T. THEORY TYPE – EmI

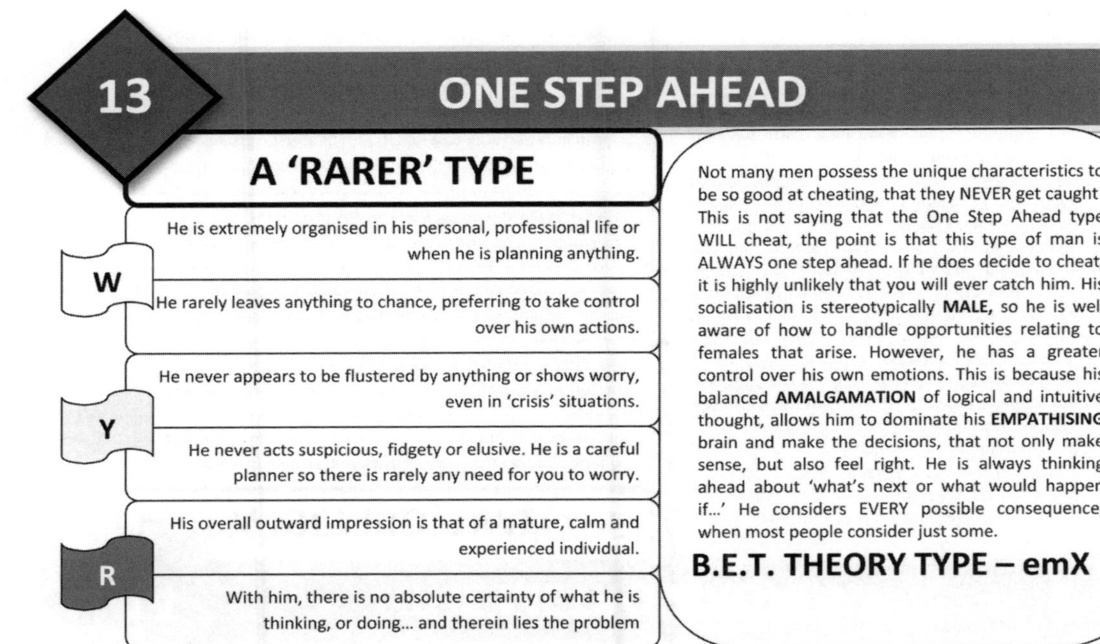
13
ONE STEP AHEAD
A 'RARER' TYPE
W
He is extremely organised in his personal, professional life or when he is planning anything.
He rarely leaves anything to chance, preferring to take control over his own actions.
Y
He never appears to be flustered by anything or shows worry, even in 'crisis' situations.
He never acts suspicious, fidgety or elusive. He is a careful planner so there is rarely any need for you to worry.
R
His overall outward impression is that of a mature, calm and experienced individual.
With him, there is no absolute certainty of what he is thinking, or doing… and therein lies the problem
Not many men possess the unique characteristics to be so good at cheating, that they NEVER get caught! This is not saying that the One Step Ahead type WILL cheat, the point is that this type of man is ALWAYS one step ahead. If he does decide to cheat, it is highly unlikely that you will ever catch him. His socialisation is stereotypically MALE, so he is well aware of how to handle opportunities relating to females that arise. However, he has a greater control over his own emotions. This is because his balanced AMALGAMATION of logical and intuitive thought, allows him to dominate his EMPATHISING brain and make the decisions, that not only make sense, but also feel right. He is always thinking ahead about 'what's next or what would happen if…' He considers EVERY possible consequence, when most people consider just some.
B.E.T. THEORY TYPE – emX

14 THE METROSEXUAL

A 'GET RID' TYPE

W

He may be viewed as narcissistic. Overly concerned about his physical image and may use several 'beauty' enhancements.

Has always been attractive or has undergone a drastic physical change since his youth, and is now considered attractive.

Y

May be condescending or belittle others, privately or publicly, about their preferences, dress-sense or company they keep.

He has a taste for the finer things in life. He is materialistic, superficial and will only be seen in certain places.

R

He places value on superficial friendships/relationships, where he gains something, that makes him look better in others' eyes.

He can be intelligent and/or sarcastic. He is always aware of his surroundings, using it to make 'behind the back comments'.

In essence, the Metrosexual possesses many outstanding qualities. The **BALANCED** brain and dominating **AMALGAMATED** thought processing gives him constructive understanding of situations. He can empathise with other people and use adaptable thought processes. But he has one detrimental flaw, which brings everything down. NARCISSISM! If somebody appeals to his ego, his vanity takes over, his narcissistic tendencies consume him and he basks in the euphoria of somebody else's adulation. It is the ultimate compliment for him, but although he may feel he looks great on the outside, really he lacks intrinsic confidence. He may not feel that he matches the stereotypical ideals of his **MALE ENVIRONMENTS**. He may hide aspects of his 'natural' self, to create an appealing image and seek self-worth elsewhere.

B.E.T. THEORY TYPE – bmX

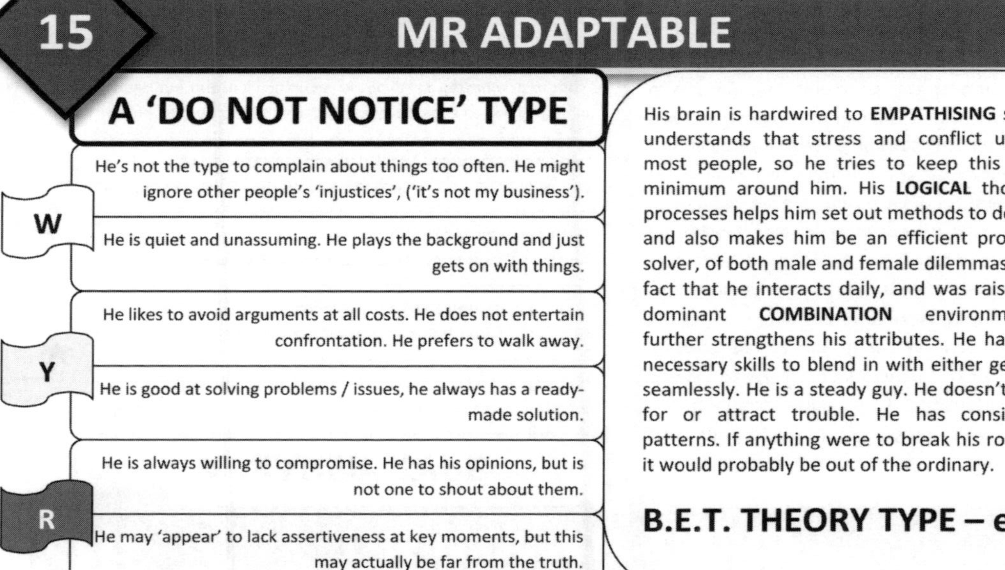
15
MR ADAPTABLE
A 'DO NOT NOTICE' TYPE
W
He's not the type to complain about things too often. He might ignore other people's 'injustices', ('it's not my business').
He is quiet and unassuming. He plays the background and just gets on with things.
Y
He likes to avoid arguments at all costs. He does not entertain confrontation. He prefers to walk away.
He is good at solving problems / issues, he always has a ready-made solution.
R
He is always willing to compromise. He has his opinions, but is not one to shout about them.
He may 'appear' to lack assertiveness at key moments, but this may actually be far from the truth.
His brain is hardwired to EMPATHISING so he understands that stress and conflict upsets most people, so he tries to keep this to a minimum around him. His LOGICAL thought processes helps him set out methods to do this and also makes him be an efficient problem solver, of both male and female dilemmas. The fact that he interacts daily, and was raised in dominant COMBINATION environments, further strengthens his attributes. He has the necessary skills to blend in with either gender seamlessly. He is a steady guy. He doesn't look for or attract trouble. He has consistent patterns. If anything were to break his routine it would probably be out of the ordinary.
B.E.T. THEORY TYPE – eCI

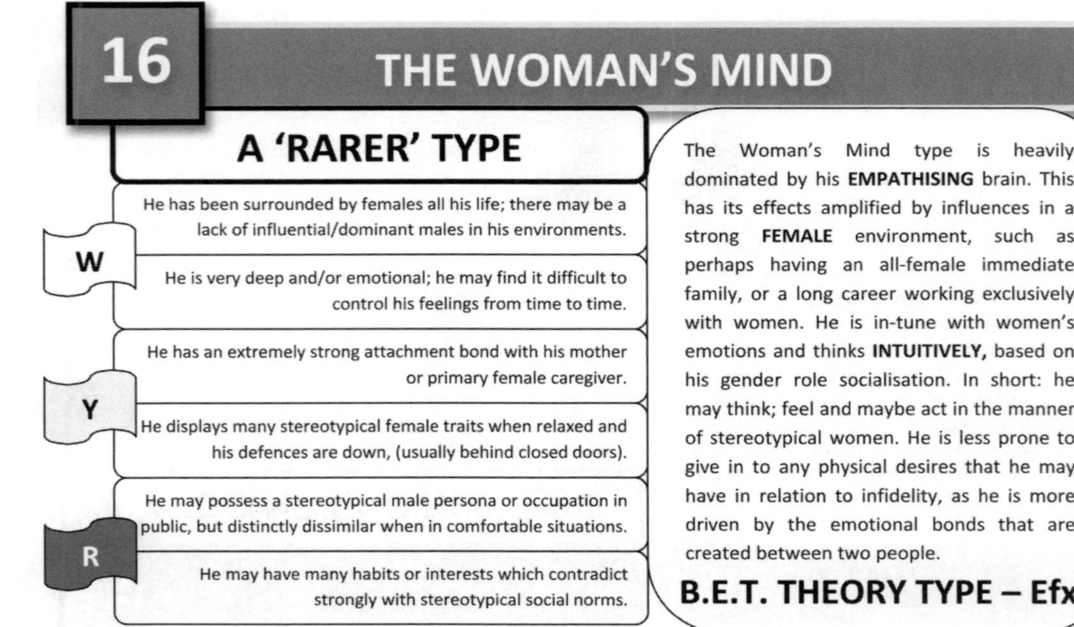
16
THE WOMAN'S MIND
A 'RARER' TYPE
He has been surrounded by females all his life; there may be a lack of influential/dominant males in his environments.
He is very deep and/or emotional; he may find it difficult to control his feelings from time to time.
He has an extremely strong attachment bond with his mother or primary female caregiver.
He displays many stereotypical female traits when relaxed and his defences are down, (usually behind closed doors).
He may possess a stereotypical male persona or occupation in public, but distinctly dissimilar when in comfortable situations.
He may have many habits or interests which contradict strongly with stereotypical social norms.
W
Y
R
The Woman's Mind type is heavily dominated by his EMPATHISING brain. This has its effects amplified by influences in a strong FEMALE environment, such as perhaps having an all-female immediate family, or a long career working exclusively with women. He is in-tune with women's emotions and thinks INTUITIVELY, based on his gender role socialisation. In short: he may think; feel and maybe act in the manner of stereotypical women. He is less prone to give in to any physical desires that he may have in relation to infidelity, as he is more driven by the emotional bonds that are created between two people.
B.E.T. THEORY TYPE – Efx

17 BACK AND FORTH

A 'COMMON' TYPE

W

He clearly has a lot of intelligence and/or common sense in social situations. He puts most of his points across well.

He is passionate and energetic about his interests and hobbies, although this may not be the case with other responsibilities.

Y

He has strong goals and beliefs and always has good intentions. He has a genuinely good heart.

He makes huge contradictions at times, in the things he says and/or does.

R

He sometimes forgets important or significant proclamations he has made about himself or others, which has big impacts.

He is the type to be thoughtful, sweet and romantic, but regularly let you down with the promises that really count.

The Back and Forth man is pulled by ideas of tradition on one hand and a form of modern individuality on the other. His dominant **BALANCED** brain sways him between stereotypes of male and females ideals. He has thoughts and notions of everything being socially constructed, (reality is of your own making), and then being stereotypically buffoonish or hypocritical at other times. This may be caused by discrepancies in his **LOGICAL** thought processes, and the way he views his heavily influenced **FEMALE** environments. Gender role socialisation may play a huge role in his perceptions. What he ***knows,*** and what he ***believes,*** may be two totally different things. It is the transitional periods in between these lapses of thought that can make the back and forth type appear contradictory. He blows hot and cold between being an ideal man and an absolute pain.

B.E.T. THEORY TYPE – Bfl

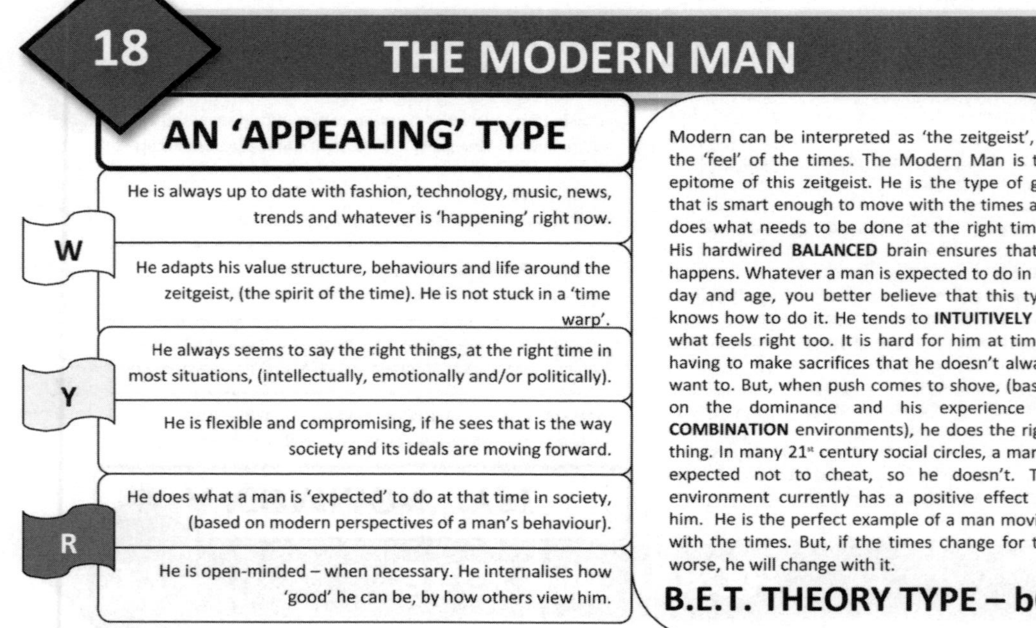

18 THE MODERN MAN

AN 'APPEALING' TYPE

W

He is always up to date with fashion, technology, music, news, trends and whatever is 'happening' right now.

He adapts his value structure, behaviours and life around the zeitgeist, (the spirit of the time). He is not stuck in a 'time warp'.

Y

He always seems to say the right things, at the right time in most situations, (intellectually, emotionally and/or politically).

He is flexible and compromising, if he sees that is the way society and its ideals are moving forward.

R

He does what a man is 'expected' to do at that time in society, (based on modern perspectives of a man's behaviour).

He is open-minded – when necessary. He internalises how 'good' he can be, by how others view him.

Modern can be interpreted as 'the zeitgeist', or the 'feel' of the times. The Modern Man is the epitome of this zeitgeist. He is the type of guy that is smart enough to move with the times and does what needs to be done at the right times. His hardwired **BALANCED** brain ensures that it happens. Whatever a man is expected to do in his day and age, you better believe that this type knows how to do it. He tends to **INTUITIVELY** do what feels right too. It is hard for him at times, having to make sacrifices that he doesn't always want to. But, when push comes to shove, (based on the dominance and his experience of **COMBINATION** environments), he does the right thing. In many 21st century social circles, a man is expected not to cheat, so he doesn't. The environment currently has a positive effect on him. He is the perfect example of a man moving with the times. But, if the times change for the worse, he will change with it.

B.E.T. THEORY TYPE – bCi

19 THE APPRECIATOR

AN 'APPEALING' TYPE

W

He grew up with a strong-willed mother/female caregiver who will have instilled in him the same strong will.

He has the utmost respect for women and women's rights.

Y

He will tend to have a very clean home, car, habits, workplace, clothes etc and takes pride in his outward appearance.

He values the differences between men and women, he may place 'deserving' women on a pedestal.

R

His attempts to do things 'correctly' is a living 'tribute', by him, that acknowledges the way his mother/caregiver raised him.

He is very selective in choosing his partners, but when he does, he treats them like a queen.

The Appreciator understands women; their emotions, their struggles and their strengths. He embraces them and does not see them as threat, or something to take advantage of. This is mostly based on the combination of his dominant brain hardwired to **EMPATHY,** which is supplemented by the **FEMALE** environments he is used to. **INTUITIVELY**, he thinks and makes decisions based on these influences. Disrespect of another female is symbolically seen as a disrespect of his mother. The ultimate person in his life! Another woman may not sit on a pedestal as high as mum does, but he is unlikely to ever mess around on you either.

B.E.T. THEORY TYPE – Efi

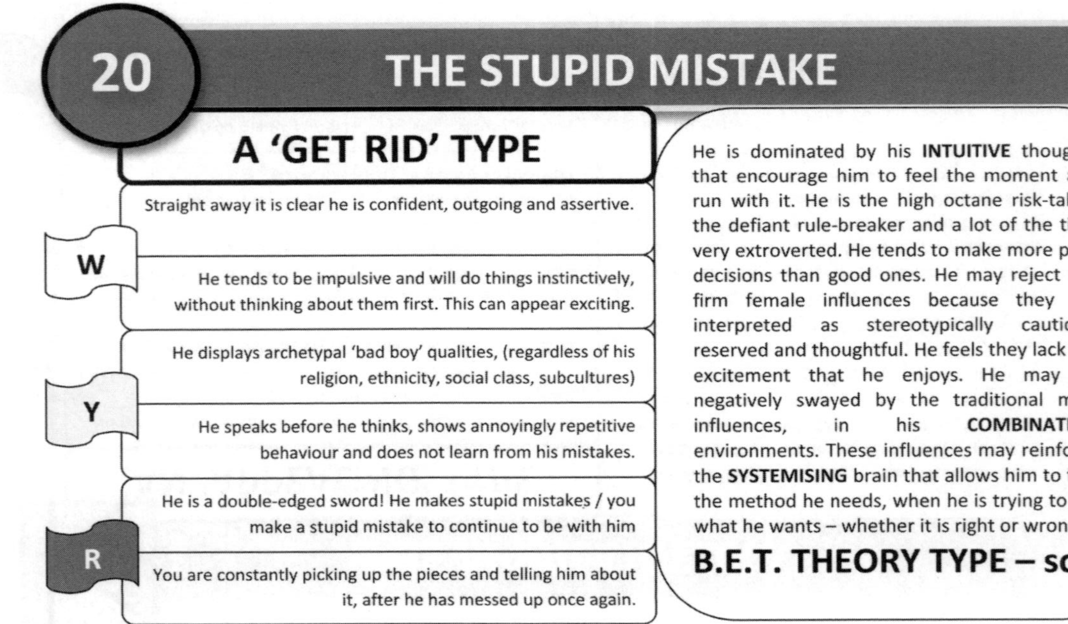

20 THE STUPID MISTAKE

A 'GET RID' TYPE

Straight away it is clear he is confident, outgoing and assertive.

W

He tends to be impulsive and will do things instinctively, without thinking about them first. This can appear exciting.

He displays archetypal 'bad boy' qualities, (regardless of his religion, ethnicity, social class, subcultures)

Y

He speaks before he thinks, shows annoyingly repetitive behaviour and does not learn from his mistakes.

He is a double-edged sword! He makes stupid mistakes / you make a stupid mistake to continue to be with him

R

You are constantly picking up the pieces and telling him about it, after he has messed up once again.

He is dominated by his **INTUITIVE** thoughts that encourage him to feel the moment and run with it. He is the high octane risk-taker; the defiant rule-breaker and a lot of the time very extroverted. He tends to make more poor decisions than good ones. He may reject any firm female influences because they are interpreted as stereotypically cautious, reserved and thoughtful. He feels they lack the excitement that he enjoys. He may be negatively swayed by the traditional male influences, in his **COMBINATION** environments. These influences may reinforce the **SYSTEMISING** brain that allows him to find the method he needs, when he is trying to get what he wants – whether it is right or wrong.

B.E.T. THEORY TYPE – scI

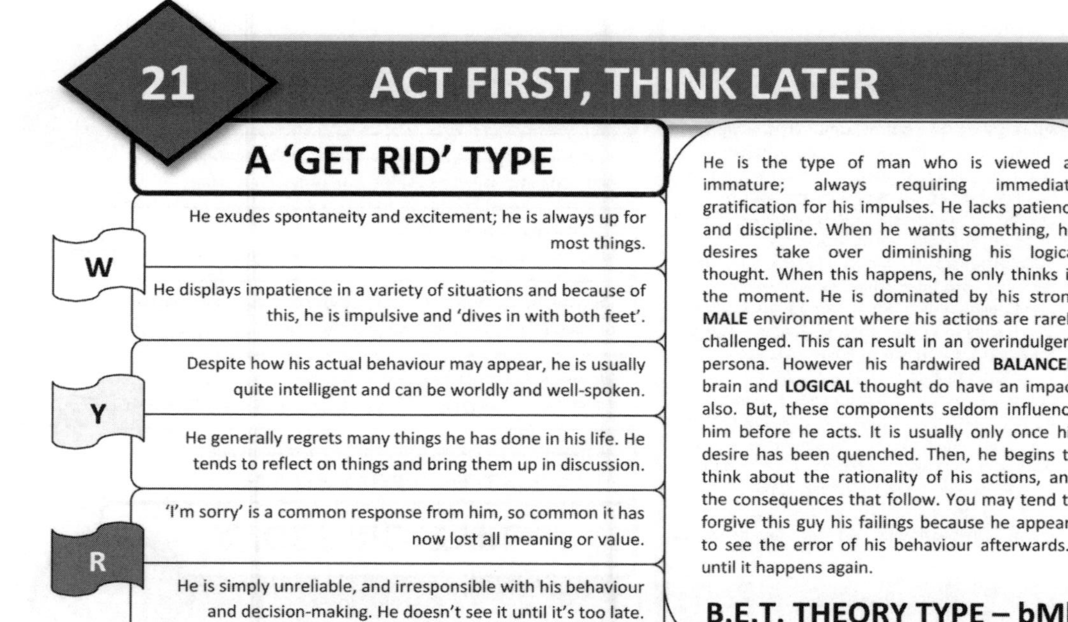
21
ACT FIRST, THINK LATER
A 'GET RID' TYPE
W
He exudes spontaneity and excitement; he is always up for most things.
He displays impatience in a variety of situations and because of this, he is impulsive and 'dives in with both feet'.
Y
Despite how his actual behaviour may appear, he is usually quite intelligent and can be worldly and well-spoken.
He generally regrets many things he has done in his life. He tends to reflect on things and bring them up in discussion.
R
'I'm sorry' is a common response from him, so common it has now lost all meaning or value.
He is simply unreliable, and irresponsible with his behaviour and decision-making. He doesn't see it until it's too late.
He is the type of man who is viewed as immature; always requiring immediate gratification for his impulses. He lacks patience and discipline. When he wants something, his desires take over diminishing his logical thought. When this happens, he only thinks in the moment. He is dominated by his strong MALE environment where his actions are rarely challenged. This can result in an overindulgent persona. However his hardwired BALANCED brain and LOGICAL thought do have an impact also. But, these components seldom influence him before he acts. It is usually only once his desire has been quenched. Then, he begins to think about the rationality of his actions, and the consequences that follow. You may tend to forgive this guy his failings because he appears to see the error of his behaviour afterwards... until it happens again.
B.E.T. THEORY TYPE – bMI

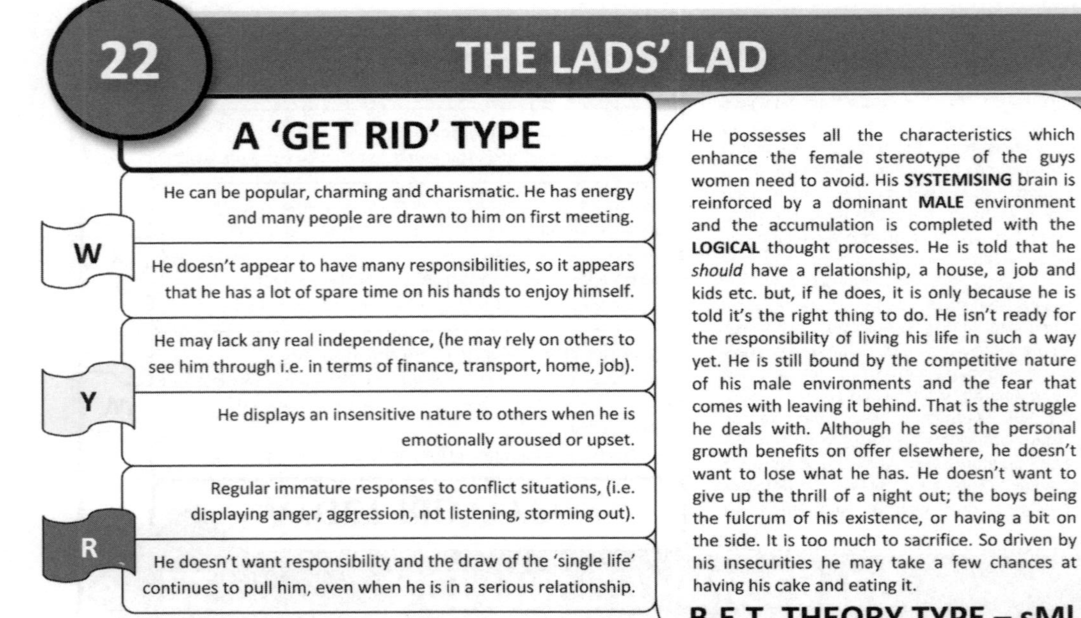
22
THE LADS' LAD
A 'GET RID' TYPE
W
Y
R
He can be popular, charming and charismatic. He has energy and many people are drawn to him on first meeting.
He doesn't appear to have many responsibilities, so it appears that he has a lot of spare time on his hands to enjoy himself.
He may lack any real independence, (he may rely on others to see him through i.e. in terms of finance, transport, home, job).
He displays an insensitive nature to others when he is emotionally aroused or upset.
Regular immature responses to conflict situations, (i.e. displaying anger, aggression, not listening, storming out).
He doesn't want responsibility and the draw of the 'single life' continues to pull him, even when he is in a serious relationship.
He possesses all the characteristics which enhance the female stereotype of the guys women need to avoid. His SYSTEMISING brain is reinforced by a dominant MALE environment and the accumulation is completed with the LOGICAL thought processes. He is told that he should have a relationship, a house, a job and kids etc. but, if he does, it is only because he is told it's the right thing to do. He isn't ready for the responsibility of living his life in such a way yet. He is still bound by the competitive nature of his male environments and the fear that comes with leaving it behind. That is the struggle he deals with. Although he sees the personal growth benefits on offer elsewhere, he doesn't want to lose what he has. He doesn't want to give up the thrill of a night out; the boys being the fulcrum of his existence, or having a bit on the side. It is too much to sacrifice. So driven by his insecurities he may take a few chances at having his cake and eating it.
B.E.T. THEORY TYPE – sMI

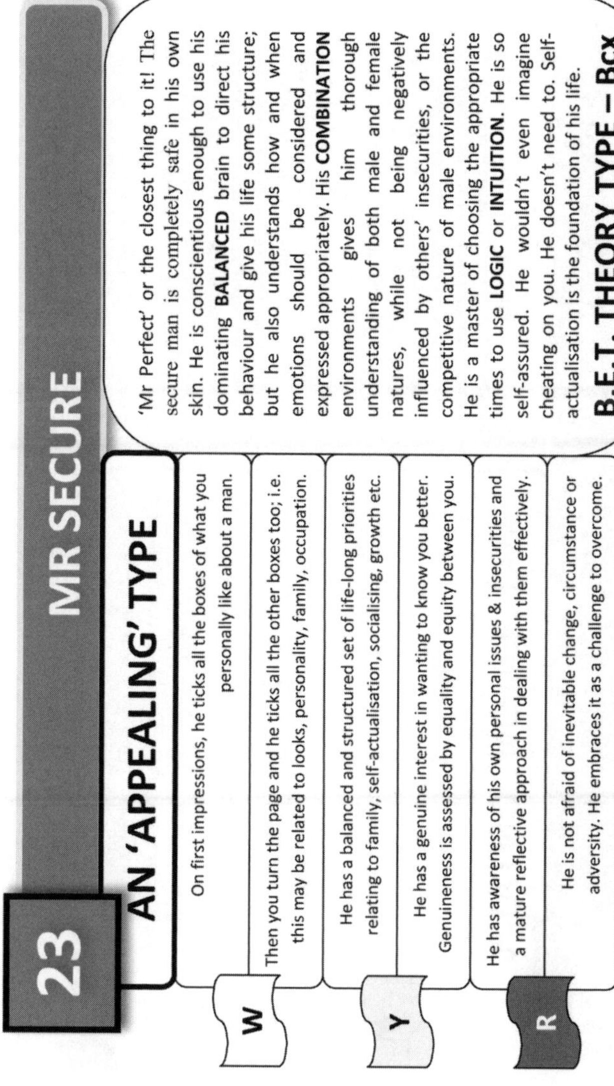
23
MR SECURE
AN 'APPEALING' TYPE
W
On first impressions, he ticks all the boxes of what you personally like about a man.
Then you turn the page and he ticks all the other boxes too; i.e. this may be related to looks, personality, family, occupation.
Y
He has a balanced and structured set of life-long priorities relating to family, self-actualisation, socialising, growth etc.
He has a genuine interest in wanting to know you better. Genuineness is assessed by equality and equity between you.
R
He has awareness of his own personal issues & insecurities and a mature reflective approach in dealing with them effectively.
He is not afraid of inevitable change, circumstance or adversity. He embraces it as a challenge to overcome.
'Mr Perfect' or the closest thing to it! The secure man is completely safe in his own skin. He is conscientious enough to use his dominating BALANCED brain to direct his behaviour and give his life some structure; but he also understands how and when emotions should be considered and expressed appropriately. His COMBINATION environments gives him thorough understanding of both male and female natures, while not being negatively influenced by others' insecurities, or the competitive nature of male environments. He is a master of choosing the appropriate times to use LOGIC or INTUITION. He is so self-assured. He wouldn't even imagine cheating on you. He doesn't need to. Self-actualisation is the foundation of his life.
B.E.T. THEORY TYPE – Bcx

24 UNDER THE THUMB

A 'DO NOT NOTICE' TYPE

He is willing to give up his friends, (male and female), for the relationship very quickly.

W

He appears to lack assuredness and assertiveness in any decision-making process (with you!).

The direction of **your** life dictates the **focus** of his life.

Y

He is not confident in arguments, confrontation or conflict (with you!).

He is willing to give in to some very unreasonable requests from you, (even in relation to close family members).

R

Nine times out of ten you get whatever you want from him, it is not uncommon for people to refer to him as a 'doormat'.

He is used to doing as he is told. His dominating **BALANCED** brain suggests that he is not rigid. His **FEMALE** environments may have been bereft of significant or defiant male influences. He is very obedient, possessing traits of an authoritarian personality. Others look at him as too soft. He deals with things **INTUITIVELY** and this is synced to his respect for rules and authority. He may not possess the strength of character to stand up to intimidating characters and can lack confidence in social situations because of this. This is especially so with people who have leverage over him. He is not assertive and may be subjected to people taking advantage of his generous nature, in both the workplace and his personal relationships. This sometimes borders on bullying. Women take advantage of him in relationships, because he allows it. He may complain at his circumstances on occasion, but this is rarely with conviction. He is all talk.

B.E.T. THEORY TYPE – Bfi

25 THE CHAMELEON

A 'GET RID' TYPE

W

He is a charismatic, charming and effective communicator. A very good listener with a believable persona!

Initially, it may appear that he does not have any 'long-term history' i.e. he may move house a lot or no long-term exes.

Y

You discover he is talented at telling stories or pulling the wool over other people's eyes.

He is intelligent, with a high level of social aptitude, (also he has the gift of the gab).

R

He appears and disappears frequently, maybe due to 'working commitments'. He may have a secret.

Too many lies have caught up with him. You find too many holes in his stories, – and perhaps a history of disillusioned exes

When in Rome, do as the Romans do. Loosely translated - this type of man will be whatever the girl wants him to be; whatever she wants to see, hear or experience at that time. His dominating **COMBINATION** environments allow him to adapt efficiently, understanding the behaviour of both men and women well. He can relate to the person's needs and fit seamlessly with them. This is until it becomes time to move to the next girl, and be who she wants him to be. His hardwired **EMPATHISING** brain enables him to spot cracks in women's emotional armour; because of this he doesn't tend to cheat in a one-night stand manner, preferring rather to cater towards their weakness. His thought processes are such a fluid concoction of **LOGIC** and **INTUITION.** His stories are always believable and you never really know who he is. You may find he is living a lie i.e. a dual life with a relationship/family elsewhere.

B.E.T. THEORY TYPE – eCx

26 THE ENIGMA

A 'RARER' TYPE

W

On first impressions he displays regular unpredictable behaviour or overly 'normalised' behaviour.

He is ***secretive'***, NOT unknowingly closed or defensive. He is well aware of it and may openly admit he has secrets.

Y

He is passionate and emotional. This may include the occasional unexpected and irrational outburst.

He unexpectedly reveals a personal disclosure, then confuses you by 'shutting down' or acting like it never happened.

R

The explanations he gives you for his feelings may appear confusing and need a certain level of decoding.

Even when you feel like you know everything about him, you realise you know nothing at all that really matters.

The Enigma cannot be defined, tied down or explained. He is unique. His behaviours may be erratic and unpredictable. He may reveal information to you, (or somebody else), which you find difficult to clarify or understand. The outcomes of his actions may be totally unexpected. Dealing with him can be a very confusing and emotionally draining experience. He is conflicted within himself, due to his **EMPATHISING** brain and his dominating **LOGICAL** thought processes being at polar extremes. He may seek solace and comfort in **FEMALE** company; the rare times he shows appropriate expressive behaviour is here. This type of man needs to find some form of introspective understanding to move forward. He doesn't even seem to understand himself.

B.E.T. THEORY TYPE – efL

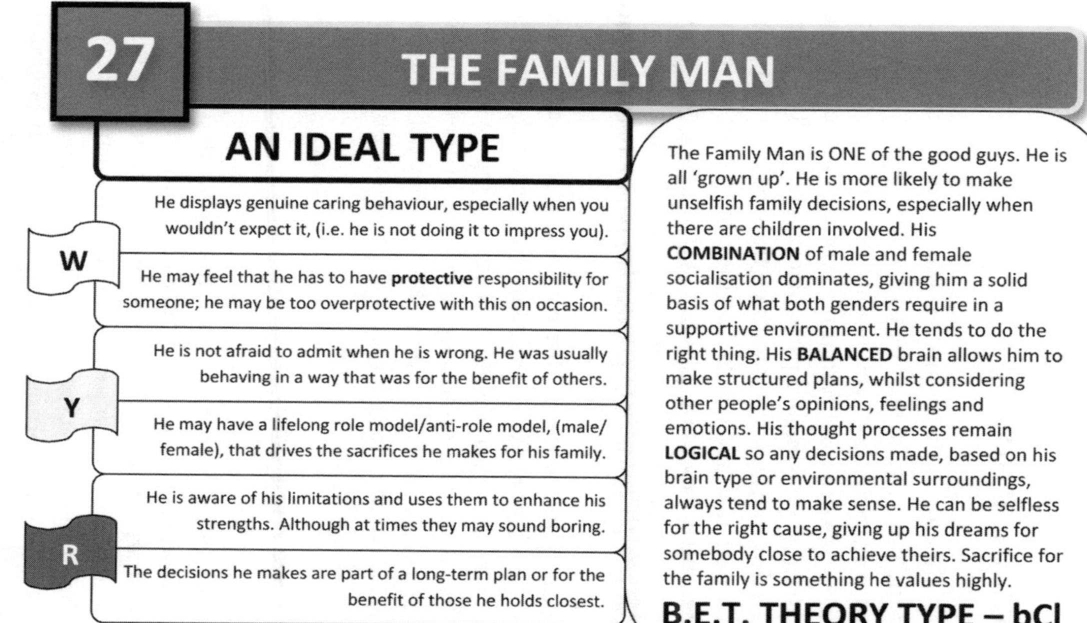

27 THE FAMILY MAN

AN IDEAL TYPE

W

He displays genuine caring behaviour, especially when you wouldn't expect it, (i.e. he is not doing it to impress you).

He may feel that he has to have **protective** responsibility for someone; he may be too overprotective with this on occasion.

Y

He is not afraid to admit when he is wrong. He was usually behaving in a way that was for the benefit of others.

He may have a lifelong role model/anti-role model, (male/female), that drives the sacrifices he makes for his family.

R

He is aware of his limitations and uses them to enhance his strengths. Although at times they may sound boring.

The decisions he makes are part of a long-term plan or for the benefit of those he holds closest.

The Family Man is ONE of the good guys. He is all 'grown up'. He is more likely to make unselfish family decisions, especially when there are children involved. His **COMBINATION** of male and female socialisation dominates, giving him a solid basis of what both genders require in a supportive environment. He tends to do the right thing. His **BALANCED** brain allows him to make structured plans, whilst considering other people's opinions, feelings and emotions. His thought processes remain **LOGICAL** so any decisions made, based on his brain type or environmental surroundings, always tend to make sense. He can be selfless for the right cause, giving up his dreams for somebody close to achieve theirs. Sacrifice for the family is something he values highly.

B.E.T. THEORY TYPE – bCl

Chapter 22 – The Shape-shifters

I WILL CHANGE HIM…

When it comes to relationships, some women feel extremely confident and powerful in their own capabilities. It is assumed that if you treat somebody how you would like to be treated yourself then relationships are easy! And if not, you can make a partner do what you desire; behaving in a particular manner will surely entice them. With this in mind, some women truly believe they can pick a man with 'potential' and mould him into the man of their dreams. Some try to turn a bad boy into Mr Perfect. However, as stated before, changing a man is not within a woman's capability.

No woman is responsible for the behaviour that her partner displays.

It can easily be forgotten that we are not accountable for the actions of other adults. When infidelity has occurred, there are too many women that beat themselves up, asking 'what did ***I*** do wrong?', 'what could ***I*** do to stop him?' etc. If they continue to believe that it was their fault that he cheated, they will destroy their ***own*** self-esteem. Even though they may profess in public that ***he*** in fact destroyed it with his actions.

A MAN CAN CHANGE

B.E.T. theory outlines that there are twenty-seven different types of men. However, with the interactive nature of the brain, environment and thought processes, there is hope that his 'type' can change, if his behaviour patterns are consistently negative. With the fact that a man can change his environments and, if he so wishes, his thought processing strategy (although obviously he cannot change his brain), it is clear that an individual's B.E.T. theory 'type' can change as a consequence. This process is named here as 'shape-shifting'.

Sometimes it's easiest for a man to change his environment. For example, he could just pack up and move to another town or stop socialising with his regular group of peers. On occasion, it's easier for a man to change his thought processes, by consciously eliminating any negative preconceptions that will precipitate any cheating behaviour. However, as the two components influence each other, a man's thought processes can get in the way of changing his environment and vice-versa. The combination of such factors can limit, (or alternatively enhance), a man's ability to shape-shift.

When men struggle to overcome cheating behaviour, many women state that they aren't as mature as women. Age is symbolically linked with the word 'maturity'. Everyone has heard that women mature faster than men. However, this all depends on the definition of 'maturity'. It's true that women tend to grow into their adult bodies faster, and perhaps learn to express themselves emotionally and communicate verbally much quicker too. Nevertheless, men do not normally judge maturity by these concepts. But, age ***is*** a factor in a man's ability to shape-shift.

You could say that men have three 'ages':

- **A biological age** – this doesn't signify anything apart from how long they have been on the planet. Some men have an older biological age but have experienced very little (and vice versa for other men).
- **A physical fitness age** – this is how a man feels within his own body and how age limits the ability to engage in physical activities i.e. sports, sex or moving heavy equipment.
- **A cognitive age** – an intellectual age in relation to the development of their attitudes, thoughts and values. This manifests in the appropriateness of their behaviour and the selection of their decisions in any given situation.

All of these 'ages' influence possible shape-shifting. His biological age is about how much life experience the person has garnered, which can influence his relationships. In discerning a man's physical fitness age, a woman can reveal how able he feels to compete physically, (i.e. sports), and sexually in comparison with other men. Remember being 'manly' is a central feature to most men. Discerning his cognitive age will uncover his attitudes and behaviour patterns, and whether he feels ready enough for commitment and responsibility, (this is what is commonly regarded as his level of 'maturity').

BE REALISTIC

Every man possesses the ability to change. However, just because a man's environment and thought processes can ***potentially*** adapt, it doesn't mean that he ***will***. Human beings are creatures of habit, meaning many will be reluctant to shape-shift. They may act like they ***want*** change but most people don't really like change as much as they say, especially if it is unexpected. However, some men are more willing than others to become a different type of man. For example, a teenage 'Opportunist' (sm**I**), may cognitively grow and become an adult 'Thinker' (**S**fi), simply by changing his perception of the environment and the peers that he interacts with. He stops chasing around every woman, and also relies more on his systemising brain rather than his gut feelings.

Only a small percentage of men will shape-shift by choice. A small minority will be forced to change by uncontrollable circumstances. However, the majority of men will remain the same. Environmental influences that have become automatic, through years of socialisation, are difficult to break; the interacting thought processes even more so. It's rare that someone would give up any regular behaviour, especially if it has brought them success in the past. Some men just love the attention a new woman can give.

ONE METHOD FOR A MAN TO INITIATE CHANGE

One psychological theory, which a man can apply to initiate a change in behaviour and thoughts, is Azjen's *'Theory of Planned Behaviour'*. The theory states that any action shown by an individual is an integration of their 'Behavioural Intentions'. A person's behavioural intentions are linked to their schemas and cognitions and consist of three components:

1) Their '***Attitudes***' towards the behaviour, (i.e. 'Relationships are better when partners don't cheat on each other.').

2) Their '***Subjective Norms***': what others will think of them, ('My friends will respect me if I have a monogamous relationship.').
3) Their '***Perceived Behavioural Control***': how much belief, (self-efficacy), they have in themselves to complete the behaviour, ('I know that I have the willpower to turn down opportunities to cheat on my partner.').

These three components, in a man's thinking, lead to his behavioural intentions and what he 'plans' to do. This should, ultimately, result in being able to predict his actual behaviour.

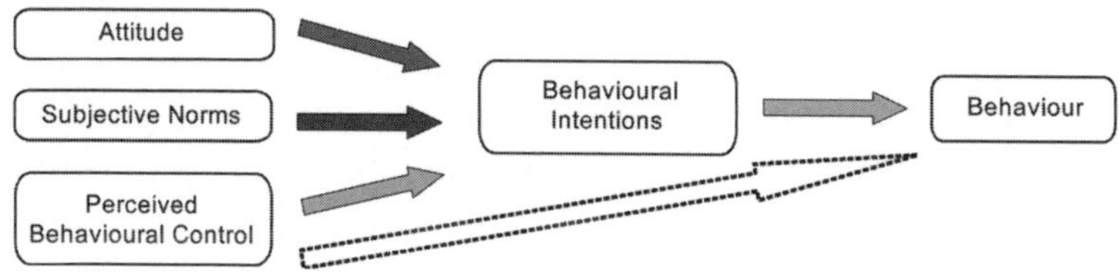

Figure 7 – Azjen's Theory of Planned Behaviour

As can be seen in Figure 7, the additional arrow between the 'Perceived Behavioural Control' and the behaviour suggests that this component is the most influential of the three that comprise the 'Behavioural Intentions'. The Perceived Behavioural Control can have a ***direct*** impact on behaviour. The man has to ***believe*** that he can achieve the goal (i.e. to change and/or adapt his behaviour) in order for him to be successful. Without the belief in his own capabilities to achieve his goal, he is likely to fail (no matter how much positive coercion he receives from his partner). Again, it's obvious that there must be a conscious choice on his behalf. Nobody can make this decision for him.

WHY MEN SHAPE-SHIFT

There are a few simple reasons why a man would want, or have to shape-shift:

- **The idealistic view;** true love and commitment – if a man is in love with a woman who will keep him on his toes, and fulfils most of his needs, he will want to keep ***her***. He is prepared to do whatever is necessary.

- **The pessimistic view;** the environment – if the environment he functions in is stigmatising, it can place reputations and stereotypes upon people. These can potentially have a negative impact upon an individual's life. Some men get to the point, where they no longer want to live with the consequences their environment has created for them. They choose to let it go.

- **The optimistic view;** cognitive re-structuring – if a man recognises that certain thoughts, and their subsequent behaviours, are not productive for the way he wants to live, he can make a mature decision. In order for him to grow, he has to 'outgrow' the thoughts that restrict any positive behaviour.

- **The realistic view;** necessity – time waits for no man, and some men just feel 'too old' to continue the behaviour they once took for granted. They ***have*** to change; there is little they can do about it.

- **By accidental response to circumstances** – although it wasn't in their plan or control, some men unwittingly respond to unexpected situations, and before they know it, they have become a different 'type'.

MISTAKEN IDENTITY

As discussed earlier, (especially in chapter 5 – the common types), some types of men are often mistaken for others, as both demonstrate similar behaviours. By looking through the 'sure fire' signs (Chapter 21) you must now understand how easy this is to do. This is a regular occurrence with both men and women. The errors in identification, between the different types of men occur because they may share environmental influences, (i.e. friends, hobbies, social groups) or use the same thought processing strategies; for example, having similar views on topics such as marriage, children and cheating. This often leads to different types incorrectly being viewed as the same.

Another way mistaken identity occurs is by women, (and men), sharing stories amongst their peers, (usually about alleged infidelity or promiscuous behaviour), which incorrectly labels men. It is easy to negatively stereotype ***people***, however, this should be avoided. Behaviours, on the other hand, ***can*** be identified as negative. There is nothing wrong with being dissatisfied with the ***behaviour*** a person shows. We can then work on identifying patterns of behaviour to distinguish between similar types, in order to make better relationship 'BETs' in future.

The table below lists the common mistaken identities for all twenty-seven types. Being aware of this, a woman should be able to differentiate more easily between one type of man and others. Using the 'sure fire' signs to compare the characteristics of each should help. The table also shows the shape-shifting possibilities each type may be receptive to, whether this is positive or negative. Again, this can only occur if the man in question makes a conscious, and sustained, change to the influencing components in his B.E.T. theory combinations.

THE SHAPE-SHIFTING TABLE

The types who are <u>more prone</u> to cheat (regardless of the relationship situation)

Type of Man	Code	Similar to / sometimes confused with	Can shape shift into	Type (possible changes)
The Manipulator	sf**L**	The Back and Forth	Positive	The Thinker (**S**fi)
			Negative	The Charmer (s**F**x)
The Stupid Mistake	sc**I**	Act First, Think Later	Positive	The Visionary (sc**X**)
			Negative	The Manipulator (sf**L**)
The Opportunist	sm**I**	The Chameleon	Positive	The Thinker (**S**fi)
			Negative	The Lads' Lad (s**M**l)
The Disdainer	s**M**x	The Enigma	Positive	The Thinker (**S**fi)
			Negative	The Lads' Lad (s**M**l)
The Lads' Lad	s**M**l	Act First, Think Later	Positive	The Rationaliser (sc**L**)
			Negative	The Opportunist (sm**I**)

The average types who <u>may or may not</u> cheat types (dependent on the relationship situation)

Type of Man	Code	Similar to / sometimes confused with	Can shape shift into	Type (possible changes)
The Charmer	s**F**x	The Sucker for Love	Positive	The Thinker (**S**fi)
			Negative	The Manipulator (sf**L**)
The Rationaliser	sc**L**	The Thinker	Positive	The Visionary (sc**X**)
			Negative	The Stupid Mistake (sc**I**)
The Visionary	sc**X**	The Rationaliser	Positive	The Thinker (**S**fi)
			Negative	The Stupid Mistake (sc**I**)
Guilty Conscience	**E**ml	Easily Influenced	Positive	The Swinger (em**I**)
			Negative	One Step Ahead (em**X**)
One Step Ahead	em**X**	The Modern Man	Positive	Mr Adaptable (e**C**l)
			Negative	The Enigma (ef**L**)
Mr Adaptable	e**C**l	The Guilty Conscience	Positive	The Girlfriend (**E**ci)
			Negative	The Chameleon (e**C**x)
The Chameleon	e**C**x	The Family Man	Positive	The Guilty Conscience (**E**ml)
			Negative	The Enigma (ef**L**)

Type of Man	Code	Similar to / sometimes confused with	Can shape shift into	Type (possible changes)
Act First, Think Later	b**M**l	The Lads' Lad	Positive	Under the Thumb (**B**fi)
			Negative	Back and Forth (**B**fl)
Sucker for Love	bm**I**	The Charmer	Positive	Mr Secure (**B**cx)
			Negative	Act First, Think Later (b**M**l)
The Metrosexual	bm**X**	The Swinger	Positive	Mr Secure' (**B**cx)
			Negative	Easily Influenced' (**B**fx)
Easily Influenced	**B**fx	Under The Thumb	Positive	The Family Man' (b**C**l)
			Negative	Back and Forth' (**B**fl)
The Modern Man	b**C**i	Mr Secure	Positive	Mr Secure' (**B**cx)
			Negative	Back and Forth' (**B**fl)
Back and Forth	**B**fl	The Manipulator	Positive	The Family Man' (b**C**l)
			Negative	Under the Thumb' (**B**fi)

The types who are <u>less prone</u> to cheat (regardless of the relationship situation)

Type of Man	Code	Similar to / sometimes confused with	Can shape shift into	Type (possible changes)
The Thinker	**S**fi	The Rationaliser	Positive	The Visionary (sc**X**)
			Negative	The Opportunist (sm**I**)
The Appreciator	**E**fi	The Charmer	Positive	The Guilty Conscience (**E**ml)
			Negative	One Step Ahead (em**X**)
The Swinger	em**I**	The Metrosexual	Positive	The Guilty Conscience (**E**ml)
			Negative	The Chameleon (e**C**x)
The Woman's Mind	**E**fx	The Girlfriend	Positive	The Appreciator (**E**fi)
			Negative	The Enigma (ef**L**)
The Girlfriend	**E**ci	The Woman's Mind	Positive	Mr Adaptable (e**C**l)
			Negative	The Chameleon (e**C**x)
Under the Thumb	**B**fi	The Easily Influenced	Positive	The Modern Man (b**C**i)
			Negative	Easily Influenced (**B**fx)
The Family Man	b**C**l	The Modern Man	Positive	Mr Secure (**B**cx)
			Negative	Back and Forth (**B**fl)

Type of Man	Code	Similar to / sometimes confused with	Can shape shift into	Type (possible changes)
Mr Secure	**B**cx	Any Type	Positive	The Family Man (b**C**l)
			Negative	Act First, Think Later (b**M**l)

The Enigma (unpredictable and unexplainable)

Type of Man	Code	Similar to / sometimes confused with	Can shape shift into	Type (possible changes)
The Enigma	ef**L**	The Disdainer	Positive	The Appreciator (**E**fi)
			Negative	The Chameleon (e**C**x)

Chapter 23 – Sleeping with the enemy

★★★★

Hope is the one human emotion that gives you the strength to keep going. To persevere through the madness you cannot explain while still believing you're doing the right thing.

Some women are so lucky, I thought to myself. *They stumble across an appealing type and there's no need for their man to shape shift*. I'll admit, I waited a long time for both Nick and Cameron to yield to my needs, but they never did. Maybe I was young and idealistic, searching for something that wasn't there, however sometimes all you can do is hope. Even though there's nothing ***we*** can do to mould a man the way we would like.

Nevertheless, there will always be those women that believe in the fairy tale ending. They ***always*** retain hope, even when it seems there is none there. They believe, and in some cases, wait in anticipation for him to change. They put up with all kinds of nonsense and behaviours, trusting that love will conquer everything, even a 'poisoned apple'. Then we have those modern, independent women with the 'plan'. She uses every tool, skill and attribute she possesses to coerce him into position. The anticipated shape-shift is just reward for her endeavour or enterprise. *I was caught in the middle of these two extremes,* I thought.

Some women however, are relentless in their pursuit, (whether it is a planned or fairytale ending), although it rarely seems to bear fruit. Take Claire, for example. She methodically plans the 'restriction of sex' or 'giving the cold shoulder' techniques if she doesn't get what she wants or until he realises what she wants. However, I had come to realise that this is more alienating than illuminating. Don't get me wrong, these tactics can be used once in a while, but some women rely on them, as their ***only*** tool in trying to initiate a man to change. In reality however, it seems that this may just make using the justification schema a little bit easier for some men. Especially, for those average types who don't normally 'step out of line'. It's just another excuse to vindicate finding someone else, rather than to change.

I doubted that either Nick or Cameron really possessed the potential to change; Cameron, maybe. So where did that leave me? I'd finished the book, and no doubt, there would be an inevitable fight between the girls over who'd get it next. I might just, keep it and they can buy their own.

What did Michael want us to do with this information? He had made it clear that we shouldn't become an army of bunny boilers, scrutinising every male interaction. However, his book seemed to snatch away our hope, our idealistic vision of living 'happily ever after'. It really didn't seem romantic, or spontaneous, to be thinking this much about things all of the time. But perhaps, in piercing the bubble, Michael was offering us a more realistic hope. In cutting to the chase, we were able to recognise a good thing when we saw it; no more silly games, kidding ourselves or taking things for granted.

I returned his smile across the table. Did he know what I was thinking?

It was Michael's last day in town and I hadn't hesitated at his offer to share the evening together. The taxi had dropped me off at the elegant Italian restaurant across from his hotel. From the moment I'd arrived, the depth of the conversation had been excellent. It began with me asking about his plans for the future and how his seminar went, (which seemed to be a roaring success). However, something nagged in the back of my mind. The evening was quickly passing into the late hours, but I still needed to know more about Michael, 'the man'. Why had our paths crossed again? He definitely had abundant potential, and I was becoming consumed by it, but I knew that it was time to make or break – if I wanted to see him again.

I had to make a strong impression so I dug deeper. When Michael revealed that he found it difficult to show his emotional side to others, I let out a little yelp inside. After feeling like ***I*** was the one constantly exposed, he was finally letting me in. He wasn't just a psychologist, studying people every minute of the day. He was a normal person with flaws, emotions and insecurities like the rest of us. But I didn't know whether to hug him or run away. What was he implying here? That he was emotionally stunted? That he too had been broken by a partner that he had placed all his trust in? Or that he was just too busy for the expressive drain that is a relationship? Had his environmental experiences made him feel this way? Or was he in possession of a rigid systemising brain that had always thought practically?

Talking about his weaknesses made me re-consider my own. I still regretted many relationship decisions I had made… and my methods of handling situations. Cameron and Danielle sprung to mind. I supposed I still didn't really know what I wanted. I mean, ***really*** wanted. When I thought about it honestly, I too am a little present hedonistic myself. Before now, I'd never really perceived my own flaws as much. Maybe it was ***me*** who overly enjoyed the adrenaline-charged chase. That would explain why things hadn't worked with Maurice. We all claim to want the idyllic relationship, but once I had it, would I still crave excitement? My eyes were opening. I presumed that was the first step to finding the right 'type' for me.

I had never considered the difference in my relationships between things like 'honesty' and 'truthfulness'; nor when we mistakenly use the word 'jealousy' when actually we really mean we are 'envious'. Michael believed we could gain some significance from every experience; whether they were positive, negative or confusing.

"We can always reflect on what we have done and strength can be gained as a consequence of ***using*** this knowledge" He said.

"I believe aiding our personal growth is the most important thing in our individual journeys. Nobody's perfect, but ***everybody*** can improve." Michael said, as I took another sip of my drink and slowly processed his words. No conversation in recent memory had made me question my worldview as much. Reigniting my 'friendship' with Michael was exhilarating as well as liberating.

After finishing our meal, we continued the conversation across the street in his hotel bar. We were just 'going with the flow', but I was armed with Michael's knowledge. There was no obvious flirting, and I consciously refrained from touching him with the clichéd 'hand on the arm after a joke' routine. Although I couldn't help that my body language was magnetically gravitating towards him. He knew how to make a woman feel at ease, without even doing anything.

As he ordered another bottle of wine, Michael smiled at the young, attractive waitress. She smiled back, and for a second I felt insecure. My mind drifted back to the first day we spoke in the bar, with the girls. The look he gave Sasha; he fancied her more than me. *Stop being irrational,* I thought. I was the one here on the date. But it still gave me the compulsion to find out once and for all whether he was worth it.

I tried to work him out. He definitely had a systemising brain. He was too planned and conscientious to possess the others. But he must have spent a long time around women. To write a book on cheating you would have to. He knew too much about how we think. The tricky thing was to decide whether he had an intuitive or logical thought processing style. An 'i', or an 'l'; according to the 'sure fire' signs, that would make him 'The Thinker', or 'The Manipulator'. I'd remembered the codes for these two types because they related to Nick. A 'Thinker' is too obvious, and he couldn't possibly be a 'manipulator' could he? I was going too fast. After all, he hadn't done anything wrong so far. I had no need to be cynical. Could he be 'Mr Secure', or was that too far of a stretch?

The bar had started to fill up with couples, after they too had finished their evening meals I presumed. Mischievously, I asked Michael to play a game, to analyse the people in the room; vividly remembering how I had felt during our last meeting at the café. Michael frowned, almost like a disappointed schoolteacher.

"You know my theory. It doesn't let you work people out like that."

"I know," I responded confidently "It's just for fun".

I think the alcohol in his system enabled him to give in more easily to my pestering. Eventually he played along, realising it was nothing serious. I also hoped that by doing so he would reveal more about himself too. Michael identified one man as 'Under the Thumb', by how his partner made his drink decisions for him, and 'The Lads' Lad' on the other side of the room, eyeing up women when his girlfriend wasn't looking.

"So are you either of those types?" I probed.

"Erm, no!" Michael's retort was instantaneous.

Well, that rules out two of them, I thought, *twenty-five more to go!*

The night was drawing to a close as our little game ended. The bar was taking last orders, but we both sensed that our conversation was nowhere near finished. Well, not for me anyway! I plotted how the evening could be stretched out – perhaps we could go for a walk; when Michael suggested.

"Maybe we could finish this conversation in my suite?"

He had caught me off-guard. If I said yes, I might have been giving the impression that I was too easy. On the other hand, would saying 'no' close the window of opportunity to see him again? I avoided answering immediately and bought myself some time, by asking Michael if he had ever cheated. He hesitated, but not in a 'guilty as charged' manner. I think he just seemed more interested to know my opinion. *Maybe to know so much about cheating, you probably needed to have some experience in it*, I thought.

"What do ***you*** think?" he asked.

"I think every guy is capable of cheating, just like every woman is." I answered.

"I agree," he replied, "but you can't let that cynicism take over your life." I knew he was referring to the idea that 'all men are the same' again.

"Sometimes we need to mentally start afresh; ***press the reset button***. We all need to clear our minds of the preconceived notions we hold from time to time. We need to free ourselves from it all. Relationships, social norms, expectations, cheating, everything; even if it is just for a moment. It's all about judging a situation without letting previous experiences get in the way. Of course, we will always create schemas; it's part of who we are. But in letting go of fears, trepidation and prejudice, B.E.T. theory works so much better."

Time was up. The book was supposed to help me be more careful with my 'BETs'; yet there I was with this big decision to make, and still having no clue which of the twenty-seven types Michael was. I knew I shouldn't do anything, but we've all been ***there*** before. Besides, I knew Michael. We had already slept together at university after all. I didn't need to take my time with somebody I already knew, did I?

It was all very confusing. I thought about what Michael said that first night in the bar. ***The chances of understanding a man increase if you were friends beforehand. But it can also leave you susceptible to confusing this man's type; thinking something that wasn't actually correct***... he wasn't kidding.

B.E.T. theory is rational. However, I always saw myself as an intuitive thinker; a feeler. I couldn't get away from thinking that relationships were about taking chances, and risks, based on what you feel is right. What was the point of being cautious and planned? It takes away the romance and spontaneity of it all. I knew I was only looking at the limitations of B.E.T. theory and none of the advantages, but nothing is ***really*** certain. Who says that relationships are supposed to be spontaneous and exciting? Is that just an illusion created by romance novels?

But maybe, I was one of the small percentages of people that you come across when something unexplainable happens. Or maybe I was just wishful thinking? Taking chances and making considered choices both sounded appealing to me. Yet, at the same time, both sounded crazy. Which did I really want? Couldn't I have both?

At this point in the evening I wasn't getting very far with my usual line of thought, so I decided to take Michael's advice and 'press the reset button', and see where the evening took me.

The hotel corridors were empty as we made our way, giggling and shushing each other. After much contemplation I decided I was fine with however this evening ended up. I still had two choices. I still had the chance to be smart with my 'BET' if I wanted to; although I could feel my present hedonistic side urging me the other way. My insecurities were swimming in my mind. Was I being too eager? Is Michael a 'get rid' type? After everything Michael had taught me through his book, was I going to disregard it all?

My argument for spontaneity seemed credible. I read a quote once that has no clear origin, but had been attributed to many authors and world leaders, that said: 'an error does not become a mistake until you refuse to correct it'. I had always interpreted this as a positive statement; allowing me not to give up on my dreams just because of any minor miscalculations. But could it be that it was just another excuse holding me back? Was it just another ruse of the mind, allowing me to make silly decisions without feeling responsible? I couldn't keep repeating the same errors I had made with so many men before. Especially when I knew what the errors were! Who was the enemy here, Michael or myself?

I stepped inside the hotel suite, knowing that I was putting myself in a precarious position. My desire to find the right guy remained strong. If I followed B.E.T. theory, I could make the right decisions, but I wasn't sure whether I wanted to! Indecision accompanied us into the room as the door closed behind me…

References

Asch, S.E. (1956). *Studies of independence and conformity: A minority of one against a unanimous majority*. Psychological Monographs, 70(9), 1–70.

Azjen, I., (1991) *The Theory of Planned Behaviour*, Organisational Behaviour and Human Decision Process, Vol. 50, p. 179-211.

Backstrom, L., Boldi, P., Rosa, M., Ugander, J., and Vigna, S., (2012) *Four Degrees of Separation*, Cornell University Library. Available at http://arxiv.org/abs/1111.4570

Bandura, A. Ross, D., and Ross,S.A (1961) *Transmission of aggression through the imitation of aggressive models*. Journal of Abnormal and Social Psychology, 63, p. 575-582

Baron-Cohen S (2002) *The extreme male brain theory of autism*. Trends in Cognitive Sciences 6 (6): p. 248–254.

Baron-Cohen, S., (2003) *The Essential Difference*, Penguin Books.

Bartlett, F.C. (1932), *Remembering: A Study in Experimental and Social Psychology*. Cambridge, England: Cambridge University Press.

Beach, F. A. and Jordan, L. (1956), *Sexual Exhaustion and Recovery in the Male Rat*, Quarterly Journal of Experimental Psychology 8: p. 121–133

Buss, D., (1989) *Sex Differences in human mate preferences: evolutionary hypotheses tested in 37 cultures*. Behavioural and Brain Sciences, Vol. 12, p 1-49.

Buss, D., (1995) *Evolution of Desire – Strategies of Human Mating*, Basic Books

Carder, D., (2008) *Close Calls: What adulterers want to know about protecting your marriage*, Northfield Publishing

Champagne, F.A., and Mashoodh, R., (2012). *Genes in context: Gene-environment interplay and the origins of individual differences in behaviour*. Current Directions in Psychological Science **18** (3): 127–131.

Dion, K., Berscheid, E., and Walster, E., (1972). *What is beautiful is good*. Journal of personality and social psychology 24 (3): 285–90

Emery, R. E., (1988) *Marriage, Divorce and Children's Adjustment*, Sage Publications.

FamilyFirstAid. [Online.] (2012) "Teen Pregnancy Statistics and Teen Pregnancy Facts" Available at http://www.teenhelp.com/teen-pregnancy/teen-pregnancy-statistics.html

Geary, D. C., (1998) *Male, Female: The Evolution of Human Sex Differences*, American Psychological Association.

Harris Interactive/Mylife.com (2012) "Connecting and Communicating Online: State of Social Media", Available at http://www.businesswire.com/news/home/20120801005524/en/National-Survey-Reveals-Consumers-Overwhelmed-Social-Media

Harrison, A.F., and Bramson, R.M., (1984), *The Art of Thinking*, Berkeley Book, New York

Jordan, A., Monin, B., Dweck, C. S., Lovett, B. J., John, O. P., and Gross, J. J. (2011) *Misery has more company than people think: Underestimating the prevalence of others' negative emotions*. Personality and Social Psychology Bulletin, 37 (1), 120–135

Kimura, D. (1999) *Sex and Cognition*, MIT Press

MacCoby, E. (1998) *The Two Sexes: growing up apart, coming together*, Harvard University Press

McDermott. R, Fowler, J.H. and Christakis, N.A. (2010) "Breaking Up is Hard to Do, Unless Everyone Else is Doing it Too: Social Network Effects on Divorce in a Longitudinal Sample Followed for 32 Years". Available at SSRN: http://ssrn.com/abstract=1490708.

Mischel, W., Ebbesen, E.B., and Raskoff Zeiss, A. (1972) *Cognitive and attentional mechanisms in delay of gratification*. Journal of Personality and Social Psychology 21 (2): 204–218

Muise, A., Christofides, E. and Desmarais, S. (2009). *More Information than You Ever Wanted: Does Facebook Bring Out the Green-Eyed Monster of Jealousy?* CyberPsychology & Behavior, 12(4), 441-444

Munsch, C., (2010) "Financially dependent men more likely to cheat". Available at http://www.livescience.com/6870-financially-dependent-men-cheat.html

Murstein, B. I. (1972) *Physical attractiveness and marital choice*. Journal of Personality and Social Psychology 22 (1): 8–12.

Pawlowski, B., Atwal, R., and Dunbar, R.I.M., (2008) *Sex differences in everyday risk-taking behaviour in humans*. Journal of Evolutionary Psychology, 6 29-42.

Ronay, R., and von Hippel, W. (2010) *The presence of an attractive woman elevates testosterone and physical risk taking in young men*. Social Psychological and Personality Science, 1, 57-64.

SecurEnvoy (2012) available at http://blog.securenvoy.com/2012/02/16/66-of-the-population-suffer-from-nomophobia-the-fear-of-being-without-their-phone/

Skinner, B.F. (1948). *Walden Two*. Toronto: The Macmillan Company.

Stewart, M., (2001) The essential factors contributing to long term relationship breakdown

Strauss, W., and Howe, H. (1991) *Generations.* New York, NY: Harper Perennial.

Volbrecht, M., Lemery-Chalfant, K., Aksan, N., Zahn-Waxler, C. and Hill-Goldsmith, H., (2007) *Examining the Familial Link between Positive Affect and Empathy Development in the Second Year*, Journal of Genetic Psychology. 2007 June; 168(2): 105–129.

Watson, J. B. (1930) *Behaviorism (Revised edition)*, Chicago: University of Chicago Press.

Whitehead. S. (2004) *The Many Faces of Men*. Arrow.

Wolfinger, N.H. (2005) *Understanding the Divorce Cycle: Children of Divorce in their own marriages*. Cambridge University press p. 11 – 14

Zimbardo, P., and Boyd, J., (2008), *The Time Paradox,* Free Press.